BY CHRISTOPHER STIFFLER

ECONOMICS
IN-OTHER-WORDS

Contents

Preface

Have you ever read something so complicated you had no idea what it said? It taxed your mind just to keep up. Three clauses into a sentence, you had already forgotten what the first clause said. Frustration and a bit of helplessness crept into your gut. You thought, "is writing supposed to make you feel stupid?" You were drowning in the words and looking for a lifeline. Typically, that lifeline is the "in other words," a simplified statement that gives your mind an easy-to-follow example, one that paints a picture in your mind.

If you look up "in other words" in an online thesaurus, you'll get a long list of synonyms: *put differently, namely, put another way, said differently, in short, in other terms, which means, that is, another way of saying, said otherwise, put the matter another way, otherwise speaking, simply put.* Each of those phrases is used to introduce a statement that repeats what has been said in a simpler way.

Here's an example:

The idiom "moral hazard" is used to describe a correlation between the incidence of the insured event and the possession of insurance for that event. *In other words, people with fire insurance are more likely to burn down their house than people without fire insurance.*

"Incidence of the insured event" is hard to see in your mind. It's conceptual and intangible. But then comes the help, the "in other words." People with fire insurance were more likely to burn down their houses. You can picture a house ablaze. It's tangible. The example makes a concrete link to a previously too-abstract and overly vague concept.

Examples are necessary to paint a picture in the mind of the audience. Even the best rhetorical argument or explanation is useless unless anchored with a concrete and relatable example. Despite the abundance of options to further explain a concept, "in other words" seems to be infrequently used in teaching economics. The result is that brilliant ideas become hard for students to digest.

Why squander students' attention spans by having them struggle to decipher abstract concepts? It's hard to see in your mind's eye a tendency, framework, context, issue, strategy or variable; they are meta-concepts. But it is easy to visualize a hockey player in a fight or a screaming baby on an airplane. The goal of this book is to hack away those abstract concepts and replace them with tangible mind's-eye-illuminating examples.

I learned this first-hand observing a high school physics teacher's course as a requirement for an education class. The situation helped shape me as a teacher. I sat in the very back of the classroom beside a student that couldn't care less about physics. For 88 out of those 90 minutes, that student didn't pay attention to a single word the physics teacher said. Newton's 2nd law that "force equals mass times acceleration" wasn't getting through to this kid. But for one brief moment, the teacher got his attention with a simple object: a plastic shopping bag.

What's "mass times acceleration"? The concept was too abstract to picture, especially as an equation.

It wasn't until the physics teacher pulled out a plastic grocery bag filled with canned soups that the inattentive student perked up. The teacher walked the soup cans safely across the classroom, then laid the bag on the floor. The cans didn't rip the bag when walking. Then the teacher suddenly and swiftly jerked the bag upward and the cans ripped through the bag. The mass of the cans didn't change, but the acceleration did, which meant the force did.

Here was the example that showed F=MA in a way that was comprehensible. The ripping plastic bag was worth a thousand "in-other-words" words to this student. The student even blurted out that the same thing happened to him when he was carrying his grandma's groceries a few weeks prior. A real-world example can lasso a disinterested audience in, and a lack of examples can drive an audience to checking their fantasy-football line ups or dating apps on their phones instead of listening.

Case in point: a memory from an undergraduate statistics course about "omitted variable bias." Lost in the professor's scribbled betas, sigmas, deltas, square terms, and x variables was the definition of omitted variable bias.

A textbook definition of omitted variable bias will say something to the effect of "the bias in estimates of the parameters in a regression analysis when the specification is incorrect by omitting an independent variable that is a determinant of the dependent variables and is correlated with one or more of the independent variables."

The definition provided no real-world connection to link to. It was hard to grasp at the mathematical *and* conceptual level.

It wasn't until a later econometrics course that I fully understood the concept. The professor was reviewing omitted variable bias, and what was memorable about her explanation was that it specifically omitted any Greek letters. Instead the professor explained omitted variable bias with an example. She said, "there is a strong correlation between ice cream consumption and accidental drowning incidents."

What about eating ice cream could directly increase the odds of someone drowning?

It wasn't the ice cream; it was *when* people eat the ice cream. People are much more likely to consume ice cream in the warm summer months; the same months they are also much more likely to be in swimming pools, lakes, and oceans. The reason there is a correlation between ice cream and drowning is because of the omitted variable of summertime. Both drowning and ice cream were related to summertime, not necessarily each other.

If you were to plot the correlation of ice cream consumption and drowning, you'd see a positive trend. But that doesn't mean ice cream causes drowning. That's the difference that economists and statisticians teach students on Day 1: correlation doesn't mean causation.

The goal of this book is to teach readers to see a pattern of events or behavior, a scheme, a mechanism, or a pricing oddity and "explain the economics behind it." I hope this book helps you learn the economic concepts to unlock the mysteries of human behavior. My writing relies heavily on analogies, examples, anecdotes, and parables or what I call the *in-other-words words*. My teaching style sees the examples and stories as gifts to the memory-challenged, uninterested and/ or hung over. An explanation without an example is hardly better than no explanation at all. Many of the economic ideas in this book are drawn from my own experiences in Colorado.

My examples are meant to generate new ones in the mind of the reader---in the same way that once you learn a new word, you suddenly start seeing that word everywhere.

This phenomenon, the "frequency illusion," occurs when you learn some new idea or information and soon afterwards it crops up again and again. This occurs to new car buyers who start becoming aware of cars with a similar make and model; it's not that that number of those cars has increased, but your awareness of the vehicle model has.

The same thing happens when you start learning a concept. Previously you probably just never saw it, but now you are aware of it. In the same way I constantly see F150 trucks on the road, I hope the reader becomes cognizant of economic concepts learned in these pages. I wrote each chapter of this book with that aim in mind.

My hope is that the reader says to themselves some version of what I often hear my students say: "That's funny, Stiffler was just teaching us about price discrimination, or dominated alternatives, or prisoners' dilemma, or moral hazard in class the other day, and I ran into my own example this weekend."

Don't be surprised if you start seeing these economic concepts every day. And be careful eating ice cream at the lake.

Christopher Stiffler

CHAPTER 1:

Markets and the Magic of Marginal Thinking

One morning in the mid 1700's an absentminded man started walking around his house in Kirkcaldy, Scotland---wearing only his pajamas. Lost in concentration, he wandered onto the road and walked about a dozen miles, as the story goes. He roamed until he reached the next town where he was brought back to reality by the sound of church bells[1].

This Scottish philosopher had a good excuse in getting lost in his thoughts: he would write one of the most important books in the history of economics. His name was Adam Smith.

According to Adam Smith (1723-1790), all the goods and services all the people of a nation consume—their standard of living—is the wealth of a nation. Adam Smith didn't invent the market, but he demonstrated that free trade and unfettered markets were at the heart of wealth. The flow of goods and services between people is the aim of economic life.

Smith believed that: "It is not from the benevolence of the butcher, the brewer or the baker that we expect our dinner, but from their regard to their self-interest." A market guided by individual self-interest will lead to increased economic well-being and improve the standard of living. Individual self-interest will result in competition, and competition will result in the creation of goods that society wants at the prices society is willing to pay. How does that wizardry happen?

It's all about the freedom to exchange goods and services with one another.

Self-interest creates the motivation to produce economic value, but a world with only self-interest would be a world of ruthless profiteering.[2] The free exchange of goods wouldn't work if the bakers were lying about the weight of their bread and the brewers were watering down their beer to boost profits. What keeps things in check is competition. Self-interest alone creates a shop owner who charges way too much for goods. But add in some conflict between other self-interested shop owners, and you've got competition. If one shop-owner charges too much or waters down the beer, the buyers will go elsewhere.

What is guiding everyone's private decisions to serve the needs of the public? No one is commanding people to make society a good place. No one tells the brewer what type of hops to use in the IPA or how much beer to brew. The brewer makes that calculation based on what will make a profit.

"Mind your Ps and Qs." The flavor of this expression is to mind your manners or be on your best behavior. As with any saying there's disagreement on the phrase's origins. One theory is that the saying comes from pubs in the 17th century when bartenders would keep watch on the patrons' alcohol consumption by remembering how many pints (p) and quarts (q) they had consumed.

In the economist's world, when we hear Ps and Qs, we think of *prices* and *quantities*. Competition and prices ensure that the quantities or amounts of a good are produced according to what society wants. Those prices send signals and provide incentives to both buyers and sellers.

The market provides a way for firms and consumers to decide where scarce resources go. Market prices (Ps) are signals that provide incentives. Prices allow communication between sellers and buyers: inducing more buyers with lower prices and inducing more sellers when prices rise. This dynamic can be seen in Uber's surge pricing when there's a massive demand for rides and a limited supply of drivers: the price per ride increases to help lure Uber drivers who are off-duty back into the market. Prices create the ability to allocate resources to where they are valued most, and thus the market mechanism will change the allocation of resources to fit its desires. It produces the right amount of Q.

The person earning money to benefit themselves also benefits society because in order to earn income from labor in a competitive market, that person must produce something others value. This helped create Adam Smith's lasting metaphor: the *invisible hand*. "By directing that industry in such a manner as its produce may be of greatest value, he intends only his own gain, and he is in this, as in many other cases, led by an invisible hand to promote an end which was no part of his intention."

Robert Heilbroner summed up Smith's philosophy like this: "Don't try to do good, says Smith. Let good emerge as the by-product of self-interest."[3] Self-interest and competition, paired with prices in a free market, accomplish the good.

Smith wanted to find the best way to organize society to boost welfare. Therefore, anything that impedes the market's ability to provide the greatest number of goods at the lowest prices, will also lessen total welfare. So, Smith was generally in favor of smaller government, but certainly saw a role for government in an economy.

In fact, Smith saw three distinct roles for government: to provide national defense, to provide a justice system, and to produce public goods like roads and education. Smith was against government interference with the magic of the market mechanism. He recognized the inherent tradeoffs with government intervention in the market, as well as the tradeoffs government itself must make.

That's another idea central to the economists' method of thinking: there are trade-offs. Because we live in a world with limited resources, we must make choices. And there's no better saying that embodies those tradeoffs than the old "guns vs. butter" argument.

Guns vs. Butter

It's a good bet that when I tell someone born before 1970 that I teach economics, more often than not, they respond with "guns and butter." This is because most people who have taken Econ 101 were drilled with that phrase as an example used to explain a country's decision to split limited resources between buying military goods or civilian goods.

"Butter" symbolizes non-defense goods a country buys such as schools, parks, and social welfare. The "butter" goods increase the happiness of a country's citizens at home. "Guns" represents defense spending or security goods such as army troops, ships, and tanks. The more we spend on national defense (guns), the less we can spend on consumer goods (butter). Guns protect us from foreign aggressors, while money spent on "butter" improves our standard of living. These two goods represent a tradeoff: every dollar spent on tanks means one less that could be spent on bike paths.

The phrase "guns and butter" has been used by politicians and journalists to demonstrate the opportunity costs (the alternative opportunities that are sacrificed to make a choice) of war. Although unclear, it's thought that William Jennings Bryan, then secretary of state to President Wilson, was the first to use the term to show his disappointment with spending government funds on war instead of spending it on the welfare of the American people.

In 1953, President Dwight D. Eisenhower gave a speech shortly after the death of Soviet leader Joseph Stalin that likened military spending to stealing from the American people. To demonstrate the high opportunity cost of war, Eisenhower articulated it in tradeoff terms:

> *Every gun that is made, every warship launched, every rocket fired signifies, in the final sense, a theft from those who hunger and are not fed, those who are cold and are not clothed.... The cost of one heavy bomber is this: a modern brick school in more than 30 cities. It is two electric power plants, each serving a town of 60,000 population. It is two fine, fully equipped hospitals....*[4]

How much to spend on defense compared to consumer goods isn't an all-or-nothing proposition. Rather it's a decision about how much of each to spend limited public funds on. In this way, Eisenhower's speech also embodies another idea that serves as a foundation of economic thinking: marginalism.

Thinking at the Margin

Decisions aren't always all-or-nothing. Many of the choices we make involve asking, *"How much?"* not just *"Do we do it or not?"* Many of our decisions involve some marginal analysis, even if we don't realize it. We're asking ourselves if we want a little more or a little less of something. This is different than all-or-nothing decisions. All-or-nothing thinking says, "I eat pancakes, or I don't eat pancakes." Marginal thinking says, "Do I have the third pancake after eating the second?"

Here's a conundrum that makes sense when you think at the margin: I decided to buy premium gasoline when it was

$2.69 but not when it was $2.59 a gallon. Why would it make sense for me not to buy something at one price but then buy it when it got more expensive?

This example occurred as I was preparing for a 330-mile road trip to Ouray, Colorado, to ice climb, and I was filling up my denim blue F-150 with gas. After swiping my credit card at the pump, I had a choice between the lower-octane 85 grade gasoline for $2.09 a gallon and the higher-performance 87 grade for $2.59 a gallon. However, before I selected my gasoline grade, I had to ask myself, "Was an extra 50 cents per gallon worth it to get a higher engine performance?"

I reasoned that the extra 50 cents price wasn't worth it; I put in the 85 grade.

On my return drive to Denver, I stopped in Frisco, Colorado, to put some gas in the tank. Gas is more expensive in the mountains. This time, my choice was 85 octane for $2.39 or 87 grade for $2.69. I went with the performance 87 grade this time.

But wait? A week earlier I didn't buy the 87 grade gas when it was $2.59 but I did when it was $2.69? Why choose performance grade gas when it was more expensive?

Remember, economists think at the margin. At the Frisco gas station, the differential between 85 and 87 grade was only an extra 30 cents, compared to an additional 50 cents back in Denver. Notice the difference between: "Is $2.59 worth it for performance?" and "Is an extra 50 cents worth it for engine performance?" That's the difference between *full cost thinking* and *marginal thinking*.

Sometimes you can get the wrong outcome when you don't think at the margin.

In *The Undercover Economist*, Tim Hartford describes college parties that sell all-you-can-drink tickets, which entitle the buyer to unlimited beer, as a related way to understand marginal costs vs. average costs.[5] Suppose that for $20 you can drink all night; there's no additional cost for the next beer. But let's say college administrators want to crack down on the overconsumption of alcohol. So, they decide to raise the price of drinking to $30 for all-you-can-drink. But that didn't stop overconsumption, in fact, it probably made it worse.

Their economic reasoning was only partially correct. They rightly understood that overconsumption of alcohol was a problem, and they rightly reasoned that raising the price of drinking could lower demand for tickets and thus consumption, so they raised the full cost of drinking at the event, but they didn't raise the price that affects the decisions students make *at the margin*: they did not change the marginal cost of the next beer. Once you paid the upfront cost, it was still $0 for the next beer whether the overall ticket was $20 or $30.

Think of a partier who only values the next beer at $2. Under the all-you-can-drink-for-one-upfront-cost method, the cost of the additional beverage is $0. Since $2 of benefit exceeds $0 of cost, that beer gets consumed. But if that same rational person had the decision to pay an additional $5 for a beer that only gave them $2 of value; they wouldn't take it. So, increasing the cost *at the margin* would be a better way to lower consumption. This could look like a $20 cover fee that covers the first three beers for free then each additional beer in $5 extra. This way that 4th beer does have a marginal cost.

Gym memberships suffer from the opposite effect. Say you want to increase consumption of a certain good such as the number of times you do bicep curls and run on the treadmill each month. Paying the monthly-unlimited visits for $40 is the better option than the $5 per visit method. If you have a marginal cost of $5 to go to the gym every day, you'll need to get at least $5 of benefit from it. So, if you're struggling for motivation to work out, adding an extra $5 worth of cost to that decision isn't the way to go. You'll get more of something when the next incremental cost is $0 instead of $5.

Businesses, like consumers, are also making decisions at the margin. Firms must decide if the additional (marginal) revenue they receive from increasing their production is worth the cost of making those additional items (more in Chapter 4).

Economists' Models

The development of marginalism is connected with the theory of rent. The best-known version of the theory of rent goes to David Ricardo (1772-1823). Ricardo was addressing the reason why the price of wheat had soared while rents on agricultural land had also soared. At first glance, it would be tempting to conclude that the price of wheat was going up because the landowners were charging high rents to the farmers to cultivate the land. But Ricardo showed that it actually was the complete opposite. In so doing, he used a little marginal analysis of his own.

To explain how rent develops, Ricardo used an example of an island with varying degrees of productive land. The example went like this: suppose there are 100 acres of really fertile land (Grade A) and 100 acres of semi-fertile land (Grade B). The people in this newly settled area will first farm all the most fertile land (Grade A). Initially, let's say only 80 acres of Grade A land is needed to feed everyone, leaving 20 acres unused. No farmer would be willing to pay anything to cultivate Grade A land from landowners since there is a sufficient supply of it. Therefore, no rent will be paid to the owners of Grade A land at this stage. Rent can only be charged when land is scarce.

But then consider what happens when the population increases and there is a need to grow more grain. Once all 100 acres of Grade A land are used up, they start farming Grade B land. But Grade B land has a lower crop yield. Let's say that with the same effort, 50 bushels of corn can be grown on an acre of Grade A land, but only 40 bushels will grow on Grade B.

What will happen now? The farmers stuck on Grade B farmland would see an opportunity to pay the landowners of Grade A land for the chance to cultivate that land. This is when rent occurs.

How much will the landowners be able to raise the rent on Grade A land? Ricardo showed the answer to that by focusing on the differential in productivity between certain land and the land at the "margin." If the difference in the productiveness of the two types of land (Grade A compared to Grade B) is 10 bushels of grain per year, then rent will also be 10 bushels of grain a year. Why not more and why not less rent?

Well, if the landowner tried to charge more, the profit-calculating farmer would leave and farm the less productive land in which they'd make more profit. If the landowner charges less than 10 bushels, then another farmer would gladly step in and offer more. Rent will be equal to the difference in grain yield between Grade A land and Grade B land. Economists use the term "marginal" land because it is at the edge of being cultivated and not cultivated. With rent on Grade A land at 10 bushels, it makes no difference to the farmers whether they grow on Grade B land or Grade A land. Once land is scarce and Grade B land is needed for growing, Grade A landowners can start charging rent.

To reiterate: if a landlord decided to charge less to a certain farmer to use that land, that farmer will get outbid by other farmers for the opportunity to cultivate that land. On the other hand, if the landlord charges too much, then no farmer would find it profitable to farm that land in the first place. You can see Adam Smith's ideas of self-interest and competition backing Ricardo's logic here.

Ricardo's big implications were that higher food prices translate into higher rent, and not the other way around[6]. Rent is not part of the price of corn. All units of corn will be sold at the same price whether it was grown on the fertile soil or the dry, less-productive soil. But the corn that is grown on the fertile soil will generate rent. As Ricardo wrote "...corn is not high because a rent is paid, but a rent is paid because corn is high." The land at the margin is central; everything is relative to the marginal land.

Of course, an economy isn't just farmers and landowners making corn on an island, but these simplified abstractions give economists a guide to making the real world more comprehensible. Ricardo's example might be oversimplified for the complicated real world, but it illustrates an underlying truth. I think about Ricardo's example and the underlying trend every time I walk by the line of people spilling out the door at lunch time at Chipotle in downtown Denver. Its prime location and ample foot traffic mean there are many businesses that would be willing to pay for that location. Knowing this, the landlord can play them against each other, which gives the property owner a ton of room to jack up the rent because they know they have "Grade A land."

The simplified model shines a light on the process at work. And this is a lot of what economists try to do. They sift away many of the complications of everyday life to show the underlying process. Models zero in on the key topic we want to examine. Economic thinking is about modeling the basic patterns and principles of decision making that operate behind the curtain of a more complicated world. Ricardo's simple strands of logic—building up long chains of cause and effect from a simplified starting point—became a key method of the economics discipline.[7]

If we first understand the dynamics of a simplified world, it helps us understand a complex one. This is the economic methodology—the way economists approach problems. It's this method that economists combine with simplified models. Perhaps the most important of those simplified models is supply and demand.

Alfred Marshall's Scissors

The backbone of any introductory economics course is the supply and demand model. The demand curve links the prices consumers are willing to pay with the quantities that people want to buy. It's a line on a graph. The demand curve slopes downward because as prices increase, people want less. When prices are cheaper, people want more. The supply curve links the price and quantities that a firm or business makes. The supply curve slopes upward because higher prices make firms more willing to make and sell that product and because the higher price covers the increased production cost (more on this in Chapter 4).

What determines the price of a good — the supply or the demand?

Well, it's both.

One of the big insights in economic theory is that prices and quantities are determined simultaneously by supply and demand. The English economist Alfred Marshall (1842-1924) took Adam Smith's competition philosophy and made it into a model. The algebra and diagrams learned in Econ 101 are, by and large, a product of Marshall's work.

And Marshall's ideas are a large product of mountain excursions. As an economist in Colorado who does his share of pondering in the backcountry mountains, I appreciate how Marshall developed his theories during mountain walks in the Alps and backpacking for days with a rucksack full of texts. From those alpine walks, Marshall recalibrated the focus of economics: this theory combined the hypotheticals of the nameless individuals and the small representative firm with the self-adjusting and self-correcting way of the economic world.

He compared supply and demand to the upper and lower blades of a pair of scissors, saying: "We might as reasonably dispute whether it is the upper or the under blade of a pair of scissors that cuts a piece of paper, as whether value is governed by utility or cost of production."[8]

Using supply and demand, Marshall solved a central problem in economics known as the "theory of value," which basically meant finding the value of a product and the distribution of income from its sale between the people who made the product.

Marshall's supply and demand departed from what the classical economists assumed. Adam Smith and other classical economists thought price as value was mainly determined by the cost of production. Many classical economists in Adam Smith's time believed that value was determined by the amount of labor that went into its production.

But just because labor went into making a product, doesn't mean people would want to buy it. I could spend all day dipping broken light bulbs in chocolate. What would their value be? I doubt people would be willing to pay for chocolate-covered light bulb shards. So, there must be more to the determination of value than just the cost of production. This is where English economist and logician William Jevons (1835-1882), who developed the idea of *marginal utility*, enters the story. To understand the concept of marginal utility, it's helpful to think of pancakes.

Imagine eating silver dollar-sized pancakes. The first butter-topped, syrup-covered pancake is amazing. It gives you a ton of happiness (or utility, as economists call it). But as you eat more pancakes, the pleasure and enjoyment you get from those carb-laden breakfast delights starts to diminish. The fifth pancake just isn't as awesome as the first.

Comedian Mitch Hedberg summed up the diminishing marginal utility of pancakes in one of his one-liners: "You can't be like pancakes – all exciting at first, but by the end, you're {explicit} sick of 'em!"

This tendency for the marginal utility to fall as you consume more of an item is known as the *principle of diminishing marginal utility*. It's a central concept in explaining why the demand curve is downward-sloping: you should only willingly pay a price equal to your marginal satisfaction. If you're sick of the fifth pancake, you obviously wouldn't pay very much for it. That's why the demand curve slopes downward: you might value the first pancake at $2, but you only value that fifth pancake at 14 cents.

This way of reasoning by thinking at the margin became the foundation of a whole new approach to economics. And today it's the basic method taught to economics students. Now, economists don't believe real people take the time to calculate the marginal utility of every decision, but you also make sure you spend your limited money in a way that you're happy with. Marginal utility is a way of making those decisions into a model that is simplified enough to explain and sometimes predict behavior.

Jevons and the marginalists were focused on a consumer's marginal satisfaction and willingness to pay (demand). Adam Smith and the classical economists were primarily concerned with the production side of things (supply). Alfred Marshall put them both together and developed what became known as *neoclassical economics*. Put succinctly, Marshall refurbished classical economics with marginalism.[9] His largest contribution to economics was to combine the classical writers' cost of production theory with the marginalists' demand theory into the famous "Marshallian cross." Today, we call it supply and demand. These now famous graphs appeared in Marshall's 1890 textbook, which modern microeconomics textbooks still rest upon. The basis for neoclassical economics' theory of value was the *equilibrium price* maintained by the forces of supply and demand. This is best understood with the aid of a simple graph.[10]

The market is in equilibrium when the demand for the item exactly equals the supply. In graphical terms, it's where the supply and demand curves intersect. The magic of the equilibrium price is that it is the price level at which firms want to make the same amount of goods that consumers are willing to buy. The market is in equilibrium at $5. At $5, there are 40 willing buyers and 40 willing sellers. It's the intersection of the supply and demand curves.

Market Equilibrium

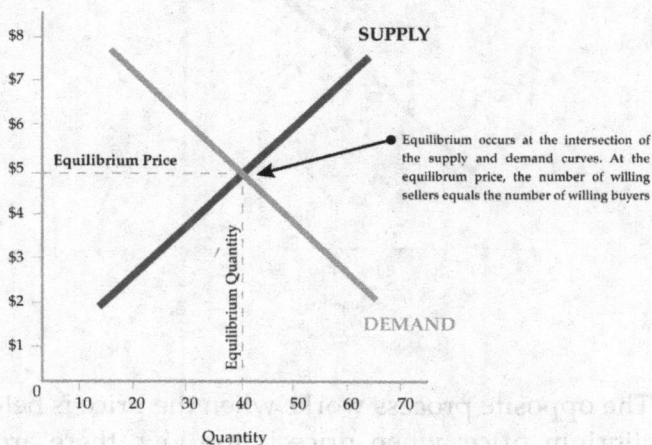

Equilibrium occurs at the intersection of the supply and demand curves. At the equilibrum price, the number of willing sellers equals the number of willing buyers

To see why equilibrium is such a sweet spot, it's helpful to think of situations when the number of buyers and number of sellers are at a mismatch.

If price is higher than the equilibrium price, at $6, the number of sellers exceeds the number of willing buyers.

At this price, there would be a surplus: suppliers are more willing to sell the product than the number of consumers willing to pay for it. In a surplus situation, sellers have an incentive to cut their price to lure in more buyers. As sellers lower the price, it moves back toward the equilibrium price.

Excess Sellers

Quantity Demanded < Quantity Supplied

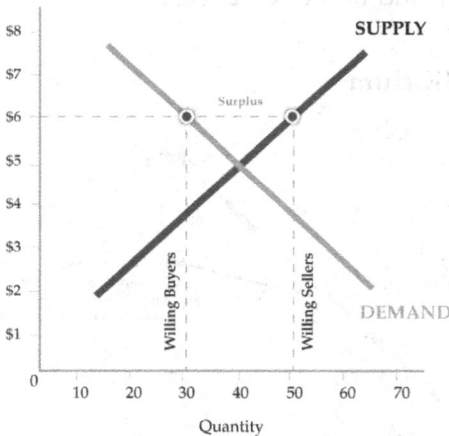

The opposite process works when the price is below the equilibrium price: when price is too low, there are more willing buyers than sellers. This results in a shortage. As buyers are chasing a limited amount of the good, sellers will respond by raising prices. These actions will cause the price to rise, which, in turn, will discourage some buyers. With freely adjusting prices, the market will naturally correct shortages.

Excess Buyers

Quantity Supplied < Quantity Demanded

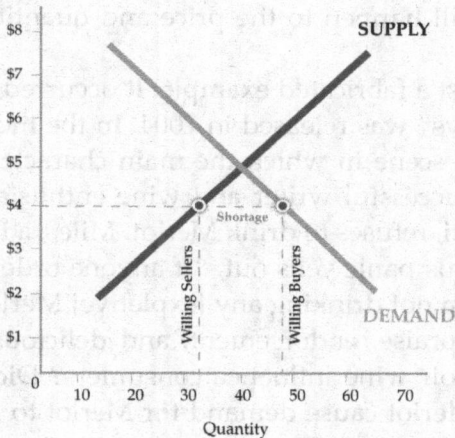

Here is Adam Smith's invisible hand in action. Producers decide how much to make and at what price to sell those items. Consumers will try to buy those items. Sometimes there might be too much of the good supplied if the price is too high, and suppliers will lower the price to encourage more buyers. Sometimes there will be too much of the good demanded if the price is too low, and suppliers will raise the price and consequently discourage more buyers. But over time, these differences will be corrected. The activities of buyers and sellers move the market toward equilibrium. And once equilibrium is reached, there isn't any pressure to change the price.

From equilibrium, we can use this model to predict what will happen when there is a change in either the supply or demand in the market. A quick supply and demand sketch can quickly tell you what will happen with both the price and quantity of a particular item if there is, say, an increase or decrease in demand.

Say, for example, consumers suddenly have an increased desire for Pinot Noir and a sudden decrease in their appeal for Merlot, even though this is not prompted by a change in prices. What will happen to the price and quantity of each type of wine?

This isn't just a fabricated example. It occurred when the movie "Sideways" was released in 2004. In the movie, there is a memorable scene in which the main character Miles, a depressed, unsuccessful writer and wine enthusiast played by Paul Giamatti, refuses to drink Merlot. Miles, a Pinot Noir fan, in an anxious panic yells out, "If anyone orders Merlot, I'm leaving. I am not drinking any {expletive} Merlot."

Did Miles' praise, endorsement, and delicious description of Pinot Noir wine influence consumers? Did his condemnation of Merlot cause demand for Merlot to fall? How did the motion picture influence the price and quantity for both varietals of wine? A quick supply and demand diagram can quickly tell you the market's prediction.

Market for Pinot Noir

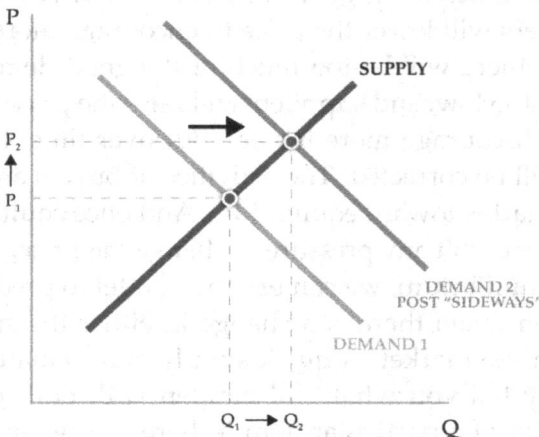

The increase in demand causes the equilibrium price and quantity to rise

An increase in the demand for Pinot Noir should cause both an increase in price and quantity sold.

If the film had altered consumers' wine buying patterns, the changes in the demand curve for Merlot would shift, causing a decrease in the price and quantity of Merlot. Double check yourself with a quick sketch.

Market for Merlot

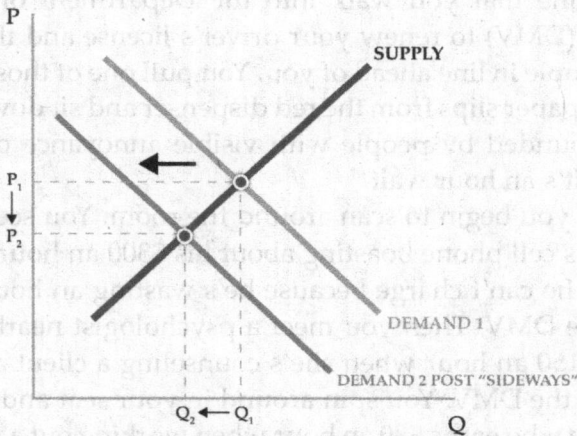

The drop in demand causes the equilibrium price and quantity to fall

A research study looked at wine data from 1999-2008, which coincided with periods before and after the release of the motion picture to see if there was a "Sideways" effect on each wine varietal's price and quantity sold. They found that the "Sideways" effect had a negative impact on Merlot consumption while increasing Pinot Noir demand. The price of Pinot Noir rose, while the price of Merlot fell. The movie also caused a general increase in overall wine consumption.[11]

Opportunity Cost and Comparative Advantage

If Adam Smith gets credit for describing how market forces operate and explaining the theory of self-interest and competition in creating the market mechanism that governs society, then David Ricardo receives the glory in explaining why there's a role for everybody in improving the efficiency of the economy by focusing on their comparative advantages and by using markets to trade.

Imagine that you walk into the Department of Motor Vehicles (DMV) to renew your driver's license and there's a sea of people in line ahead of you. You pull one of those "take a ticket" paper slips from the red dispenser and sit down. You are surrounded by people with visible annoyance on their brows—it's an hour wait.

Then you begin to scan around the room. You see a lawyer on his cell phone boasting about his $300 an hour billing rate that he can't charge because he's wasting an hour waiting at the DMV. Then you meet a psychologist nearby who bills at $150 an hour when she's counseling a client and not sitting at the DMV. You spin around in your seat and meet a masseuse who earns $80 an hour when working out a muscular knot on a client and even a panhandler who can make $10 an hour asking for spare change. All of them are making $0 this hour because they are stuck waiting to get their driver's licenses renewed.

You and the lawyer, psychologist, masseuse, and panhandler must wait an hour to get your paperwork done to legally drive. None of you is better at waiting, that is, no one can "wait faster" than another: it's an hour for everyone. To the person unfamiliar with an economist's way of viewing the world, it might initially seem that no one is better than anyone else in the waiting room at waiting that hour.

But the economist thinks another way. To an economist, the question "Who is the best at waiting the hour?" is quickly translated in their minds into "Who *gives up the least* to wait that hour?"

The economist's understanding of cost compares the alternative opportunities that are sacrificed to make a choice. Economists call what they give up the "opportunity cost" of waiting that hour. The lawyer sacrifices the chance to make $300 during that hour if billing a client instead of waiting. The psychologist gives up $150. But the panhandler only gives up $10 to wait an hour. The panhandler has the lowest opportunity cost. Economists would say that the panhandler has a "comparative advantage" in waiting.

Someone has a comparative advantage in something if they can produce it at a lower cost than others. But having that comparative advantage doesn't mean they are the best at something. Someone can be unskilled at doing something and still have a comparative advantage at it! But focusing on that advantage, that unskilled worker can improve the situation for everyone.

I learned this firsthand as an unskilled undergraduate student who had a role in working with a very skilled economics professor. When I was an undergrad, I worked as a research assistant with Professor Volker. He was digging into longitudinal data to investigate the married-man wage premium to discover the reason why married men make more money than similarly situated single men. Did the higher wage increase marriage chances? Or did getting married spur the men to make more money? What happens first? To answer that question, we needed to track the wages of the same guys over time and see what happened to those wages once they got married. It required a lot of statistical analysis, which in turn needed a bunch of hours of code writing.

Professor Volker could code much better than I could. What took me three hours to create lines of code only took Volker one hour. He was clearly better than me at coding, in fact, three times as good. But that doesn't mean there wasn't a role for me in coding. Even though Professor Volker was better than me at coding do-files to run through the statistical package STATA, I was still valuable to him. *Because it came down to opportunity cost.* I had a much lower opportunity cost to spend my time coding than Volker did. So, I actually had a comparative advantage in coding compared to Professor Volker even though he was better at it in absolute terms. Volker could use that hour that he didn't have to code and do something he was even better at, such as writing research grants or writing the text of the research paper.

Opportunity cost can also explain why college enrollment, particularly two-year degree college enrollment, increases during a recession. The opportunity cost of a college education is the income/wages you could be earning by working instead. As the availability of high paying jobs increases, so does the opportunity cost of going to college.

Consider two scenarios:
- A. The choice between going to college or working after high school for $12 an hour.
- B. The choice between going to college or working after high school for $20 an hour.

Notice the price of college (in terms of explicit dollar cost, i.e., tuition) hasn't changed, but the opportunity cost has. The "what do I give up" has changed with more and better jobs available to high school graduates. During economic downturns, there are fewer high-paying jobs for high school graduates available. This means the opportunity cost of college falls during a recession. Like any good, as it gets cheaper (less costly), we demand more of it. Jobs disappear and college enrollment rises.

Opportunity cost and comparative advantage can also explain other paradoxes. For instance, why do poor countries have more maids and housekeepers than rich countries? If one country has more rich households, shouldn't that country also have more maids and butlers? But, what other jobs are available in that country?

For example, the United States has far fewer domestic servants than India because India has many more low-skilled workers who have fewer job options. A higher opportunity cost means fewer butlers. To say it another way: it's hard to afford a butler who could earn $50 an hour working another job.[12]

Another way of grasping a rather counter-intuitive concept like comparative advantage and opportunity cost is to think about why superheroes shouldn't be rescuing kittens from trees. The superhero has a huge opportunity cost on their time. They could be flying and rescuing people from burning buildings. Instead, the boy/girl scout should be rescuing kittens from trees because while the boy/girl scout doesn't have superpowers, they don't have to give up as much.

But why? If it takes a boy or girl scout 30 minutes to do it, it could take a superhero only 10 seconds. So, shouldn't the superhero rescue the kitten? And the answer is still probably no. And it's all because of what a superhero could do with the extra 10 seconds — what the superhero gives up in that short time. Maybe the superhero could use their super lungs to blow out a fire that will burn down a building. Giving up that opportunity to rescue a kitten from a tree doesn't seem worth it in those types of opportunity cost terms.

Since the superhero can do more in those 10 seconds than the girl scout can in 30 minutes, the girl scout has a comparative advantage in rescuing kittens. It takes the girl scout much longer, but she doesn't have to give up as much! Just because someone is better than another in performing a specific task, it doesn't mean the most efficient person should always do it. It would be best to focus on the comparative advantage. To do so, you *don't compare absolute advantages you instead focus on opportunity costs*.

Trade and Markets

Because of the magic of comparative advantage, everyone stands to gain from trade. Even the most disadvantaged worker has something to offer, in the same way the lowest-skilled panhandler has something valuable to offer.

Pause and think about how this exponentially expands the opportunity and benefits of exchange/trade. You don't have to be the best at anything to gain from specialization and trade. Without trade, what a person consumes is limited to the amounts that an individual can make. Trade expands things, enabling each person to consume more.

This concept is at the heart of economics, and it was David Ricardo who solved a problem that even eluded Adam Smith. Smith addressed the benefits of trade in his opus *The Wealth of Nations (1776)*, writing:

> *If a foreign country can supply us with a commodity cheaper than we ourselves can make it, better buy it of them with some part of the produce of our own industry, employed in a way in which we have some advantage.*[13]

Smith also wrote: "...never attempt to make at home what it will cost him more to make than to buy. The tailor does not attempt to make his own shoes, but buys them of the shoemaker...."

If England can make a good at a lower cost than Portugal and Portugal can make another good at a lower cost than England, clearly it makes sense for each country to trade for the relatively cheaper good. Both countries will gain from trade, and both counties will consume more by specializing in what they do best and then trading. In the same way, the tailor is much better at sewing shirts than the shoemaker. It makes sense for the person who is best at sewing to do the shirt making and the one who is the best cobbler to do the shoe making. Each country/person can consume more as a result of specialization and trade.

Trade is just an indirect way of producing goods for consumption. The notion of roundabout production through trade was the stepping-stone that led to one of the most important ideas in economics: the theory of comparative advantage,[14] a concept for which we give the most credit to David Ricardo. At the age of 27, David Ricardo read and was inspired by Smith's *Wealth of Nations*. Ricardo wrote his first economics article when he was 37. His economic insights came in the time of the English Corn Laws.

The Corn Laws were trade restrictions on imported food and grain enforced in the United Kingdom in the 1800s. The laws made grain grown outside the UK more expensive for its consumers. Their design was to keep grain prices high in favor of those producing home-grown wheat, oats, and barley. So, England's consumers paid higher corn prices because the cheaper imported grain was forbidden or heavily taxed (import duties), while the domestic corn producers made more money. David Ricardo opposed the Corn Laws in favor of free trade.

So, let's take a step back and ask, "What is the difference between Adam Smith's idea of trade and Ricardo's?" Economists today would say it comes down to the difference between "absolute advantage" and "comparative advantage," best grasped through a numerical example.

Consider a subdivision in which each house has a backyard with a space of 100 square feet in which to plant fruits and vegetables. Each neighbor also plants 50 vegetable seedlings each spring. To accomplish their spring planting, each neighbor must till their 100 square feet of soil then plant their 50 sprouts.

First on the block is Doris, who, being very dexterous with a hand trowel, is a good planter. Doris can plant three plants a minute. But her back muscles give her fits. Doris isn't as good at swinging a garden hoe, so tilling up the soil is a slower process for her. Doris can till five square feet of soil per minute.

Next to Doris is Dan, who is the gardening opposite of Doris. Dan's good with a garden hoe; he can till six square feet of soil per minute, but he can only plant two plants per minute.

It takes Dan 41.66 minutes to prepare the soil and plant his garden if he works by himself. It takes Doris 36.66 minutes to till and plant her garden working alone. (See math below).

Smith's Example

Productivity Per Minute

	PLANTS	SOIL TILLING	
DAN	2 Plants	6 sq. ft.	Dan is better than Doris at tilling and Doris is better than Dan at planting
DORIS	3 Plants	5 sq. ft.	

DAN	50 plants/ 2 plants-per-minute	=	25 minutes
	100 sq.ft./ 6 sq.ft.-per-minute	=	16.66 minutes
			41.66 MINUTES TOTAL
DORIS	50 plants/3 plants-per-minute	=	16.66 minutes
	100 sq.ft./ 5 sq.ft.-per-minute	=	20 minutes
			36.66 MINUTES TOTAL

Notice that Doris is better than Dan at planting (three plants per minute instead of two). Dan, however, is better at tilling (six square feet per minute over five square feet per minute). What would happen if each focused on the task s/he is best at and then trade for the other task?

Smith's Example with Specialization and Trade

Productivity Per Minute

	PLANTS	SOIL TILLING	
DAN	2 Plants	6 sq. ft.	By focusing on the task in which they have a comparative advantage, both neighbors finish quicker.
DORIS	3 Plants	5 sq. ft.	

DAN	200 sq.ft./ 6 sq.ft.-per-minute	=	33.33 minutes
			33.33 MINUTES TOTAL
DORIS	100 plants/ 3 plants-per-minute	=	33.33 minutes
			33.33 MINUTES TOTAL

If Dan tills both his plot and his neighbor's soil while Doris focuses on doing all the planting, each neighbor is done in less time than if they'd each tilled and each planted their own garden. Again, the numbers show the benefits of specialization and trade.

But would specialization and trade still work if one neighbor was better than Doris at both tilling and planting?

Let's say over the winter, Dan moves his family back to North Carolina, and a new neighbor moves in next to Doris. His name is Derrick, and he's in great shape. Derrick can plant four plants a minute and till a whopping 10 square feet of soil in a minute. Derrick is better at both planting and tilling than Doris.

If both work by themselves, it takes Derrick 22.5 minutes, and it again takes Doris 36.66 minutes like last year.

Ricardo's Example

Productivity Per Minute

	PLANTS	SOIL-TILLING
DERRICK	4 Plants	10 sq. ft.
DORIS	3 Plants	5 sq. ft.

Derrick is faster
in both
planting and tilling

DERRICK	50 plants/ 4 plants-per-minute	=	12.5 minutes
	100 sq.ft./ 10 sq.ft.-per-minute	=	10 minutes
			22.5 MINUTES TOTAL
DORIS	50 plants/3 plants-per-minute	=	16.66 minutes
	100 sq.ft./ 5 sq.ft.-per-minute	=	20 minutes
			36.66 MINUTES TOTAL

Is there still room for specialization and trade? By Smith's logic, Derrick has nothing to gain from trading with Doris. He's better at both activities, so how could Derrick possibly benefit from trade? *Wouldn't that mean he'd have to trade for a good that he, himself, is already better at producing?* That's seems counterintuitive. But that's the magic that Ricardo demonstrated in 1817.

What happens if each gardener focuses on the task where they have a comparative advantage? Because Derrick is more efficient in both planting and tilling, we say that he has an *absolute advantage* in both tilling and planting. So, at an initial glance, it doesn't seem it would benefit Derrick to trade with someone worse at both tilling and planting. But that's not what's important. We need to look at the opportunity cost between the two. (The same way we looked at the opportunity cost of the panhandler from the DMV at the beginning of the chapter). We need to focus on what each *gives up*.

If Doris spends a minute tilling, she can prepare five square feet of soil. If she used that minute to plant, she'd be able to plant three sprouts. Doris is *relatively better at planting* because she doesn't have *to give up as much soil tilling per plant*. For every seedling she plants, she trades off 1.67 square feet of soil tilling (five square feet per minute/three plants per minute = 1.67). But Derrick must trade off 2.5 square feet of tilling for each plant he puts into the ground (10 square feet per minute/four plants per minute = 2.5). So even if Doris is worse in absolute terms in both tilling and planting, she still has a comparative advantage at planting.

Let's see the math when they each focus on their comparative advantage with Doris doing all the planting and Derrick doing all the tilling.

Ricardo's Example with Specialization and Trade

	Productivity Per Minute		
	PLANTS	SOIL TILLING	
DERRICK	4 Plants	10 sq. ft.	Derrick is faster in both planting and tilling
DORIS	3 Plants	5 sq. ft.	But Doris has a *comparative advantage* in planting because Doris can plant at a lower *opportunity cost*. For every plant she plants she trades off 1.67 square feet of tilling. Derrick must trade off 2.5 square feet of tilling for each plant Derrick puts into ground.

DERRICK	200 sq.ft./ 10 sq.ft.-per-minute	=	20 minutes
			20 MINUTES TOTAL

DORIS	100 plants/ 3 plants-per-minute	=	33.33 minutes
			33.33 MINUTES TOTAL

Notice that Derrick is also better off from specialization and trade, doing all the tilling in 20 minutes instead of tilling and planting his own garden in 22.5 minutes. Doris doesn't need to be better than Derrick at anything for there to be gains from trade. She just needs to focus on her *comparative advantage*. If each focuses on their comparative advantage, they can each get done planting more quickly, i.e., they each gain from trade. An economist would say that Derrick and Doris increased output by specializing, even though Doris was less competent at both tasks.

Here's the power of Ricardo's insight: You don't need to be better than your trading partner at anything to still benefit from trade. The numerical gardening example was hardly different from the example Ricardo wrote about 200 years ago, except he used the example of England and Portugal producing cloth and wine.

Ricardo showed numerically that if England specialized in producing cloth and Portugal produced wine, the total output of both goods could grow. Although inferior in production, this also meant England would benefit from trade because England still had a comparative advantage.

The English political economist Robert Torrens (1780 – 1864) first flirted with the crux of comparative advantage in 1815. He pointed out that trade can still be beneficial between counties even if one country was better at producing every good.[15] David Ricardo put the finishing touches on the theory of comparative advantage and gets most of the credit for fully developing the idea in his book *Principles* with the famous numerical example of cloth and wine traded between England and Portugal. Working through a two-good example between two countries was the best way to prove it.

Ricardo's example was different and more nuanced than Smith's. Instead of assuming, as Adam Smith did, that

England is better at producing one good and Portugal is more productive in the other good, Ricardo started by assuming *Portugal was better at producing both goods*. Based on Adam Smith's thinking, it would appear there was no way trade would work.[16] It initially seems counterintuitive: why would you import a good from another country when you can already produce that good at a lower cost at home? Or conversely, how could a country gain from trade if that country was inferior at making all goods? But trade allows you to focus on the production of a good you're even better at producing.

Here are the big takeaways from the Ricardian model said in several different ways. First, trade boosts welfare. That is, each trading partner gets more than what they could produce on their own. Or in Ricardo's words, trade "increases the amount and variety of the objects on which revenue may be expended." And both parties can benefit from trade even if one trading partner is better at producing everything. The Ricardian framework shows that if we want to maximize total output in the world, then we should have each country focus on its comparative advantage and allow people to trade freely; trade makes the most efficient use of the world's scarce resources. It all comes down to comparative advantage and opportunity cost.

You can also use the concept of opportunity cost and comparative advantage to illustrate why trading could improve the situation at the DMV. The panhandler might not be able to write legal opinions, provide great counseling or give professional massages, but it'd be wrong to say the panhandler didn't have a role in improving the market. What would happen if a "market for waiting" would arise? What if the panhandler offered to wait the hour for the lawyer? There's room here for a mutually beneficial trade.

Say the panhandler offered to wait the hour in line for the lawyer for $50. Wow. That initially seems expensive, but it sounds like a deal if the lawyer could pay $50 to make $300. If the lawyer could bill a client in that extra hour, he'd make $300 for a cost of $50, making him $250 better off. The panhandler would be happy with that transaction as well since the hour wait is only costing him $10 for a chance to make $50 that hour. So, the lawyer pays $50 in cost to get $300 in benefit. The panhandler gives up $10 to make $50. Everyone wins. The transaction would make both parties better off.

And here's another important concept at the center of economic thinking: people weigh costs versus benefits. If the benefits exceed the costs, that action/transaction will improve the person's happiness. To see what I mean, let me ask you this: would you buy a $20 bill for $10? Of course, you'd be $10 better off. But you wouldn't buy a $20 bill for $30; the costs would exceed the benefit. You're implicitly asking yourself, "Will this benefit or cost me?

Everything in economics has a cost and benefit. If attending the new Quentin Tarantino movie at the theater is worth $20 to you in joy, and you only have to pay $10 for the ticket, that transaction is the same as buying a $20 bill for $10. It boosts your welfare. Sellers use the same logic: as long as they can sell an item for a price that's more than it costs to make, the sellers are good with that transaction.

In a free market, consumers don't buy things if they're worth less to them than the price. In the same way, people don't sell items that are worth more to them than the asking price. So, when a transaction occurs, it must involve a willing buyer and seller. It's a mutually beneficial sale. This also means that the sale improves efficiency; it makes both buyer and seller better off (or at least not worse off, and it also doesn't impact a third party). Every transaction makes the trading partners better off.

Those who have an absolute advantage can do even better by zeroing in on those skills they are best at and then buying other goods/services from those who produce them at a comparatively lower cost. That is, the lawyer makes money writing legal briefs and trading for someone to "wait an hour." Likewise, the psychologist specializes in counseling sessions, then uses her income to buy her clothes, skis, and coffee.

In this way, trade is a roundabout way of producing things more efficiently. Trade makes people better off while also making the most efficient use of the world's limited resources. For example, suppose a country is *relatively* better at making cloth. It makes sense to put more resources into fabric and to export some of the material to pay for imports even if that country might be better in absolute terms at making those items.

Think for a second about a world without trade.

Every person in the world would only be able to consume strictly what they, themselves, were able to produce. The psychologist would have to grow her own coffee beans and sew her own clothes and fashion her own skis. That could take weeks. It would be a waste of time that the psychologist could use to do something far more productive. In a world with specialization and trade, the psychologist can make the income in a couple of hours that she can use to buy coffee, clothes, and skis. Think of trade as a magical machine that can convert an hour-long counseling session into clothing or software into wine.

All these welfare-enhancing trades/transactions occur because of the magic of the market and of price equilibrium, with its demand-and-supply curve diagram: the simplest and most widely used tool in microeconomic analysis. It gets used to

- show how price adjustment ensures equilibrium.
- show the impacts of changes in tastes, incomes, technology, input prices and prices of related goods.
- demonstrate how price ceilings and price floors cause shortages and surpluses.
- compare a competitive market to a market dominated by a monopoly.

And, it is used as a quick way to predict the direction of the change in quantity and price when one curve shifts. But how big are those changes when a curve shifts? That question all boils down to how steep each curve is. It's a concept that Alfred Marshall also perfected and added to economic texts called "elasticity," which is the topic of the next chapter.

CHAPTER 2:

How Responsive Are Marijuana Users to Price Changes: Price Elasticity of Demand

In the fall of 2012, the University of Denver campus hosted a presidential debate between the incumbent president, Barack Obama, and rival candidate, Mitt Romney. The presidential debate, however, was only one of the reasons the national news media shifted their eyes to Colorado during a big election year. The other reason involved what was on the bottom of Colorado voters' ballots that fall: Amendment 64, which asked voters whether they wanted to legalize the sale of recreational marijuana.

In the summer of 2012, I had just started working as a research economist for a think-tank in Denver. And one of my first research projects was to answer a policy question: "How much tax revenue would be generated in Colorado if the state legalized recreational marijuana and taxed it?" (A lot of the potential revenue was promised to schools.) The final goal was producing the statistic that went on the Pro-Amendment

64 campaign commercial that ran during the Broncos' football games, the "Yes on 64" TV spot.

The campaign relied heavily on the message that Colorado should legalize recreational marijuana, tax it and use that revenue to pay for schools. So along with B-roll shots of smiling teachers showing geometry to happy children on a chalkboard, there was my statistic: "Marijuana tax revenues post-2017 could top $100 million annually" with a tiny footnote on the screen referencing my study. Vote yes on Amendment 64!

To get to that final figure that went into the campaign commercial, I had to build a model to estimate the total consumption of marijuana in Colorado if it were legalized. Under the legalized scenario, I anticipated that the price of pot would fall from its current street price. The Law of Demand tells us that the quantity demanded changes inversely when the price changes. But how big is that change in consumption?

One of the factors in that model was the responsiveness of marijuana users to pot prices, as well as to changes in availability and legal status. To get to the final statistic that would be used for commercials, I needed to know the *price elasticity of demand* for cannabis.

Price Elasticity of Demand (Ed) = Percentage change in quantity demanded / Percentage change in price

Ed = % change in Qd / % change in P

If a 10% increase in price would cause a 5% reduction in sales, then the elasticity is -0.5.

$$Ed = -5\%/10\% = -0.5$$

Similarly, if the price elasticity of demand is -2.0, then a 10% increase in price would lead to a 20% loss in sales.

- Greater elasticity means that demand for a good or service is more responsive to price changes

- Less elasticity means that demand for a good or service is less responsive to price changes

To calculate price elasticity, then, you need to know how much the quantity demanded will change when the price changes.

Economists further make a distinction between demand curves based on their magnitude of elasticity (which is closely related to the steepness of the demand curve). Demand is inelastic when the elasticity is less than 1 in absolute terms. With inelastic demand, the quantity demanded changes proportionally less than the price changes, that is, consumers are relatively insensitive to price.

Elastic demand is the opposite: with values above 1, the quantity demanded changes proportionally more than price changes, that is, consumers are relatively sensitive to price.

(A quick side note: Because demand curves are downward sloping—the law of demand says there's a negative relationship between price and quantity—price elasticities in theory are always negative. But we often express them in absolute terms, so -0.2 is the same as 0.2).

The premise of my research was simple: figure out how many ounces of cannabis would be consumed in a year if it were legalized and then multiply those ounces by the taxes per ounce.

I started with survey data from the 2010 National Survey on Drug Use and Health to estimate that 12.9% of Colorado adults 21 and older were current marijuana users.[17] By applying that portion to the adult population and then assuming an average of 3.5 ounces would be consumed per year per user, I derived the total number of ounces of cannabis being consumed in Colorado in 2012 before it was legal.

But that amount would change once cannabis was legalized. I had to account for both

- shifts in the cannabis demand curve, due to factors other than price, and
- movement along the cannabis demand curve, due to changes in price.

I expected the demand for marijuana to increase because of factors such as changes in attitudes, preferences, perceived health risks, and the ease with which legalized marijuana would be available: you'd be able to buy it at the store right next to Chipotle instead of in a back alley. These are consumer behavioral changes based on factors irrespective of price that would shift the demand curve. These are known as *exogenous*, or nonprice, effects on consumers' demand.

A Shift in Demand for Marijuana

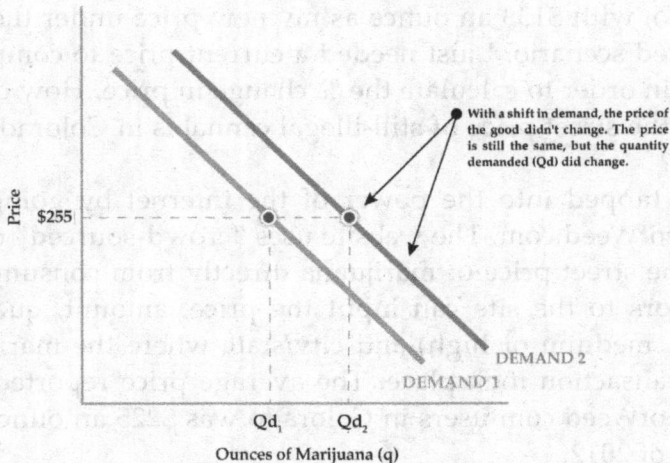

With a shift in demand, the price of the good didn't change. The price is still the same, but the quantity demanded (Qd) did change.

Price

$255

DEMAND 2
DEMAND 1

Qd₁   Qd₂

Ounces of Marijuana (q)

I still had to estimate the change in price and the change in the quantity demanded in order to estimate price elasticity, see how legalization would create movement along the cannabis demand curve, and come up with actual numbers.

First, I estimated the change in price that could be expected, so I had to find the price before and after legalization. I expected that the production cost of marijuana would fall for two reasons.

- Workers would no longer need to be paid a higher premium for performing illegal activity.
- Legalization would permit economies of scale as growers could expand their operations without worrying about attracting police attention.

There would also be some cost increases due to the burden of meeting regulatory requirements. After accounting for growing costs, fees, producer mark-up, retailer mark-up, transportation, distribution costs, and taxes, I estimated that the legalized price of marijuana would be $133 an ounce if Amendment 64 passed.[18]

So, with $133 an ounce as my new price under the legalized scenario, I just needed a current price to compare it to in order to calculate the % change in price. How did I find the street price of still-illegal cannabis in Colorado in 2012?

I tapped into the power of the internet by going to PriceofWeed.com. The website uses "crowd-sourced" data on the street price of marijuana directly from consumers. Visitors to the site can input the price, amount, quality (low, medium or high) and city/state where the marijuana transaction took place. The average price reported by PriceofWeed.com users in Colorado was $225 an ounce in May of 2012.

A Drop in Price of Marijuana

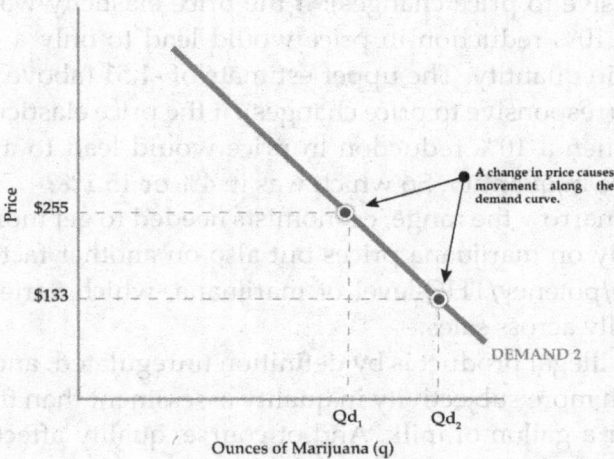

A change in price causes movement along the demand curve.

DEMAND 2

Price

$255

$133

Qd_1 Qd_2

Ounces of Marijuana (q)

A reduction from $225 to $133 would be a 51% drop in price. I could use that to predict how much quantity demanded would change if I knew the price elasticity of demand for marijuana consumers. But what was that elasticity? How sensitive are cannabis users to prices? I began to look at the economic literature to figure that out.

The first paper on the price elasticity of marijuana was published in 1972 when Charles Nisbet and Firouv Vakil sent out mail surveys to college students at UCLA.[19] The data was collected from an anonymous mail questionnaire of 926 UCLA students, who reported how much marijuana they purchased and at what price. They were also asked how much marijuana they would purchase in the future after hypothetical price changes. Nisbet and Vakil concluded that the price elasticity of marijuana was between -0.40 and -1.51.

That's a fairly large range—too large for making good predictions. The lower estimate of -0.40 was inelastic (unresponsive to price changes): if the price elasticity was -0.40 then a 10% reduction in price would lead to only a 4% increase in quantity. The upper estimate of -1.51 (above 1) was elastic (responsive to price changes): if the price elasticity was -1.51, then a 10% reduction in price would lead to a 15.1% increase in quantity. So which was it: 4% or 15.1%?

To narrow the range, economists needed to get more data not only on marijuana prices but also on another factor: the quality/potency/THC-level of marijuana, which varied dramatically across sales.

An illegal product is by definition unregulated, and there is much more subjectivity in quality assessment than there is, say, for a gallon of milk. And of course, quality affects consumers' willingness to pay a price or to even purchase the product.

As more and more studies tried to perfect estimates on marijuana price sensitivity, they began to distinguish between low-quality and high-quality marijuana. But even that wasn't perfect, because it brought in subjective judgment. Some users might report their quality assessment before using it, others reported after they sampled its potency, and still others likely reported their statistics while they were using it.

Fortunately, the power of large samples helps overcome this limitation. Any error caused by each user's subjectivity should be random and therefore shouldn't bias the results if a large enough sample could be obtained. But getting large datasets is tricky. Regrettably, the local drug dealer doesn't keep great records, and even if they did, that data wouldn't be easy to obtain. Estimating the price elasticity of a then-illicit-substance like marijuana is a lot more difficult than, say, estimating the price elasticity for milk, for which data is readily available. (The price elasticity of whole milk in one such study was pegged at -0.43.)[20]

So, who does have the data on drug prices that researchers use to calculate the demand for cannabis? The U.S. Drug Enforcement Administration does. The DEA has data on marijuana prices from the undercover agents and local narcotics officers who buy drugs. Of course, a covert drug enforcement sting's first priority is not collecting the data necessary to build the demand curve for marijuana, its focus is on busting drug dealers—although it would be interesting to picture what economists would have been whispering in the ear of undercover cops on a marijuana bust.

To obtain better data on drug use, researchers turned to the National Household Survey on Drug Abuse and another survey entitled "Monitoring the Future" that asked students in the U.S. their attitudes toward and usage of drugs and alcohol. The surveys typically asked respondents to answer

"Yes, I do consume marijuana" or "No, I do not consume marijuana," and then researchers used statistical techniques to tease out how much price influenced whether those people answered "yes" or "no."

Economists use the term "participation elasticity" to describe this relationship between price and consumption, to differentiate it from price elasticity, which describes the relationship between price and quantity consumed. One study estimated the participation elasticity of annual marijuana participation in the U.S. over the 1980s and 1990s at a range of -0.06 to -0.47, ultimately pinning it down to -0.30.[21] So, a participation elasticity of -0.30 would mean a 10% fall in the price of pot increases *the number of new marijuana consumers* by 3%. (10% multiplied by -0.30 = 3%).

Another paper in 2007 looking at the participation elasticity of marijuana among Australian youth found a participation elasticity between -0.31 and -0.70, with their preferred estimate at -0.50.[22] Such an elasticity meant a 10% fall in the price of marijuana increases the number of people starting to use marijuana by 5%.

But answering the question of how many would consume marijuana is not the same as figuring out *how much would be consumed*. Participation elasticity, looking at the price that attracts new users, is different from price elasticity at different price points. Price elasticity measures the responsiveness of existing users.

Another weakness in using participation elasticity was the fact that the majority of marijuana is consumed by heavy users. For example, Caulkins and Pacula found that 26% of users account for 71% of total purchases of marijuana.[23] Therefore, studies that look only at participation elasticities, which focus on how prices will induce more people to become cannabis users, overlook the price sensitivity of the majority of marijuana buyers.

So, to understand the potential size of the marijuana market in Colorado and the potential tax revenue that could be generated from taxing it, I needed to know how much would be consumed. I needed the conventional price elasticity.

I was heavily influenced by the work of Clements and Zhao whose work on marijuana suggested full demand elasticity of -0.4 for marijuana.[24] In the end, I used a price elasticity of demand of -0.22, which was more inelastic than most studies and was therefore a more conservative estimate. An elasticity of -0.22 meant that the price drop from $225 an ounce to $133 an ounce (a 51% drop in price) would lead to a roughly 11% increase in total marijuana consumption in Colorado. (51% price drop multiplied by -0.22 = 11% increase in Q).

Once I settled on a price elasticity of demand to use in my projections, I was able to estimate how much more marijuana would be consumed once it was legal. All that was left was to multiply that by the taxes per ounce and get that TV commercial made.

And the projections from 2012 that I made with those elasticities baked in (marijuana pun) were close to the actual tax revenue that was collected two years later. I estimated that the excise tax of 15% imposed on the marijuana growers would generate $24.1 million in the first year. In the first state fiscal year, (FY 2014-15, which ran from July to June) Colorado collected $24 million from the excise tax on Colorado marijuana growers, just barely under my estimate.[25] I was sure to mention this in my annual performance evaluation.

Price Elasticity and Total Revenue

If you are not a research economist, you most often want to know price elasticity so you can predict sales numbers based on a price change. You can choose whatever percentage increase in price you want, then multiply it by your elasticity to predict how much sales will change. So, suppose you are wondering what will happen to your sales if you increase the price of the crafts you sell on Etsy by 10%. Now suppose you also know the price elasticity of demand for your crafts is -1.2. Take the 10% price increase and multiply it by -1.2 to predict that sales will fall by 12% (10 × 1.2=12).

Price elasticities can help you predict how sales may rise or fall when you change price. But their powers don't stop there. Price elasticity can also help you answer these two questions: When should you raise your prices to bring in more total revenue? And, when should you lower your prices?

And it all depends on whether your customers are highly responsive to price changes or not very responsive to price changes. That's the same way of saying, it depends whether the demand for your product is *elastic* or *inelastic*.

This was a lesson I had to teach transit advocates in 2015.

In January 2016, the Regional Transit District (RTD) that provides buses and light rail train service for the eight counties around Denver was set to raise its fare prices from $2.25 to $2.60. Anticipating this price increase, a coalition that included advocates for individuals experiencing homelessness, for low-income students, and for people with disabilities wanted to find ways to mitigate the burden of the fare increase on low-income riders. So, they started by hiring an economist to provide the budget analysis and be the "numbers person" for the coalition. I was that economist.

Over the course of several months of meetings in the summer of 2015, I heard many versions of the same recurring statement that went something like, "Why doesn't RTD just lower its fare price? This will lead to so many more riders that

RTD will generate more revenue than before. It'll be good for our clients and good for RTD!"

There's nothing inherently wrong with the logic of that statement. There are cases where dropping prices can lead to more total revenue. Unfortunately, transit is not one of those cases. The net effect of the price change on RTD's revenue all depends on whether transit riders have elastic demand (very responsive to price) or inelastic demand (not very responsive to price).

Remember that price elasticities with values greater than 1.0 (in absolute value) are considered elastic. Price changes cause a greater-than-proportional change in consumption. On the other hand, price elasticities with values less than 1.0 (in absolute value) are labeled inelastic. Changing prices on inelastic goods will lead to a less-than-proportional change in consumption.

The following diagram is a quick math example to show the relationship of total revenue and price elasticity of demand. In both markets, if the price of the good is $7, then 10 items will be bought. In both markets the total revenue is $70 ($7 × 10 = $70).

But now consider what happens when we raise the item's price to $8. In the inelastic case, a dollar price increase only drives away one buyer. In this case, total revenue is ($8 × 9 = $72) which was higher than when we initially priced at $7. Total revenue goes up as price increases if there is inelastic demand for the good.

But look what happens from the same dollar increase in a more elastic market. At $8, only five consumers buy the item. Total revenue in the market with elastic demand ($8 × 5 = $40) has gone way down.

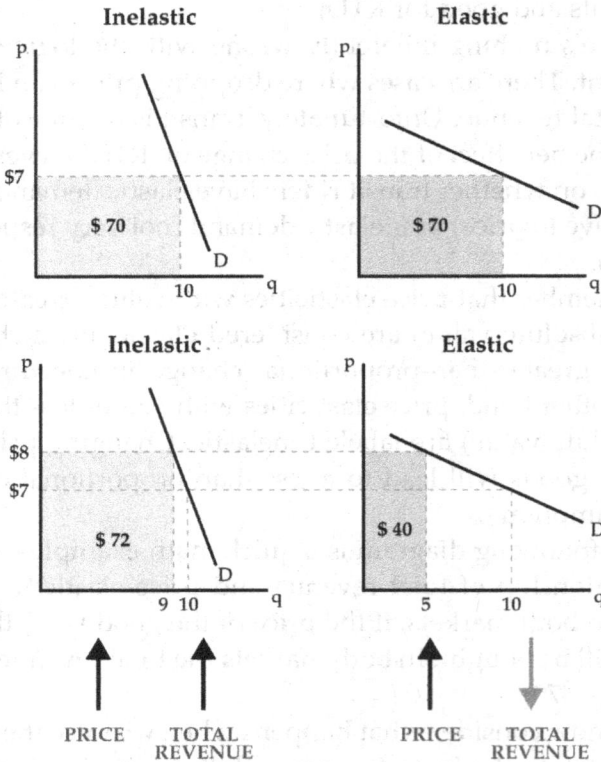

Inelastic

$7

$ 70

10 q

Elastic

$ 70

10 q

D

Inelastic

$8

$7

$ 72

9 10 q

D

Elastic

$ 40

5   10 q

D

PRICE   TOTAL
REVENUE

PRICE   TOTAL
REVENUE

And that's the big punchline:

- *if you are faced with elastic demand, you want to lower prices to increase total revenue.*
- *If you are faced with inelastic demand, you need to raise prices to increase total revenue.*

Returning to our transit example, the only way that decreasing prices would lead to an increase in total revenue for the Regional Transportation District in Denver would be if transit riders had a price elasticity that was *elastic* (i.e., greater than 1). If transit riders are very responsive to price, then a small drop in fare prices will lead to a great increase in ridership. If this were the case, the loss in revenue from lowering prices would be more than made up for by a big increase in fare sales. But this isn't the case.

I had to burst the advocates' bubble. Overall, transit elasticities are inelastic, generally between the range of -0.2 and -0.4. There was no way that decreasing the price of bus and train tickets would increase total revenue for RTD. Using a transit elasticity of -0.4, a 10% drop in fare price would only mean a 4% increase in ridership. The loss in revenue resulting from a 10% drop in price outweighs the additional fares brought in by the increase ridership of only 4%, so total fare revenue goes down.

So RTD would need to raise their fare price to generate more revenue. How would that impact certain types of riders? Well it depends how elastic their demand is.

To see what I mean, think about the *determinants of price elasticity of demand*, which are the factors that influence the magnitude of change in quantity demanded in response to a price change. The determinants of price elasticity of demand are factors that make shoppers more or less responsive to prices.

Most of the variation in the price elasticity of demand boils down to three questions:

1) Are there other close (in proximity and in approximation) substitutes available for that good or service?
2) What proportion of a consumer's income is spent on the good or service?
3) How much time has passed since the price change?

Goods with close substitutes have more elastic demands when prices of these goods go up, a consumer can easily find other options. Goods that don't have close substitutes, or where their substitutes aren't readily available, tend to have inelastic demands. You can see this by looking at ski rental prices at large ski resorts compared to small ski resorts.

In Steamboat Springs, Colorado, famous for its trademark "champagne powder" snow, there are more than a dozen different ski rental shops in town. And many of those ski shops are right at the base of the mountain next to the chairlifts. All ski and snowboard rental shops charge almost the same price for their rental gear. Why?

If Christy Sports charges $7 more per day for the intermediate ski rental, it only takes a skier a minute to walk to Terry Sports to buy a rental package from them. If Terry Sports is too expensive, then you leave and go to Powder Pursuits, another rental shop (another substitute). The demand for rentals at Christy's is fairly elastic because rental shoppers have many options. Christy Sports, with many competitor firms in walking distance, doesn't have much room to raise its rental prices. The demand curve for a good with many substitutes will be flatter than the demand curve for a good that has few substitutes.

Now compare Steamboat Springs to a small mountain resort like Monarch, which only has one ski rental at the base of the ski mountain. Sure, there are other options; Mt. Shavano Ski and Snowboard shop is 11 miles down the road from the ski base and Salida Mountain Sports is 22 miles back down Highway U.S. 50.

But if you already bought your lift ticket to ski Monarch and you realize that the ski rentals are $7 more expensive at the Monarch base than you thought, are you really going to drive 30 minutes round trip to get your ski rentals at another shop? No, and especially not if there's fresh powder! The demand for rentals at Monarch tends to be more inelastic than that of Steamboat. Skiers and snowboarders aren't going to drastically change the magnitude of their quantity demanded due to the lack of a nearby substitute. The rental company at Monarch can raise prices without fear of losing too many equipment renters.

The availability of substitutes also helps explain why popcorn at movie theaters is so expensive: there are no other nearby popcorn vendor options.

It also explains why the price elasticity of gasoline is inelastic: you can't put orange juice in your car and expect it to run — there just aren't too many substitutes for gas. Now, there are substitutes for driving a personal car, like public transportation, but that is dependent on these options being available in your area.

Because of the limited availability of substitutes, drivers are not very responsive to changes in price at the pump. The current price elasticity of gasoline is estimated to be in the range of -0.02 and -0.04. This means a 25 percent to 50 percent increase in the price of gas only decreases automobile travel by 1 percent.[26]

The second major determinant of price elasticity of demand is the proportion of your income you spend on a good.

After my lecture one morning I stopped by the gas station to grab a pack of gum. I noticed the pack of gum was $1.20, 20 cents more than earlier that year — a 20% increase in price! But did I care? Did I change my consumption because of that 20 percent price hike? Heck no. The pack of gum was such a small part of my overall budget that I continued to consume the same amount, even after the price increase. I wasn't responsive at all to the price change.

Compare the way I reacted to a change in gum prices to how I reacted when I learned my heating bill was increasing by 20 percent per month. My $200 a month heating bill is a much bigger portion of my budget. A 20 percent increase in my heating costs induced me to change my actions. I set the temperature of the house a few degrees lower, and I decided to wear sweatshirts more often at home. Consumers are more responsive to price changes on goods that are a larger part of their budget.

The third major determinant of price elasticity of demand is time frame. For many items, the more time people have to adapt to new prices, the more responsive they are.

For example, a commuter paying for parking downtown who realizes the daily parking rate just went up $6 a day can't suddenly decide not to pay for parking at 7:50 a.m. —10 minutes before they need to be at the office. They are stuck paying the extra parking price. But once the weekend comes, the commuter has time to get on Craigslist and buy a used road bike as a cheap alternative to driving and paying for parking. Given some time, the commuter can plan and implement some changes in how they consume. This also explains why the short-run demand curves for transit tend to be more inelastic (less responsive) than long-run demand curves for public transit. Individuals have greater constraints on their ability to alter behavior in the short run, and it takes some time for them to be aware of the price change and adjust accordingly.

Now back to Denver's transit fare change in 2015.

Transit elasticities differ depending on factors like type of transit rider, trip type, time of day, and general geography. Any differences in elasticities can be explained by the availability of substitutes, timing, or income.

Let's look first at the difference between *transit-dependent riders* and *choice riders*. Transit-dependent crowds tend to be nondrivers, people with disabilities, elderly people, and kids. Transit-dependent riders can't easily access other modes of transportation—they have no substitute—and thus, these riders must rely on the bus or train regardless of the price. Choice riders, on the other hand, have other options available for transportation, such as biking or driving their own cars.

To use the economist's language, choice riders have more *available substitutes* when it comes to transportation. The price elasticity of goods with a variety of substitutes tends to be more elastic; hence choice riders have more elastic demand. This also means that transit-dependent riders have more inelastic demand, which means they'll continue to purchase the bus fare even at a higher cost.

The population of riders who are most impacted by fare increases are the ones who can't easily find other alternatives. Transit-dependent riders who lack substitutes are the most impacted by an increase in price.

This is a good time to note that having *more elastic* demand is not the same as having a demand elasticity > 1. For example, transit riders traveling during off-peak times tend to be more price responsive than on-peak riders. Peak hours are generally between 6 a.m. to 9 a.m. and 3 p.m. to 6 p.m. The average fare elasticity of off-peak travel in one study was

-0.42 compared to on-peak of -0.23.[27] Both elasticities are less than 1 (in absolute value), so both are inelastic. In both cases, an increase in price would lead to an increase in total revenue. Yet peak-transit users' demand is still *more inelastic* than off-peak riders' demand.

Even less responsive to price than on-peak-transit-riders are disabled riders. A study of transit ridership in Sacramento, California, concluded that the fare price elasticity of disabled riders was -0.161.[28]

People's elasticity for transit varies based on a number of other factors related to timing, income, and overall substitutes. Transit riders on shopping trips tend to be more responsive to price than riders traveling for work. Riders aged 17-64 are more responsive than riders over 64. Leisure trips have more elastic demand than work trips. Riders on short bus trips are much more responsive to price than riders on long trips. For example, trips under one mile had a demand elasticity of -0.55, while for trips over three miles, the demand elasticity dropped to -0.29[29]

Elasticities are Not Only for Price

Economists can use elasticities to measure the proportional change in any one variable relative to its impact on another variable. These other elasticities help transportation planners to answer a wide range of questions like:

- Will changes in public transit service lessen the amount of vehicle traffic and emissions of private automobiles?
- How will higher taxes on automobile fuel impact vehicle miles traveled and pollution?
- How do bike prices influence car commuters?
- What do parking fees and toll roads do to bus ridership?

Notice that we are not talking about the relationship between the price of the bus ticket and bus ridership, we are examining the relationship between the price of parking for private automobiles and bus ridership. For example, if increasing parking costs by 10% led to a 3% increase in the transit demand, then the cross-price elasticity between parking and transit ridership would be -0.3.

Cross-Price Elasticity of Demand (Ed) = Percentage change in quantity demanded of good A / Percentage change in price of good B
Cross-Price Ed = % change in Qd_A / % change in P_B

Cross-Price Elasticity works just like Price Elasticity, except it denotes the proportional relationship between the price change of one item and the consumption of another good.

The relationship between fare price and transit consumption isn't the only relationship that transit planners are interested in. Many factors other than price influence ridership decisions. To understand those dynamics, we need to look at cross-price elasticities with factors other than price.

With transit, wait time, which represents an added cost to consumers, is one of the bigger factors.

Let's say you live in the foothills about 18 miles southwest of Denver. Your office is located in downtown Denver, and your commute via public transportation takes about 55 minutes. That commute requires you to transfer buses. The wait time between buses each day is normally five minutes. Then you learn that, due to a new bus route, your wait time to transfer buses will be 15 minutes instead of five. Will you still continue to ride public transportation to work? How you change your consumption of transit in response to journey time can be captured by journey-time elasticities. Journey-time elasticities denote the proportional change in demand for proportional change in some time measurement.

An analysis of transit riders in the Seattle area showed that transit riders were more sensitive to changes in travel time than to the costs of transit fares.[30] Findings like this suggest to city planners that growth in transit use, and a decrease in pollution from automobiles, could be achieved through more competitive travel times on buses, trains, and ferries.

The Department of Transportation in the United Kingdom provides guidance documents that give advice on calculating a cost-benefit analysis for transport projects.[31] These documents help transportation planners forecast the potential costs and calculate the direct impacts on transportation users. If we put another lane on this road, how much will traffic increase? If we add an extra bus that runs every 10 minutes instead of every 20 minutes, how will that boost ridership?

To answer those questions, you should base your forecast on past rider experiences, which are synthesized down into elasticities.

For example, the guidance for travel time elasticity of demand for transit is -0.58. That means a 10% decrease in journey-time would lead to a 5.8% increase in transit ridership. The faster the trip, the more likely you are to ride transit. Notice the inverse relationship between time and transit ridership. That's reflected in the negative sign of the journey-time-elasticity of demand for transit. As travel time goes down, ridership goes up.

These elasticities can get even more detailed. Is the time spent on the bus different from the time spent waiting at the bus station? How about the time it takes you to walk to the station? This is why more and more research papers are looking at the difference in transit user behavior between wait time, headway time and walking time. All of those are a component of the journey-time elasticity or what transit researchers call Generalized Journey Time Elasticities (GJT). More and more studies are getting better at calculating the elasticity of wait time[32].

A rule of thumb in transit wait time literature is that passengers value wait time approximately twice as much as in-vehicle time.[33] This means reducing time spent waiting at the bus station will deliver a bigger response in ridership than reducing the same time spent on the bus/train actually moving. If they have to wait, people prefer it if they are moving towards their destination. Of course, that might be a little different in Colorado if transit riders are mixing some cannabis with their coming bus.

CHAPTER 3:

Jam Jars, Ikea Boxes, Odysseus and a Hard-of-Hearing Salesman: Behavioral Economics

If you happened to be in the market for a new outfit and stumbled into the Drubeck Brothers Clothing Shop in the 1930s, you'd be the subject of multiple sales ploys aimed at convincing you to buy an expensive suit—and you'd leave the store feeling good about it. Why? Because those Drubeck brothers knew a thing or two about consumer psychology.[34]

Whenever the salesman, Sid, had a new customer trying on new suits, Sid would claim to have a hearing problem and request the customer speak louder. "What was that? You'll have to speak up," Sid would say as he fitted a custom wool suit on his customer in front of the three-sided mirror. Sid would give the suit-seeker a number of options on thread, buttons, and hem design, all the while feigning that he was losing his hearing.

Once the customer found a suit he liked and had tried it on, Sid would call to his brother, "Hey Harry, how much for this suit?" Looking up from the task he was working on, Harry would call back, "For that great wool suit? $42." Sid, pretending not to hear would cup his hand over his ear to hear better and ask again, "Hey Harry how much for the custom wool suit again?" Once again, Harry would reply "$42."

Sheepish about his poor hearing, Sid would turn to the costumer and report, "Harry says it's $22." Having deceptively anchored the price of $42 in the mind of the shopper, many shoppers were quite motivated to buy the $22 suit and get out of there before the other brother noticed the "error"!

Harry and Sid knew the power of relative pricing. The brothers' tactics rely on many of the principals, biases, and mental quirks that would be studied by behavioral economists several decades later.

You see, Sid and Harry knew that most people like the feeling of getting a bargain (transactional utility), but determining that bargain requires a comparison to another figure (anchoring, framing, priming). As clothing salesmen, they knew that getting the customer to try on the suit gave them a better chance of making a sale (endowment effect and loss aversion). They knew that they'd boost their sales if their customers had at least a small role in the creation and customization of their suit (IKEA Effect), but they also were cognizant not to bombard their clients with so many choices that they might risk anxiety and regret in not making the best choice (decision paralysis). They might even throw in a free belt with the purchase of a new suit (power of free).

But none of the Drubeck Brothers' sales tricks would work on the type of people or rational agents assumed by Standard Economic Theory. This is because Standard Economic Theory starts with these specific assumptions about human behavior: agents in the models have well-defined preferences, they make optimal choices based on these preferences, which implies they have perfect cognitive capacities and willpower. The agent's primary motivation is self-interest. These assumptions define the type of agent assumed in traditional economics' model: *"Homo economicus."* Assuming this type of person in their models helped economists provide a framework for modeling human behavior.

Homo economicus wouldn't be influenced by the Drubeck Brothers' hard-of-hearing shtick. *Homo economicus,* who is completely rational, selfish, and can readily and effortlessly solve difficult optimization problems (making best choices based on available budget)[35], would intrinsically know the costs and benefits of the suit. The idea of "getting a great deal" wouldn't factor in. Nor would *Homo economicus* value the suit more once they try it on.

Yet actual human beings are influenced by marketing gimmicks and sales tricks all the time. The discipline that tries to incorporate some of these mental quirks is called Behavioral Economics, and it purports that we are far less rational than traditional economic models suggest. Behavioral economics says people don't make decisions in a vacuum. They are influenced by all sorts of ambient forces.

The goal of this chapter to is extrapolate the findings from behavioral economics (basically psychology plus economics) to other contexts in our daily lives. The chapter should help you begin rethinking what leads people to make the decisions they do. At the end of the chapter, you'll be more aware of those mental quirks to influence how you make decisions and maybe pick up some tricks of your own to make better decisions, or perhaps become more aware of others using your own mental foibles against you. And you'll soon discover how many of the Drubeck Brothers techniques show up in your daily life.

What is Behavioral Economics?

Behavioral Economics explains the world through grounding its reasoning in empirical hypotheses about human acts, rather than making deductions from assumptions made about rational choice. In other words, Behavioral Economics begins with collecting facts then moves to theory, whereas traditional economics starts with the axiom that people are completely rational and then builds from that point.

Behavioral Economics attempts to introduce into economics the theoretical and methodological approaches of psychology and sociology. Consequently, Behavioral Economics benefits from being able to test its predictions either with laboratory or field experiments. Experiments help isolate the forces that shape our decisions, and extrapolating from those findings allows us to improve our lives. In this way, Behavioral Economics offers a set of tools to assist people in making wiser decisions.

Dan Ariely says behavioral economics is about "figuring out the hidden forces that shape our decisions, across many different domains, and finding solutions to common problems that affect our personal, business, and public lives."[36]

Behavioral Economics research shows that the methods we use to make choices are not as simple or as single-minded as the classical economists assume. Unlike traditional economic theory, Behavioral Economics doesn't assume that people are sensible and calculating robots. Instead, actual humans make choices because of habits: we think automatically, and we sometimes even avoid making choices altogether because it causes us stress. Humans rely on mental shortcuts or rules of thumb in making decisions. Behavioral Economics works to identify the irrelevancies that influence people's decisions that wouldn't sway the type of rational agent assumed in traditional economic models. As Nobel Prize winner Richard Thaler puts it bluntly: people are dumber and nicer than neoclassical economics assumes.

Economic Theory's Detour around Psychology

Most of the ideas in behavioral economics aren't new, they have just been ignored during neoclassical theory's century-long detour. In Adam Smith's day, economics and psychology were branches of the same subject: moral philosophy. In *The Theory of Moral Sentiments*, Smith discusses how humans make decisions from two realms: one of emotion that involves fear, anger, and love and another involving reason. In the same work, Smith even wrote about loss aversion (arguably the flagship concept of behavioral economics) in 1759 saying "pain is, in almost all cases, a more pungent sensation than the opposite and corresponding pleasure. The one almost always depressed us much more below the ordinary, or what may be called the natural state of our happiness, than the other ever raises us above it."

The neoclassical economists of the 20th century made a break with psychology compared to the moral philosophers and economists that came before them. It was after World War II that economists began intensive focus on *Homo Economicus* with all its calculating rationality.

During this time, economists increasingly adopted a mathematically inspired description of the world. And you can't blame them. Statistics, mathematicians, physicists, and economists played an unprecedented role in the Allied effort during World War II. Their tools had many war-time uses, like routing ships across the ocean and cracking the German codes. After the war, the momentum carried over with the hope that the logical, statistical, and mathematical approach would transform other fields as well. And at that time, psychology didn't have the scientific rigor it does today. Between 1940 and 1980, the main lines of development in economic theory attempted to build on the mathematic approach and extend the scope of the rationality-based model.[37] However, not everyone fully accepted the deductive reasoning that laid the foundation for what economists dubbed "rational choice."

Herbert Simon, who won a Nobel Prize in Economics in 1978, was one of the early critics of people's information-calculating abilities. He suggested the term "bounded rationality" to portray a human's problem-solving ability. Instead of the robot brain of *Homo economicus* with perfect foresight, complete information, and the wherewithal to solve complex optimization problems, Simon thought that people might rely on rules-of-thumb in making decisions rather than trying to accurately calculate the best choice.

Simon suggested that the perfect rationality assumption of *Homo Economicus* be amended for cognitively limited agents: " . . . the task is to replace the global rationality of economic man with the kind of rational behavior that is compatible with the access to information and the computational capacities that are actually possessed by organisms, including man, in the kinds of environments in which such organisms exist."[38]

Said another way, humans can't spend all day collecting the information necessary to make the decision on whether to buy "cage-free" eggs or not. We make choices that are satisfactory instead of optimal. That work opened up several lines of inquiry in economics to try to answer the questions:

- "How do humans actually make decisions?"
- "How do we amend traditional economic theories of rationality to incorporate those findings?"

But at this point, the evidence about how people make decisions wasn't quite there, though it was growing. However, any momentum that existed against theories of rational choice was swiftly halted by Milton Friedman's "as if" argument.

In a 1953 essay, Friedman used an excellent analogy to brush aside questions about the realism of rational choice's assumptions.[39] The analogy involved billiards players making pool shots. Those pool players don't have advanced degrees in mathematics and aren't solving complex multi-variate calculus problems based on Newtonian physics. Nevertheless, Friedman argued, even though they don't set up equations each time they take a shot, they act *as if* they do, so it should be fine to make predictions about their behavior as if they do.

Friedman argued that all behavior can be modeled as if decision-makers were solving complex optimization problems. In other words, even if those neoclassical economic assumptions weren't realistic, they are still good as long as they actually predict behavior. The brilliant economist and communicator Milton Friedman basically used the billiards analogy and two words "as if" to end the debate about the realism of assumptions in economics, at least, for 30 years.

Another line of defense in guarding economic theory's assumptions was the "errors are randomly distributed with mean zero" argument,[40] which essentially said, "Sure, people don't make every decision like an expert, but their small errors will wash out in the aggregate." So, for example, if Thomas's prediction is 5% too high and Amanda's is 5% too low, they will cancel out, leaving the model unbiased on average. Thus, not everybody has to make perfect calculations, but in a free market, rational behavior would prevail.[41] Deviations from that theory are just short-lived errors.

To be like *Homo economicus,* you don't have to make perfect forecasts, but they should be unbiased. In other words, *Homo economicus's* forecasts can be wrong, but they can't be continuously wrong in a predictable direction. The psychologists began to show that humans are continuously wrong in a predictable direction. Said another way, Thomas was always 3% too high and so was Amanda. Their errors don't cancel out in the aggregate.

Behavioral Economics in that sense tries to understand how people are predictably biased in their choices/judgment. If humans are using rules-of-thumb in their decision process—and there are biases associated with those rules-of-thumb—then they can lead to systematic biases that won't cancel out in aggregate.[42] Basically, behavioral economics wanted to amend rational choice theory to include Thomas and Amanda's predictable 3% error. They wanted to augment the rational choice model with additional descriptive theories derived from data (about people's decision-making quirks) rather than axioms.[43]

The earlier behavioral economists began collecting examples of behavior that seemed to violate economic theory's rationality model. Richard Thaler, who would win the Nobel Prize in 2017, spent much of his early career cataloguing examples when people around him violated standard economic behavior. Thaler called them "supposedly irrelevant factors," which he purported are actually quite influential in practice.

So, he collected stories of the ways actual people act differently than the calculating and rational creature assumed by economic models.

In his 2015 book *Misbehaving*, Thaler gave the example of his students getting graded out of a total of 100 points or out of a total of 137 points.[44] He noticed his students would often complain if they got a 72 (out of 100 possible points) but they hardly grumbled when they got a 96 (out of 137 possible points). If you pause to calculate that in percentage terms, 96 divided by 137 is a 70% — a worse grade than a 72%. But 96/137 isn't as easy to calculate without a calculator as 72/100. Richard Thaler's column "Anomalies," which started in 1987 in the *Journal of Economic Perspectives*, gets a lot of credit for introducing the economics profession to the field of behavioral economics.[45]

Early papers around behavioral economics established the tone or recipe that many future behavioral economic articles would emulate:[46]

- identify an assumption about behavior used by economists.
- show anomalies or evidence of the violation of that assumption.
- use that evidence to create alternative theories or modifications to the existing models.

What follows is a collection of some of the most influential examples of this playbook, many of which the Drubeck Brothers already knew.

Transactional Utility

Suppose you are craving a soda at the airport. After a three-hour, stuffy, packed plane ride, the benefit of the Diet Cherry Coke's cold, fizzy, and refreshing caffeine injection is well greater than the airport's $4 price. You figure you value that bottle of pop at $7. So, rationally, buying it would improve your happiness: like paying $4 to acquire $7. But you also dislike the idea of getting ripped off.

Instead of buying that soda, you tell yourself, "That's too much. I'm used to paying $2 for that same bottle of Diet Coke." The $4 soda bottle creates negative *transactional utility* because you know $4 is much higher than the reference price---the price you are used to paying. And caring about that difference violates rational choice theory. *Homo economicus* doesn't care about the perceived value of the deal, but humans do.

Transactional utility was developed by Nobel Prize winner Richard Thaler to describe the difference between the actual price and the price you expected to pay. The term describes the happiness that someone gets from a perceived deal or bargain. Thaler makes a distinction between Transactional Utility and Acquisition Utility. The latter is the pleasure from obtaining the product, while transactional utility denominates the value we get from the deal.

If we value an item at $15 but expect to pay $10 for it, and the store is selling it for $10, it's rational for us to buy it. We get $5 worth of acquisition utility (or consumer surplus in standard economic theory terms), but since we expected to pay $10, and we paid $10, we get no transactional utility.

Because humans think that way, sellers have an incentive to sway the perceived reference price to further fabricate the illusion of a "deal." The "my-hearing-ain't-so-good" scam swayed what price the customer expected to pay for a Drubeck Brothers suit so the customer would gain transaction utility: paying $22 for a suit they thought should cost $42.

The idea of transactional utility started with beer on a beach, as Thaler asked people how much they'd be willing to pay for a cold beer. Experiment participants saw one of two versions of the following question. Most of the text was the same except the location at which the beer would be purchased: either a resort hotel or shabby grocery store.

You are lying on the beach on a hot day. All you have to drink is ice water. For the last hour, you have been thinking about how much you would enjoy a nice cold bottle of your favorite brand of beer. A companion gets up to go make a phone call and offers to bring back a beer from the only nearby place where beer is sold (a fancy resort hotel's bar/a small, run-down grocery store).

He says that the beer might be expensive and so asks how much you are willing to pay for the beer. He says that he will buy the beer if it costs as much or less than the price you state. But if it costs more than the price you state he will not buy it. You trust your friend, and there is no possibility of bargaining with (the bartender/store owner). What price do you tell him? [47]

There isn't a difference between a beer that's bought from a run-down grocery store or a fancy resort bar. Standard economic theory says the price we are willing to pay for that beer should be the same, independent of its purchase location. Also, since you can't negotiate down the price, there is no incentive to disguise your actual willingness to pay. But that wasn't the case in Thaler's experiment. Since people expect prices at a resort to be much higher than at a rundown gas station, they don't feel ripped off paying the higher price at the resort's bar (though they may be annoyed by it). But they do feel like paying the same price for the same beer to a shabby grocery store owner is a swindle.

Participants in this survey were willing to pay more for beer from a fancy resort than from a grocery store: the median responses were $8.11 at resort and $4.59 at grocery in 2021-inflation-adjusted dollars. The big takeaway was that participants were willing to pay different prices for the same beer consumed at the same beach depending on where the beer was bought. *Homo economicus* would only care about acquisition utility and the purchase location would be irrelevant, but *Homo Sapiens* take into account the transactional utility as well — paying eight bucks for a beer from a dumpy store just doesn't seem right.

Anchoring, Priming, and Relative Prices

Do you intrinsically know what an ultralight backpacking tent is worth? Or do you first see what the generic brand costs, then calculate how much you'd spend to upgrade to a lighter (and much more expensive) tent? It's all about the contrast. By itself nothing is cheap or expensive: it's only when it's compared to something else that we make these determinations. And the price of that generic model you first see can have a lot more influence on you than you'd suspect.

The rational economic agent intrinsically knows the exact value of every item. Ambient products don't influence *Homo economicus*. But humans' willingness to pay for items can be manipulated by neighboring items and prices. And when we don't know that intrinsic value of a new item, we can be heavily manipulated by the initial *anchor*. This is because we aren't completely-calculating robots and don't do a good job thinking in absolute terms. We don't have internal value mechanism in our bodies that tells us exactly what everything is worth to us. We compare one item to another. I didn't know how much a 15-ounce ultra-light backpacking single pole tent would cost me, but I did know that my current three-pound REI tent cost $220. So, I figured the ultra-light tent must be more than $220. I was shocked to learn that that 15-ounce tent cost $615! In my tent shopping, I used a method called "anchoring and adjustment."

To understand what that is, consider this question: what year did George Washington became the first president of the United States?[48] You might not know the year off the top of your head, but you probably know that the Declaration of Independence was signed in 1776. So, you figure Washington must have been elected a few years after 1776. You start with 1776 as your anchor, then make adjustments by adding a few years to your estimate. (Washington was sworn into office in 1789, by the way).

In an often-cited example, two psychologists asked people to estimate what portion of the United Nations were countries from Africa. But before the experiment subjects could answer, a roulette wheel was spun in their view with figures between 0 and 100. The subjects were then asked if their answer about African United Nation members was higher or lower than the roulette wheel's figure. The results showed that people's estimates were heavily influenced by the arbitrary number that the roulette wheel landed on. When the roulette ball landed on 10, the median estimate was 25%. When the roulette ball stopped on 65, the median answer was 45%. Even if you know nothing about global politics, you should know that a roulette wheel's random number has nothing to do with the number of African members of the UN. Yet the data showed the roulette wheel had a big influence on people's judgment.[49]

Consider another experiment with anchoring. Estimate in your mind what 8 x 7 x 6 x 5 x 4 x 3 x 2 x 1 equals. What's your guess?

Whatever you thought, it's very likely it would be higher than if I asked you to estimate in your mind what 1 x 2 x 3 x

4 x 5 x 6 x 7 x 8 equals. They both equal 40,320. But since the first sequence starts with the big numbers---anchoring them in—people estimate the product of the first sequence higher than the second.

Anchoring experiments show that the first perception tends to linger in a buyer's mind, and that later affects their decisions. In one example, students paid more for items based upon an arbitrary auction using the last few numbers of their Social Security numbers as their anchor. That is, the arbitrary anchor of writing down a part of their Social Security numbers influenced how much they valued wine.[50] Those who had higher Social Security numbers were willing to pay much more for wine than those with lower Social Security numbers. Students with Social Security numbers in the bottom 20% of the distribution priced a bottle of wine at $8.64 on average, while those students with Social Security numbers in the top 20% said they valued that same bottle of wine at $27.91.

The listing price of a house for sale can act as an anchor. So can the initial offer thrown out in a negotiation. The suggestion of an anchor can also have a "priming" effect. Priming refers to how thoughts, emotions, and acts make further thoughts, emotions, and acts more readily accessible.[51]

If the Drubeck brothers purposely threw out luxury sounding words like "artisan fabric" and "Parisian Silk" when describing their fancy suits, they'd be tapping into priming. They'd also take advantage of anchoring and relative pricing. If a customer walked into the Drubeck clothing stores and told Harry they were looking for a suit and a sweater, which item do you think Harry would show first: the expensive suit or the cheaper-priced sweater?

If Harry and Sid want to increase the chances of selling both a suit and sweater; they'd want to lead with the suit.

Clothing store workers are taught to show the more expensive item first because once they've anchored the high price with a $500 suit, then the $150 sweater doesn't seem too bad. Studies show that a guy buying a suit will usually pay more for whatever accessories he purchases, like belts or shoes or cufflinks, if he buys them after getting the suit.[52]

Likewise, adding an expensive item to the menu will increase the sales of the then second-highest-priced item. That is, the $35 burger sounds a lot more reasonable next to the $55 steak on the menu, but that same $35 burger seems pricier if it is the most expensive item on the list. Marketers know this, which is why they often add a decoy item on the menu to sway your selection. The decoy option might be completely inferior to the other choices and may never get selected, but it is solely there to manipulate your judgment.

Dan Ariely writes about an often-recounted example of subscriptions to the *Economist* magazine.[53]

> Option 1: Annual subscription includes unlimited online access $59
> Option 2: Annual subscription to the print-only edition $125
> Option 3: Annual subscription to print edition and unlimited online access for $125

You might be uncertain as to whether the online-only edition for $59 is a better deal than the hard copy print subscription for $125, but clearly the print AND online access for the same price of $125 is unequivocally better than Option 2, which only includes the print edition.

The marketing team at the *Economist* isn't anticipating anyone buying Option 2, but they include it to drive more people to choose Option 3. Introducing the decoy creates a simple comparison and in turn makes Option 3 look better compared to Option 1. Said another way, we feel more strongly about one option after a third option is added.

Ariely presented these three options to his students, and 16% chose the $59 online only option while the other 84% chose Option 3 (print and online). No one picked Option 2. Then Ariely took away Option 2 and asked another group of students to pick between the two remaining options. But this time around, 68% picked Option 1 (print only), up from 16%, and only 32% chose print and online subscription (down from 84%). Without the decoy option, suddenly Option 3 looks less appealing.

From *Homo economicus's* perspective, this doesn't make sense. Why would the people's preferences switch when the decoy was removed? Because the decoy alters the way we humans perceive our choices.[54] With a creative and humorous twist, Ariely tested the decoy effect in the dating market and found that we find people more attractive if we see them alongside a similar looking, but less attractive "decoy."

To do this he showed students photos of attractive men and women and asked participants to pick which one they'd go out with. In the first phase of the experiment only 2 options were available. So, do you prefer to date guy A or guy B?

Then he went to photoshop and manipulated the image of one of the choices. By tweaking the nose or adding acne, Ariely created a third option, the decoy option that was slightly less attractive but readily comparable to one of the original faces. Another group of experiment subjects then were asked whom they'd prefer to date: guy A, guy B or guy B, but with acne and crooked nose. With the decoy (guy B with acne and crooked nose) present, guy B was much more appealing than guy A.

This means that when flipping through online dating profiles, your perception of someone's beauty might depend on who came before or after. Such findings are useful advice for someone in the dating market at bars who is trying to pick up potential dates: you need a slightly uglier version of yourself to stand beside![55] Your own decoy will make you look more attractive to the rest of the people in the bar.

We don't compare everything. There's a limit to what we can compare, so we don't compare things that are too different. Manipulating the price of climbing harnesses won't likely impact your mountain bike purchase, but changing the cost of nearby road bike model might influence you. This is why the pricey organic broccoli is not directly beside the regular (cheaper-priced) broccoli in grocery stores. The Drubeck Brothers could increase their sales of regular wool suits by having an extravagant vicuna fleece suit on display. The high price of the luxury suit makes the regular price look even better!

The Power of Free

If the Drubeck Brothers offered a "buy one suit, get one free" promotion or perhaps advertised a free belt with the purchase of a designer suit, they'd be tapping into the consumer psychological quirk of the "power of free," which of course wouldn't have any effect on *Homo economicus*.

One of economics' more irresistible experiments with the "power of free" involved truffle chocolates and Hersey's Kisses. The experimenters set up a stand to sell two types of chocolates: high-quality Lindt truffle chocolates and regular Hershey's Kisses. The Lindt chocolate truffles were very tasty while the Hershey's Kisses were more mass-produced and more ordinary. The customers were only allowed to purchase one chocolate—you couldn't buy both the truffle and the Kiss.

In the first round of the experiment, the Lindt truffle chocolate was set at 15 cents and the Hershey Kiss was 1 cent. After tallying up their sales, they found that 73% of the chocolate buyers went with the truffle and 27% spent their change on the Hershey's Kiss.

Then, to test whether the power of "free" might change customers choices, in a second version of the experiment, the Lindt truffle was priced at 14 cents and the Kisses were free. Notice the Lindt price was lowered by a cent from the earlier trial, so the relative price difference between the Kiss and the truffle is still 14 cents. *Homo Economicus* would calculate each chocolate's relative value based on strict economic theory's cost-benefit analysis: "Is the extra 14 cents worth the extra benefit I get from buying the truffle over the Kiss?" So economic theory should predict that, just like the earlier version, around 73% of chocolate buyers would buy the truffle.

But that's not what happened.

When the Hershey's Kiss was free, customers' preferences switched. Suddenly, Hershey's Kisses became a hit. Some

69% of customers took the Hershey's Kiss (up from 27%) and only 31% paid for the truffle (down from 73%).

Don't get confused. It's not necessarily irrational to pick up free items. But it can lead you to make sub-optimal decisions, like buying the shirts you don't really like just to get the "free one" offered in the buy-two-get-one-free deal. Or perhaps you've purchased extra items on a website in addition to the ones you actually wanted to purchase to qualify for the spend-$50-and-get-free-shipping-on-your-order deal?

This is why buy-one-get-one (BOGO) free promotions get more sales than 50% off, even though they are the same. Sure, two pairs of shoes each priced at $100 marked down to $50 is the same mathematically as buying the first at the full-price of $100 and getting the second pair free, but the "power of free" has more influence on human brains. Seeing the word "free" can cause our brains to release dopamine, which makes us feel happy. Of course, that wouldn't matter to *Homo economicus*.

Once Amazon began offering free shipping with orders over $25, sales went up in every country except one: France. The reason? France charged 20 cents (1 franc) for the discounted shipping deal instead of having it be free.[56] After all, 20 cents is basically free, right? And it's still a discount compared to paying $4 for shipping. Yet, that 20 cents made a big difference. The difference between 2 cents and 1 cent is small, but the difference between 1 cent and free is rather large. Eventually, France changed to free shipping and sales also increased, as in every other country.

Decision Paralysis

One day shoppers at a grocery store saw a display table with 24 varieties of gourmet jam. Another day, shoppers saw the same table but with only six jam options on display. More shoppers stopped at the large display but when it came time to purchase the jams, the people who saw the table with 24 different jam choices were not as likely to buy jam as those shoppers who only saw the six jam options:[57] Only 3% bought jam when bombarded with 24 varieties, but 30% bought when only six options were available. Fewer flavors on the shelf caused a drastic increase in sales.

This doesn't make sense; added options don't make anyone worse off and in fact are likely to make someone better off. But having more options can lead to regret, anxiety, and self-blame if the choice doesn't pan out. These risks/costs of anxiety appear to grow with more and more options (Makes you think if Baskin Robbins would be better off if it lost a few flavors!) Too many options can overwhelm us. Again, *Homo economicus* wouldn't succumb to decision paralysis. This is why the Drubeck Brothers wouldn't overload their customers with too many thread, button, or pocket options. Overloading them with too many suit options might cause the customer to freeze up and not buy.

Decision paralysis is also the culprit that explains why employees are reluctant to participate in 401(k) plans. When people are given more options for their retirement accounts, they are more likely to put off a decision instead of making one. And sometimes people have a tendency not to make any decision; instead, they rely on the *status quo*.

An example of the "status quo bias" shows the psychological barriers preventing people from becoming organ donors. Making a change to their policy might align better with their personal beliefs, but humans tend to default to the option originally proposed. Deviating from a default requires effort and deliberation, which then requires more responsibility, and in turn, potentially regret.

Changing from an "opt-out" choice to an "opt-in" choice was shown to boost organ donations when people make that selection when getting or renewing their driver's license.[58] This is also the reason why Google pays millions of dollars to be the default search engine on certain web browsers.[59] Users are just one click away from using Bing or Yahoo as their search engines, but they don't. They go with the status quo. People prefer things stay the same and to not have to make a decision.[60] Default wins. Be on the lookout for differences in opt-in choices: "Check this box *if you'd like* to receive offers by email" or "check this box *if* you *would not like* to receive offers by email."

Endowment Effect

What if I placed a nice coffee mug with the Colorado state flag on it in the center of the table in front of you? What would you pay for it? If you're like most people, you'd probably say something like $3 or $4.[61]

But what if I were to give you the mug. It's yours. You can hold it. You can see how it would feel to look at the Colorado "C" each time you sip your morning beverage. What if I asked you to sell it? Tell me what it's worth now. You'd probably say something between $5 and $7 now.

When it wasn't yours, you were only willing to pay $3 for it, but now that it is yours, you value it at $6. It's the same mug, but its relation to you has changed. Once you have the mug, you would have to give it up to sell it. You want more for it then.

The mug experiment showed that people demanded a higher price for a mug that had been given to them but a lower price on the same mug if they did not yet own it. Another study found hunters on average wanted $143 to sell a hunting permit they owned, yet they would only be willing to pay $31 to obtain that same hunting permit.[62]

The gap between $143 and $31 wouldn't make any sense to *Homo Economicus*. If a hunter would only pay $31 for the permit, then rationally, they'd be happy if they could sell that permit for any price above $31. For *Homo Economicus* there'd be no gap between the price they'd be willing to sell an item and the price they'd be willing to buy an item. Rationality requires those hunters to have a single evaluation of the permit, not two depending on whether they possess it or not.

The gap between selling price and buying price was dubbed the "endowment effect." The void between selling and buying prices can be attributed to loss aversion, which we will discuss shortly. Having the item in one's possession requires giving it up (foreseen as a loss), whereas having the opportunity to buy it is framed as a gain.[63] The endowment effect says that people value things greater merely because they possess them. This wouldn't make a difference to *Homo Economicus*, who would value the mug in both scenarios at the same price.

The Drubeck Brothers used the endowment effect to their advantage. They made sure their customers tried on their clothes in order to boost the customer's perceived value of the item.

Ikea Effect

The IKEA effect is slightly different from the endowment effect; it occurs when someone's invested labor leads them to inflate the product's value.

Norton, Mochon, and Ariely had students assemble IKEA boxes and fold paper origami. They found that builders of IKEA boxes or origami frogs/cranes bid more money for those products than students who had no labor involved in the IKEA box building or the paper-crane creation.[64] Whether *Homo Economicus* assembled the IKEA furniture or not wouldn't influence their evaluation, but it does for humans.

An example of this effect was apparent in the 1950s when instant cake mixes were introduced. Home chefs, proud of their baking prowess, were initially resistant to cake mixes because it made the cooking too easy and thus seemed less valuable. Cake mix sales dwindled. So, the cake mix manufactures made a few tweaks to give the bakers more ownership of their desserts: they changed the boxed mixes so that the customer had to add the eggs.[65] Requiring a little more work gave the bakers a sense of ownership over their cakes, and boxed cake mixed starting flying off the shelves.

The IKEA effect also shows that people are willing to pay a premium for products they have customized for themselves, and companies know this. I noticed this when I bought an ultralight sleeping quilt for long-distance backpacking trips. The company allowed me to create my own customized quilt with 19 different outside fabric colors and 15 different inside fabric colors. It also allowed customization with length, width, down fill type and temperature rating. I value my long 950-fill-down, 20-degree temperature-rated quilt with midnight blue-colored interior and charcoal exterior that I "created" a lot more than the off-the-shelf un-customized quilts out there. Allowing their customers to pick the thread and button would have given the Drubeck customers a sense of ownership and creation—tapping into the "IKEA Effect" and causing those Drubeck customers to value the suit more.

Confirmation Bias

Another cognitive bias that violates the way *Homo Economicus* makes decisions and judgments is the way people tend to value evidence that supports their initial hypothesis and tend to disregard data that contradicts it.

Peter Wason was the first to describe confirmation bias in 1960 by asking participants to guess at a rule about a sequence of numbers.[66] In Wason's experiment, participants were taught that the sequence 2-4-6 fit the rule. Then the participants were allowed to come up with their own three-number sequences to see if their sequence fit the rule. Once they tried enough three-number sequences, they were allowed to guess the rule.

Given the initial sequence of 2-4-6, many participants generated sequences that were even numbers increasing by two. They asked, "Does 22-24-26 fit the rule?" But participants were less likely to test sequences that might falsify what they thought the rule was: they were less likely to ask "Does 22-20-18 fit the rule?" with the hopes that a "no" answer built their theory. The subjects didn't test sequences inconsistent to their initial hypothesis.

These types of experiments showed how we deliberately search for confirming evidence. Unlike the rules from philosophers who test hypotheses by trying to refute them, humans seek out data that is already compatible with their beliefs.

One of the seminal articles on confirmation bias came as researchers at Stanford rounded up students who had opposing opinions on capital punishment. Half believed in capital punishment and thought it deterred crime.[67] The other half were opposed to it and believed capital punishment didn't have an effect on crime.

The students were then shown two studies: one study that gave data in support of capital punishment preventing crime, and the other that suggested capital punishment didn't deter crime. (Both studies were made up but were designed to deliver equally compelling data on capital punishment). Turns out that the students who had originally supported capital punishment rated the pro-capital punishment data very credible and the anti-capital punishment as unconvincing. The students originally against capital punishment did the reverse. When asked about their views after reading both studies, students who were pro-capital punishment were now even more in favor of it, and those opposed to it were even more against it. In short: they looked at the same exact data and further dug into the positions they already held before reading the data.

Confirmation bias shows that we pay attention to information that upholds our beliefs while ignoring information that challenges them.[68] This also means we don't look at evidence objectively. Confirmation bias says we tend to favor information that already confirms our hypothesis. It says we give more weight to evidence that agrees with our beliefs while undervaluing evidence that doesn't agree with our beliefs. Confirmation bias helps explain why facts don't change people's minds.

It also explains, and is exacerbated by, internet search algorithms. The internet is really good at finding evidence to support your initial hypothesis. It gets even worse as information that people see on social media is often only reflective of what users want to see.

Self-Control, Procrastination, and Temptation

Unlike *Homo Economicus*, we don't always act in ways that maximize our desired outcomes. We put off writing that essay until the night before, we don't stick to diets, we get hangovers, we pass up the heathy fruit snack in favor of the calorie-dense glazed donut and we sometimes don't get to the gym as often as we'd like.

If people were 100% rational, self-control problems and procrastination wouldn't be a problem. We'd just compute the value of our long-term objectives, compare them to short-run decisions and calculate that we have more to gain in the long-term if we make some short-term sacrifices. In other words, *Homo Economicus* probably wouldn't put off writing that paper if that meant pulling an all-nighter the next night. When facing a decision, *Homo Economicus* looks at the situation and assesses the pros and cons. We humans aren't as good at this. We often have difficulty skipping those tempting short-term rewards in lieu of long-term goals.

To understand what I mean, what if I asked what type of movie you'd like to watch tonight?

Would you pick a movie that is fun and forgettable or one that requires more effort to watch but is more edifying? Are you picking "Mrs. Doubtfire" and "The Mask" or "Schindler's List" and a documentary? What if you had to decide what movie to watch tonight after a long week to relax? What about a movie three days from now?

A study in 1999 had people pick three movies out of 24[69]. Some were what were deemed "low-brow" and some were deemed "high-brow." High-brow movies had virtues compared to low-brow movies, with long-term benefits like edification and cultural enrichment, but they involved more work because they were subtitled or required suffering through depressing plots. Meanwhile, low-brow movies were more fun, such as comedies and action films that offered more immediate and easier enjoyment.

After their movie selections, the subjects watched one movie right away, then another two days later and a third two days after that. Most chose to watch a low-brow movie right away but picked a high-brow movie to watch several days later. They saved the heavy stuff for later and picked the immediately rewarding movie to watch right away.

The same concept was tested with healthy snacks compared to unhealthy snacks. If you are asked what snack you want in a week, would you pick fruit or cake? Most people choose the healthier option for their future selves, but when the immediate decision is presented to them, the chocolate cake beats the apple more times than not.

Of course, this wouldn't matter if you had unlimited cognitive abilities, complete information and total self-control. *Homo Economicus* doesn't have any self-control problems — they'd just tally up the future benefits compared to the present costs — but we humans do.

The instructors for Navy Seal training acknowledge that people don't have the self-control assumed by *Homo Economicus* with their ring-out bell. To quit, all you need to do is ring the bell three times. The bell sits outside the instructor's office, but not all the time. To make the process of quitting convenient, the bell comes to each obstacle course, log race, ocean swim. It's always around and easy to access.

"The instructors want it to be easy to ring that bell. If you decide to quit and they start driving you back to the office, you may change your mind. They don't want that. They want it to be right in front of you at all times. They want to take advantage of that small moment of weakness you have."[70]

To fight off your impulsive short-term self, you can have your planning/long-term-self set up a mechanism to prevent your short-term self from succumbing to temptation, that is, put a mechanism in place now that will prevent your future-self from doing something. (More on commitment mechanisms in Chapter 6 on Game Theory.) The classic example comes from Homer's Odyssey when Odysseus wanted to hear the sirens' song but didn't want to be lured away to them where his ship would be wrecked. So, his planning-self instructed his sailors to plug their ears so they couldn't hear the sirens song and also tie him tightly to the mast of the ship. Had he not been tied down, Odysseus's short-term self would be lured by the sirens. He couldn't trust himself. The temptation would be too great. So, he had the ropes keeping him in place while he listened, keeping him from making a bad decision when in a tempted state.

I was able to apply what I was learning from behavioral economics literature during graduate school. When working on my master's thesis, I was struggling for motivation. So, every Monday morning, I gave $20 cash to my fellow grad student and friend, Greg, who held onto it. If I completed 20 hours of research on my thesis by the following Monday, I got my $20 back. If I did less than 20 hours of work, Greg became $20 richer and I lost that 20 bucks. I vividly remember one Sunday evening when I was four hours short of my 20-hour quota. Instead of watching the Sunday Night Football game, I hid myself in the library until 2 a.m. to make sure I got my 20 hours. Without the external motivation from Greg, I would have chosen SNF instead of the library stacks.

During my undergrad days at the University of Richmond, I had a weight-lifting partner. Most days we'd plan to work out together at 8 a.m. I had extra motivation to get out of bed and get across campus to the gym. Otherwise I was letting my workout partner down. We would sporadically see another two guys who tried to work out at 8 a.m. each day as well. They weren't as consistent, and the reason for that was that they were roommates. It was too tempting to roll over in their bunk beds in their dormitory and sleepily mumble to the other, "let's sleep in today." Their short-term selves took over.

Framing

What sounds better to you: "90% fat free" or "10% fat?" What about "a dollar a day" compared to "$365 a year?" Does the idea of paying a $50 late-fee penalty motivate you differently than the idea of getting a $50 discount for early registration? What about a plan that has a success rate of 70% compared to a plan that has a failure rate of 30%? Would you spend a $100 rebate differently than a $100 bonus? If the Steelers beat the Broncos on Monday Night Football, does "the Steelers won" mean the same thing as the "Broncos lost?"

Mathematically, the choices are the same. The descriptions of the outcomes are interchangeable. And to *Homo Economicus*, the wording wouldn't make any difference. But it does to humans. To *Homo Economicus*, choices don't depend on how a task/purchase is framed, but to humans, framing matters.

For example, imagine there is a disease that will kill 600 people, and there are two programs to address the disease. The first program saves 200 people. Under the second program, 400 will die. Which program do you prefer: the one that saves 200 people or the one that kills 400 people? People favored the first even though the outcomes of both are exactly the same.

It seems that people framed the first program as a gain from a reference point of everyone being dead while the second program is framed from the reference point of everyone being alive. Framing from a reference point matters. And that thesis arguably was what really launched behavioral economics.

The Behavioral Economists' Somewhat Unifying Model: Prospect Theory

The 1970s saw a movement of psychologists seeking to unseat *Homo Economicus* and replace them with someone who acts "more human." These behavioral economists insist that real-world human actions and behavior deviate from the completely rational way *Homo Economicus* acts.

But again, behavioral economics was quickly criticized as not having much applicability in the real world. "Sure, the results show up in a lab, but that doesn't mean they could be generalized to the real world in a real market setting," was the riposte from the rational economists. They objected to experimental techniques that lacked appropriate incentives. The anomalies that these experiments purported to show were just artifacts of experimental design rather than fundamental decision-making power. The rational choice defenders basically said you can't change the foundations of economics just because of some scant evidence from experiments involving a cherry-picked pool of undergraduate students. If people made these mistakes in the real world, someone else would realize it and benefit from those mistakes; the efficient market takes care of mistakes on average.

And, there wasn't a unified model to unite all these anomalies and anecdotes. You can't step into the ring to fight a rational choice economist without a math-heavy model. This would change in 1979 with two Israeli experimental psychologists, Daniel Kahneman and Amos Tversky (who came up with the "disease problem" that demonstrated framing).

Kahneman would in 2002 be the first non-economist to win the Nobel Prize in Economics[71]

Kahneman and Tversky invented the "disease problem" to show how choices between medical scenarios in terms of *lives saved* or *lives lost* would change participants' decisions. Kahneman and Tversky asked participants the choice between two policy options to a hypothetical disease outbreak that would kill 600 people.[72]

> *Policy A would save 200 people.*
> *Policy B had a one-third chance of saving everyone but a two-thirds probability of saving no one.*

Framed this way, participants overwhelmingly went with Policy A (72%), the less risky option: go with the sure thing of saving 200 people of those 600.

Then they re-framed the exact question about a disease outbreak expected to kill 600 people in a "loss-framed" manner. Participants had to choose between:

> *Policy A would kill 400 people.*
> *Policy B had a one-third probability of killing no one and a two-thirds chance of killing everyone.*

Framed this way, participants overwhelmingly went with Policy B (78%), the riskier option. Mathematically, the questions are the same: saving 200 people out of 600 is the same as having 400 of the 600 die. Again, when the choice is framed in terms of gains, people are more risk-averse. But when framed as a potential loss, people are more likely to roll the dice.

This got the pair thinking that maybe people respond to losses differently than to gains. So Kahneman and Tversky began to ask most questions involving gambles to see if people judged losses differently than gains. They did this with questions like the following:

Question 1: Which do you choose?
Get $900 for sure OR 90% chance to get $1,000

If you choose the $900, you're like most people. You'd rather take a sure $900 than take the risk of getting nothing for a chance of gaining $1,000.

Now consider a slightly different question:

Question 2: Which do you choose?
Lose $900 for sure OR 90% chance to lose $1,000

In this case, if you're like most people, you chose to gamble and went with the 90% chance to lose $1,000. The certainly of losing $900 feels pretty bad. With the second option, there's still a 10% chance that you'd lose nothing. You decide to make that wager.

Most people avoided the gamble in question 1 but took the gamble in question 2. They were risk-averse in question 1 and risk-seeking when it came to question 2.

It was through experiments like this that Kahneman and Tversky were able to show that humans are risk seeking when it came to losses but risk averse when it came to gains. In other words, people will take greater risks to avoid losses than to get gains.

The comparison of two scenarios also highlights the role of the *reference point* (the difference between what's considered a loss and what's a gain). Finding a *reference point* was a big break-through for Kahneman and Tversky.

If you ever were dared to jump out of a hot tub and do a snow angel in the Colorado mountain snow in 20-degree weather, you've thought about reference points. Jumping from the 104-degree hot tub water into the 82-degree swimming pool feels really cold. But laying your skin in mountain snow for 10 seconds then jumping in to that same 82-degree pool water feels really warm. The pool water is the same in both scenarios, but where you came from (reference point) matters: the same experience seems very different depending on the event that preceded it.

Now consider a different scenario:

> *You are offered a gamble on a toss of a coin:*
> *If it comes up tails, you lose $100.*
> *If it comes up heads, you win $150.*
> *Would you take the gamble?*

Mathematically, you should take the gamble! Over and over on that bet, you'd make out. But for most people, the fear of losing $100 is more intense than the promise of winning $150.

You can test yourself to see if you are risk-averse or risk-seeking by considering this wager: In a wager with a 50% chance of losing, how much would you need to win in order to wager against a loss of $100?

> If you answer $100, you are indifferent to risk
> If you answer more than $100, you are risk-averse
> If you answer less than $100, you are risk-seeking.

Kahneman and Tversky found that most participants wanted between $150 and $250. So, the *prospect* of winning $200 offsets the *prospect* of losing $100. In other words, most people wanted a $200 win (twice as much as the $100 loss) in order to accept the wager. In other words, losing something makes people twice as miserable as the same gain makes people happy. All these observations allowed them to conclude that "losses loom larger than gains" and people are *loss averse*.

The pair began to build their model, using what they had learned:

- There's a big difference between losses and gains. Losses hurt twice as much as gains.
- A loss or a gain has to be defined from some reference point.

- Diminishing sensitivity applied to wealth, that is, the subjective difference between $14,000 and $14,100 is less than the difference between $200 and $300.

Kahneman and Tversky presented these ideas graphically. Their famous "S" shaped graph contains three important ideas that distinguish how humans value decisions compared to *Homo Economicus*: diminished sensitivity, loss aversion and a reference point between gains and losses.[73]

The graph has two separate parts, to the right and to the left of the reference point. The S-shape embodies diminished sensitivity of gains and losses (the slope continuously changes as you move away from the reference point). And notice the two curves are not symmetrical. The slope abruptly switches at the reference point and gets steeper in the loss zone.

Prospect Theory

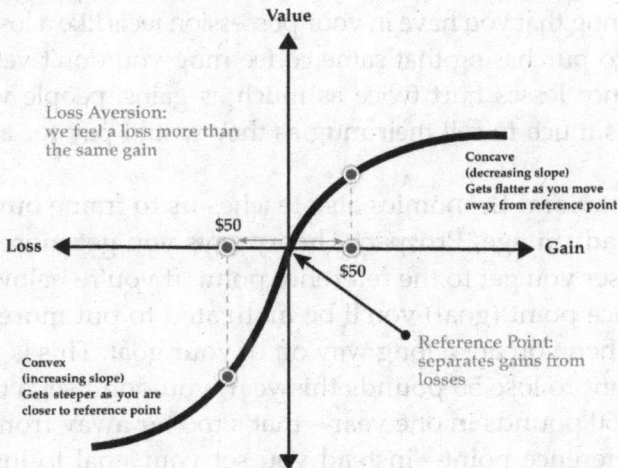

Value

Loss Aversion:
we feel a loss more than
the same gain

Concave
(decreasing slope)
Gets flatter as you move
away from reference point

$50

Loss ←——————————————→ Gain

$50

Convex
(increasing slope)
Gets steeper as you are
closer to reference point

Reference Point:
separates gains from
losses

To see what this famous "S" graph illustrates, consider two scenarios: suddenly losing $50 out of your purse compared to finding an unexpected $50 on the sidewalk. The value of the $50 depends on whether it's a loss or gain. Your happiness of gaining $50 isn't as large as the pain from losing $50. In fact, the negative value of losing $50 is twice as large (distance on y-axis on left side) as the positive value of gaining $50 (distance on the y-axis in the gain domain).

Kahneman and Tversky gave the behavioral economists a model to bring to the fight. It was published in *Econometrica*, a journal on decision theory and economics. This was important because it exposed the psychologists' ideas to economists. The article would turn out to the be most significant work the pair ever produced. It became highly impactful in the fields of finance, psychology, and economics as it explained a bunch of phenomena like how people use mental shortcuts when making a choice and how people make suboptimal decisions.

Prospect Theory supports the endowment effect that people value things more just because they possess them: giving up that coffee mug that you have in your possession feels like a loss compared to purchasing that same coffee mug you don't yet have. And since losses hurt twice as much as gains, people wanted twice as much to sell their mug as they would pay for another one.

Behavioral Economics also teaches us to frame our goals to our advantage. Prospect Theory says you get more value the closer you get to the reference point. If you're below your reference point (goal) you'll be motivated to put more effort than when you are a long way off of your goal. This is why if you want to lose 50 pounds this year, you don't set a goal of losing 50 pounds in one year—that's too far away from your goal/reference point—instead you set your goal to lose one pound per week.

Prospect Theory (particularly loss aversion) can also explain why professional golfers make more par putts of the same length and difficulty than they made birdie putts.

Golf provides a neat lab to test loss aversion since the winning score in a golf tournament is based on total number of strokes taken throughout the entire tournament. Yet each individual hole provides a reference point to par.

A field experiment in golf was tested for loss aversion in 2011 by Pope and Schweitzer who asked the question "Is Tiger Woods loss averse?" They studied not only Tiger but many PGA professional golfers with their putting statistics,[74] They showed that golfers are more likely to protect par (the stroke number a player should take to finish the hole) than they are making the same putt for birdie (a score of one less than par).

Failing to make par is a *loss*, but missing a birdie putt is a *foregone gain*. That missed birdie putt doesn't sting as bad. To *Homo Economicus*, a *foregone gain* is no different than a *loss*, but not so for golfers. The aversion to a bogey apparently makes golfers try harder.

The researchers found that golfers make birdie putts about two percentage points less often than they make comparable par putts. Their data also showed that professional golfers tend to hit birdie putts less hard — leaving more birdie putts short — than par putts. The authors figured that making birdie putts with 2% more accuracy would improve their score on average by one stroke in a 72-hole tournament.

That experiment used a large data set to statistically tease out the difference between par and birdie putts. But what would happen if you just arbitrarily changed a par five into a par four without changing the distance and difficulty? Would that change the way professional golfers approach the hole?

The U.S. Open provides such a natural experiment at the golf courses of Pebble Beach and Oakmont Country Club. Pebble Beach changed the par rating on hole No. 2 from a par five in 1992 to a par four when the U.S. Open was played there in 2000. Oakmont Country Club did the same between 1994 and 2007 on the ninth hole.

What if the psychological effect on the golfer imposed by the label of par four or five caused them to play differently? A hole labeled a par-4 or a par-5 doesn't change the game of golf. A 72-stroke play tournament crowns the winner as who scores the lowest total score (strokes) over all the holes. A label shouldn't influence a golfing *Homo Economicus*.

Prospect Theory says that golfers should work harder playing the same exact hole classified as a par four than they would playing it classified as a par five. That's what the authors found: golfers scored between 0.13 to 0.32 strokes better when Pebble Beach's hole No. 2 was a par four than when it was labeled a par five.[75] Loss aversion shows why professional golfers focus harder trying to save par because making that par avoids encoding a loss. So even people at the highest level of their profession will violate economic theory's rationality assumption.

What about economists who are at the height of their profession and who study these topics? Are people who are aware of these effects immune to their manipulation? Are they immune to framing's influence? That's the question that Simon Gachter, Henrik Orzen, Elke Renner and Chris Starmer pondered and tested at an economics conference in 2006.[76]

To test framing effects, the experimenters gave a $50 discount for conference registration fees if the participants registered early. But a $50 discount for registering early is no different mathematically than a $50 extra fee for registering late. And so, two groups received the same email about the conference, with one sentence changed.

> "We take this opportunity to remind you that the *discounted conference fee for early registration* is available until 10 July 2006"
> "We take this opportunity to remind you that the conference fee will include a *penalty for late registration* after 10 July 2006"

Half had their $50 fee framed as a penalty for late registration, and the other half had it framed as a $50 discount for early registration. What would motivate these economists: the chance to avoid a penalty or the opportunity to avail themselves of a discount? The conference attendees were also naturally divided into two types of registrations: Ph.D economic students and economic professors.

It turned out that framing did not influence the senior economists (already professors) but did sway the junior economists (Ph.D students). A third of the junior economists registered late in the discount group, but hardly any junior economists registered late when they had the $50 framed as a penalty. In other words, junior economists were more inspired to avoid a $50 late fee (loss aversion) than they were to enjoy the $50 discount. To the economists who were already professors, it didn't make a difference.

You can also use loss aversion to your advantage.

In the book "Never Split the Difference," hostage negotiator Chris Voss explains how he uses loss aversion and anchoring to his advantage. In one story, Voss relates a consulting project where he had to drastically cut the pay of his workers that were expecting a much higher rate of pay. Voss had signed up contractors who normally got $2,000 a day, but due to problems could only manage to pay them $500 a day.

Going from $2,000 to $500 is too hard to swallow. But going from $0 to $500 would be a nice win. So how do you flip it? Well, Voss started the conversation by anchoring their expectations really low — make them think that the contract might not even happen.

Voss explains, "…once I'd anchored their emotions in a minefield of low expectations, I played on their loss aversion, 'Still I wanted to bring this opportunity to you before I took it to someone else,' I said. Suddenly, their call wasn't about being cut from $2,000 to $500 but how not to lose $500 to some other guy."[77]

You can also use those mental foibles to find a better way to split the check at restaurants.

There are several ways to split a check with friends over a shared meal at a restaurant: divide it equally, itemize and charge what each person had or have one person pick up the whole tab and then alternate the payer next time.

Scrutinizing each item on the bill switches us to our business norms lens (more in Chapter 10). Suddenly we are analyzing whether Bryan ate more of the cheesecake (that we equally paid for) than I did instead of remembering how en-joyable the cheesecake actually was.

Behavioral Economics tends to favor the alternate-one-per-son-pays-for-everyone method because 1) getting a free meal causes a special feeling — remember the power of free from earlier? 2) The person paying doesn't suffer as much pain of paying as everyone would paying individually and 3) The payer might generate joy from giving a gift. Similar to the di-minishing slope from the prospect theory graph above. And all this before the headache of actually itemizing the bill.

When we pay money for something, we give up our hard-earned cash and feel some psychological pain often called the "pain of paying." But this pain doesn't increase linearly with the cost of the meal —doubled payment doesn't feel double the pain.

For example, if Tim and Kailey each divide the shared restaurant meal evenly, each would feel five units of the pain of paying (for a total of 10 pain points). But because of di-minished sensitivity, if Tim picks up the entire tab, he would suffer fewer than 10 units of the pain of paying. While Kailey suffers no units of misery because she's paying zero. So, take turns picking up the check.

Or you could also just be like the Drubeck Brothers and when the server asks who should get the bill pretend to be hard-of-hearing.

CHAPTER 4:

The Theory of the Firm and Competitive Markets

This chapter will show how microeconomics theoretically proves why market competition is best. That's a loaded statement: we'll first have to understand what "best" means from *Homo Economicus's* perspective. The short answer is that a competitive market produces what consumers want while also using society's scarce resources most efficiently. We build a theoretical model of the firm (a business selling a good or service) to prove that.

Earlier we talked about how economists use models to peel away many of the complications of everyday life to show the underlying process. For example, Ricardo assumed Portugal and England only produced wine or cloth. In this case, we'll start with a simplified view of the firm and the decisions it has to make, such as how much output to produce and how to produce that output. By doing this, we'll better understand the supply curve.

Profit = Total Revenue – Total Cost

The theory of the firm works side by side with the theory of the consumer. Consumers seek to maximize their overall utility and firms seek to maximize profit: to do so both make decisions at the margin. Consumers contend with diminishing marginal utility (remember how the third pancake is never as good as the first?), while producers deal with a similar issue in diminishing marginal productivity. We start with an idealized firm seeking to maximize profit by making some good or service.

Just like Ricardo used the "marginal land" to explain the value of rent in Chapter 1, neoclassical economics uses *marginalism* to derive the value of the supply curve. Think of it as going behind the curtain to see the production process of a bunch of individual firms that make up the supply curve for the entire market.

So, we'll start with a single firm trying to maximize its profit. Well, what's profit?

It's the difference between total revenue and total cost. OK, so what's total revenue and what's total cost?

The value that a business receives for the sale of all of its products is known as total revenue. Total revenue is the price of each good sold (p) multiplied by the quantity sold (q). The cost a business incurs in order to produce a certain level of output is called total cost. That could include the cost of making or buying the items sold, and of the overhead of running the business itself. The profit is the difference between total revenue and total cost. Here's a very simple example:

- A ski shop sells 10 snowboards at $400 each in one month, then the total revenue would be $4,000 (10 X $400 = $4,000).
- Each snowboard on average costs $250 to make, so the total cost of making those 10 snowboards would be $2,500 (10 X $250 = $2,500).
- If the cost of renting the store is $500 per month, then the total cost is $3,000.

- The profit for that month would be $1,000 ($4,000-2,500-500 = $1,000).

The firm's goal is to produce the amount that maximizes the difference between total revenue and total cost. However in figuring out that sweet spot of how much to produce, a firm may also face "diminishing marginal productivity," a concept best understood with a simplified example.

The Production Function and the Marginal Product

Alan runs a catering business. Table 1 shows how the number of meals Alan can produce per hour depends on the number of chefs he has in the kitchen. If there are no chefs, then the kitchen makes no meals.

Table 1 Chefs	Number of Meals per hour
0	0
1	3
2	8
3	16
4	20
5	23
6	25
7	26
8	22

When there is only one chef, that one chef has to do everything from cutting the vegetables to cooking the food to cleaning the dishes. Working alone, that one chef can make three meals per hour.

But when there are two chefs, they can each specialize and do different tasks, dividing their labor, and together they make eight meals per hour. Adding a third chef is even more productive: the three cooks can make 16 meals per hour.

Marginal thinking is key to understanding the decisions a firm makes when deciding how many chefs to hire, or more broadly, how many units of labor or materials to apply. Table

2 has the same data as Table 1, but it also shows the marginal product of each chef. Marginal product is the change in output coming from employing one more unit of an input. In this case, it is the extra meals made as an extra chef is added.

When the number of chefs goes from one to two, the total product (total meals) goes from three per hour to eight. So, the marginal product of the second chef is five meals per hour.

Table 2 Chefs	Number of Meals per hour	Marginal Product of Labor
0	0	
1	3	3
2	8	5
3	16	8
4	20	4
5	23	3
6	25	2
7	26	1
8	22	-4

When the number of chefs goes from two to three, the total number of meals made per hour goes from eight to 16. So, the marginal product of the third chef is eight meals. So, the third chef is more productive at the margin than the second.

But the fourth chef in the kitchen isn't as productive at the margin as the third chef was; with four chefs in the kitchen, 20 meals are made per hour. The total number of meals did increase by 4 meals with the fourth chef, but not as much as when Alan went from two chefs to three, which allowed production to grow by 8. And, as more and more chefs get crammed into the kitchen, each additional chef contributes less to the creation of meals and the production process becomes less efficient. The total number of meals still went up with the fourth chef, but at the margin, the fourth wasn't as productive as the third.

The figure below shows the production function of Alan's kitchen. *Diminishing marginal product*ivity is apparent in the slope of that production function. The law of diminishing marginal productivity states that adding a variable input of production, while another factor is fixed, will eventually result in smaller increases in output. In other words, as we add more chefs into a fixed-sized kitchen, productivity, as measured by the number of meals made by each chef, eventually decreases.

Total Product

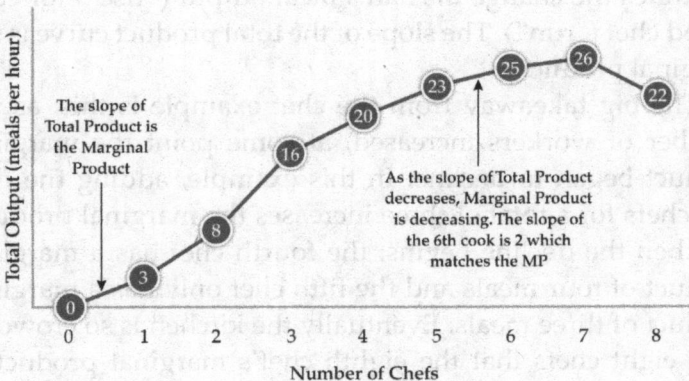

The slope of Total Product is the Marginal Product

As the slope of Total Product decreases, Marginal Product is decreasing. The slope of the 6th cook is 2 which matches the MP

Total Output (meals per hour)

Number of Chefs

Marginal Product

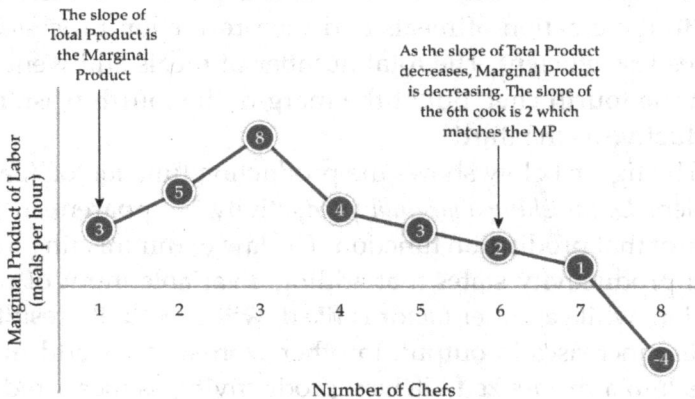

The slope of Total Product is the Marginal Product

As the slope of Total Product decreases, Marginal Product is decreasing. The slope of the 6th cook is 2 which matches the MP

Marginal Product of Labor (meals per hour)

Number of Chefs

The slope ("rise over run") of the productivity function illustrates the change in Alan's meal output ("rise") for each added chef ("run"). The slope of the total product curve is the marginal product.

The big takeaway from the chef example is this: as the number of workers increased, at some point the marginal product began to decline. In this example, adding the first two chefs for a total of three increases the marginal product, but then the decline begins: the fourth chef has a marginal product of four meals and the fifth chef only has a marginal product of three meals. Eventually the kitchen is so crowded with eight chefs that the eighth chef's marginal product is *actually* negative. This means hiring that 8th chef leads to a decline in total meals produced. Graphically, you can see this by observing how the slope of the total product curve gets flatter as more chefs are added.

With too many chefs in the kitchen, crowding has a negative effect on productivity. Everyone is in everyone's way. The eighth chef has no counter space to cut the carrots, and the dishwasher is bumping elbows with another sous-chef. It's madness. In this example, Alan could actually make more meals with seven chefs than with eight.

We have assumed that the size of Alan's kitchen is fixed, so he can only vary the number of meals by varying the number of chefs. This is a good assumption in the *short run*. After a weekend, Alan might have time to re-evaluate and decide to get a bigger kitchen. This will take a few months to build. We assume that in the *long run*, the kitchen can expand, but in the *short run*, it can't. At this point, Alan is stuck with the *short run* situation.

This is an important distinction: in the short run, new firms can't enter/exit and those existing firms have at least one fixed factor (e.g., Alan's kitchen size). In the long run, the situation can change.

The distinction between the short run and the long run isn't a specific number of days or weeks or months. Economic theory defines the short run as a period too brief to be able to vary some inputs: in the short run some factor of production is fixed.

Alan's catering business illustrated the concept of diminishing productivity, but now we turn to Simone's jewelry business to understand the various cost curves.

Moving from the Production Function to Costs

Simone's jewelry business focuses on crafting rings. She pays $100 a day to rent her workshop space. Table 3 shows that her costs change with the number of rings she makes per day. *Total Cost* can be dissected into the costs that vary with output (*variable cost*) and the costs that are independent of how much is produced (*fixed cost*).

Simone's fixed cost is her rent: she pays the flat rate of $100 to rent the workshop whether she crafts 10 rings a day or one. Often, people use the term "overhead" to describe fixed costs. In contrast, with each ring she creates, Simone incurs the cost of the raw materials that she uses, and thus materials are a variable cost.

Table 3 Number of Rings	Total Fixed Cost ($)	Total Variable Cost ($)	Total Cost ($)	Marginal Cost ($)	Average Total Cost ($)
0	100	0	100	---	---
1	100	100	200	100	200
2	100	180	280	80	140
3	100	240	340	60	113
4	100	310	410	70	103
5	100	400	500	90	100
6	100	520	620	120	103
7	100	660	760	140	109
8	100	880	980	220	123
9	100	1,200	1,300	320	144

The first four columns of Table 3 show these costs, but the last two columns of Table 3 are our main focus.

The change in total cost as each additional ring is produced is called *marginal cost*. Take a close look at the shape of the curve in the graph below that shows the shape of Simone's marginal cost curve. The second ring is cheaper at the margin than the first. In fact, each ring is cheaper at the margin until she has made four rings, but then marginal costs begin to rise, in this case, due to diminished productivity of labor.

This is graphically reflected by the rising marginal cost curve. As the number of rings crafted rises (x-axis), the costs also rise at the margin (y-axis).

Marginal Cost

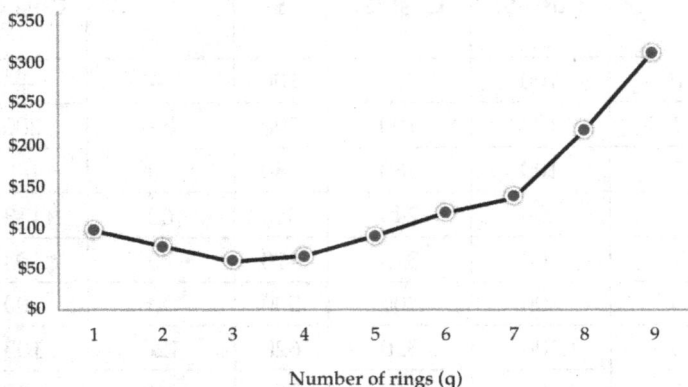

Number of rings (q)

The behavior of the marginal costs bears a direct relationship with the marginal product. Double-check this logic. If Simone hires an additional jeweler for $20 an hour, and he can make three rings per day, the cost per ring is much lower than when Simone hires one additional jeweler for $20 an hour but can only make one ring per day. More productive workers translate into falling marginal costs, while less productive workers translate into rising marginal costs.

The generic version of this is graphically represented on the next page.

Falling Marginal Product turns into Rising Marginal Costs

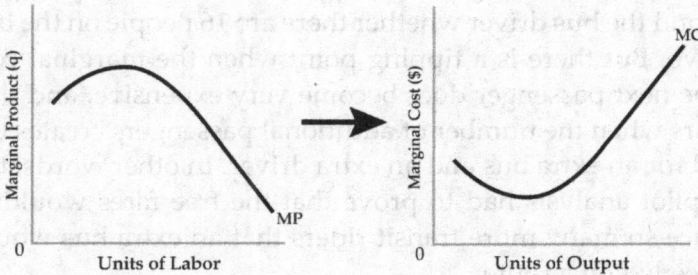

In the short run the fixed factor results in diminishing marginal product and as marginal productivity falls the marginal cost rises.

In the textbook version of the marginal cost curve, we often assume a nice smooth curve, but there are times in the real world where that marginal cost curve can have a sudden spike. I ran into a jump in marginal cost when researching public transit in Denver. It involves the city's Regional Transportation District (RTD) and a pilot program to offer free fares in Longmont, one of Denver's suburbs.

The pilot program would reimburse RTD for all the farebox revenue foregone during the trial period when free bus fares were offered. However, that wasn't the only cost the transportation district was worried about. Before the City of Longmont could try a free fare pilot program on RTD buses in the city, it had to prove RTD would not incur any additional capital or operating costs. This concern makes more sense if we think about marginal costs.

The marginal cost of adding an extra passenger on a bus with empty seats is minimal: it's a little extra gas. The added costs don't vary too much with the number of riders. The fixed costs are the big costs. That is, RTD has to pay for the bus and the bus driver whether there are 16 people on the bus or two. But there is a tipping point when the marginal cost of the next passenger does become very expensive, and that occurs when the number of additional passengers creates the need for an extra bus and an extra driver. In other words, the pre-pilot analysis had to prove that the free fares wouldn't induce so many more transit riders that an extra bus would be needed on a route.

To prove this wouldn't be the case, Longmont looked at "maximum load factors" for all the local bus runs made in Longmont per day.[78] A maximum load factor is the largest number of passengers witnessed on board at one time over the entire route. Most of the routes never got above 25% capacity at any one time. This was strong evidence there was ample capacity for increased ridership without extra buses, so RTD wouldn't bear any additional operating costs during the pilot program.

The Different Measures of Costs

Now that we understand why the representative firm eventually has an upward-sloping marginal cost curve past a certain point, we have to add some extra cost curves in order to understand how a firm decides the quantity it will produce.

Remember the firm's objective: to maximize profit: the difference between total revenue and total cost. With all this focus on the margin, there are also times we find it convenient to discuss costs on a per-unit or average basis.

Specifically, marginal cost shows the change in total cost associated with a change in output (expressed in equation form as $\Delta TC/ \Delta q$). Marginal cost is the extra cost of making one more unit. An average cost is exactly that: the average cost of making *any* one unit, or the total cost divided by the number of units made.

That also means that total cost can be found if you know the average cost per unit and how many you are producing. (If you produce 5 rings and they each cost $100 on average to make, then your total cost is 5 X $100 = $500). This helps explain why we need to know and define the average total cost curve (ATC).

Notice the U-shape of the average total cost curve below. If the marginal cost of the next ring is less than the average cost (graphically this is where the MC is below the ATC), the average cost will decrease. If the marginal cost is greater than the average cost, that next ring's cost will pull up the average. This also means that the marginal cost curve (MC) intersects the average cost curve (ATC) at its minimum. (This is important later in the chapter because this point of the minimum average total cost curve plays a key role in the competitive firm's decisions.)

Marginal Cost and Average Total Cost

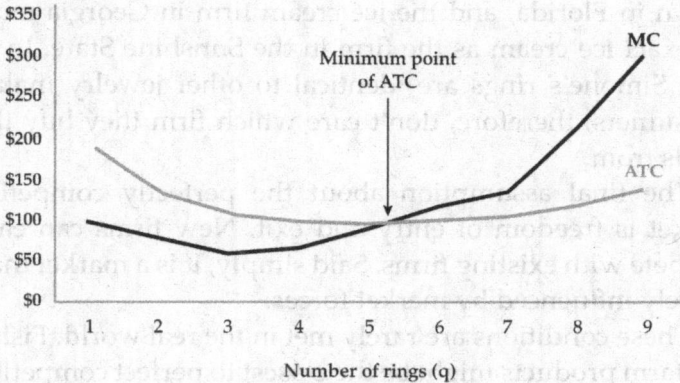

The graph shows Marginal Cost (MC) and Average Total Cost (ATC) curves plotted against the Number of rings (q) on the horizontal axis (1 through 9) and dollar amounts ($0 to $350) on the vertical axis. An arrow points to the "Minimum point of ATC."

The Ideal Bubble of Perfect Competition

To recap, our model firm is trying to maximize profit. We've shown the "law" of diminishing marginal productivity results in the rising marginal cost curve, and we've added the average total cost curve to our firm model. Now that firm must use its cost curves to answer two questions: what price to charge, and how much to produce?

The answers depend on market structure. That is, how many firms are in the market and how competitive are they?

We start with a theoretical world that's ideal for competition called *perfect competition* or *the perfectly competitive market*. This world of perfect competition can be boiled down into three conditions. First, there are many small firms and many customers. No individual producer or buyer can influence the price of the good.

The second condition is homogeneity of the product. Said differently, the products offered by each seller are identical. A Georgia watermelon is no different than a watermelon grown in Florida, and the ice cream firm in Georgia makes the exact ice cream as the firm in the Sunshine State. In our case, Simone's rings are identical to other jewelry makers. Consumers, therefore, don't care which firm they buy their goods from.

The final assumption about the perfectly competitive market is freedom of entry and exit. New firms can easily compete with existing firms. Said simply, it is a market that is entirely influenced by market forces.

These conditions are rarely met in the real world. Fishing and farm products might be the closest to perfect competition that the real world gets.

So, if this type of market doesn't really exist in the real world, why bother studying it?

The simplified model still provides an approximation of what happens in markets that are less than perfectly competitive. The Perfectly Competitive Market (PC market) is the benchmark by which all other markets are judged. It shows us what an ideally functioning market can accomplish. We show the best market, then analyze markets that deviate from it.

Under these assumptions, any individual firm must accept the price that the market determines. Economic textbooks call this representative firm a "price taker." Since each firm makes identical products, each firm must match its competitors' price, otherwise, no one would buy its good; consumers would just buy from someone else.

These assumptions simplify the analysis considerably. These firms don't differentiate their products, and they don't have control over price. Instead, the price is determined in the market by supply and demand. Under these conditions, all the firm decides is how much to produce and how to produce it.

Under these assumptions, the perfectly competitive market can be illustrated graphically. The market on the left determines the equilibrium price at $140. The right side of the diagram shows how the market price determines the demand for the individual firm. If that firm would raise the price at all, no one would buy it. Those customers would just get it from a competitor whose product is identical. The firm can also sell whatever amount it wants at the existing price, which means there's no reason to lower the price either. The representative firm in the PC market faces a perfectly elastic demand curve for its product.

The Demand Facing a Single Firm in the Perfectly Competitive Market

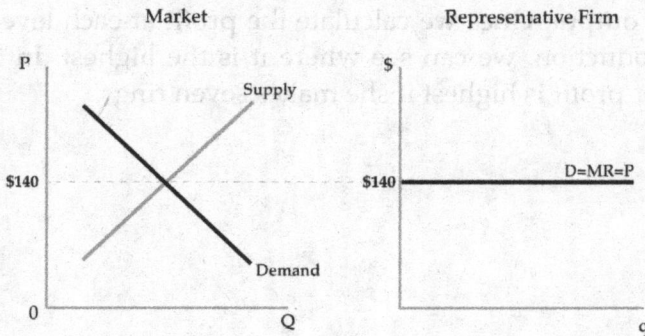

The representative firm can sell as much as they like at $140, but if they raise price above $140, the quantity demanded of that firm will be zero.

That demand curve also represents the marginal revenue (MR). Marginal revenue is the additional revenue that a firm gets when it increases output by one extra unit. If that representative firm sells one more item at $140, then the marginal revenue would be $140. Notice that's exactly what price is. The horizontal line on the right side can be thought of as the demand curve for the individual firm and also the marginal revenue curve. (That's why it's labeled D=MR=P or Demand=Marginal Revenue=Price).

Example of Profit Maximization

Let's go back to Simone's ring business and assume she operates in a perfectly competitive market. In this ideal market, the forces of supply and demand determine a $140 price. That means we can calculate Simone's total revenue (quantity of rings X $140) and compare it to her total cost. Knowing total revenue (TR) and total cost (TC) (from Table 3 above), we take the difference to determine profit. Table 4 does this at each level of output. Once we calculate the profit at each level of ring production, we can see where it is the highest. In this case, her profit is highest if she makes seven rings.

Table 4 Number of Rings	Total Revenue ($)	Total Cost ($)	Profit ($)
0	0	100	-100
1	140	200	-60
2	280	280	0
3	420	340	80
4	560	410	150
5	700	500	200
6	840	620	220
7	980	760	220
8	1,120	980	140
9	1,260	1,300	-40

There's another way to look at Simone's decision: she can find the profit-maximizing quantity by looking at the margins: the marginal revenue and marginal cost of each ring. How profitable is it to make the next ring? Table 5 is the same as Table 4, but also includes two extra columns that calculate the Marginal Revenue (MR) and Marginal Cost (MC). MR is easy to calculate, it's the change in total revenue as Simone sells an additional ring ($\Delta TR/\Delta q$). It's also equal to price. MC is the change in total cost as Simone produces an extra ring ($\Delta TC/\Delta q$).

Table 5

Number of Rings	Total Revenue ($)	Total Cost ($)	Average Total Cost ($)	Profit ($)	Marginal Revenue (Price) $	Marginal Cost ($)
0	0	100	---	-100	---	---
1	140	200	200	-60	140	100
2	280	280	140	0	140	80
3	420	340	113	80	140	60
4	560	410	103	150	140	70
5	700	500	100	200	140	90
6	840	620	103	220	140	120
7	980	760	109	220	140	140
8	1,120	980	123	140	140	220
9	1,260	1,300	144	-40	140	320

The profit-maximizing level of output can be found the long way by calculating the total revenue and total cost of each unit and then calculating profit, or it can be done with a short-cut: by looking at the margin. At the seventh ring, we see that MR = MC ($140 = $140).

Why MR = MC is Profit Maximizing

Remember, the firm is trying to decide the profit-maximizing level of output. In other words, how many "q" to make. The supply rule is simple: keep offering products for sale as long as the price they can sell for is at least as great as the marginal cost.

Look at the second ring: it costs $80 to make (marginal cost), but Simone can sell it for $140, so the production and sale of that second ring increases profit. As the MC < MR, it makes sense to sell more. Now look at the sixth ring, Simone can sell it for $140, but it still only costs $120 to make. It makes sense to continue producing and selling more rings. As long as marginal revenue exceeds marginal cost, increasing output will raise Simone's profit.

Why doesn't Simone make more than seven rings? Well, look at the marginal cost and marginal revenue of the eighth ring. It costs $220 to make, but she can only sell it for $140. She'd lose money on that ring. Producing the eighth ring would reduce profit. As a result, Simone will produce seven rings; the quantity where marginal revenue equals marginal cost.

And that's our profit-maximizing rule for the firm. The firm will set its output where MR = MC. Setting output below that level where MR > MC means sacrificing extra profit made from producing the extra units. Setting output where MR < MC means the firm is selling too much, and those last units lose money. Producing where MR = MC is the firm's profit-maximizing rule.

Profit Maximization in the Perfectly Competitive Market

So, we've determined the shortcut method for finding the profit-maximizing level of output for a firm: find where MR = MC. Now let's show what this looks like on a graph.

Determining profit on a graph can be broken down into three steps.

First, find where marginal revenue equals marginal cost to find the profit-maximizing output level. It's where the MR curve intersects the MC curve. This point we call q*.

From that point, the next step is to draw a line straight left to find the market price, because once you have price and quantity you can find total revenue. The last step is to find the total cost. This is where that q* level intersects the Average Total Cost Curve (ATC). If we multiply the average total cost by the output level, we can find total cost (TC = ATC X q*).

For example, Simone's jewelry firm finds MR = MC. Since she operates in the PC market and she's a "price taker," she must accept the market price of $140, where q = 7. Then we can see the average cost of producing each of those seven rings. It's $109. You can see the price and the ATC of making the seventh ring on the graph below.

Profit Maximization for the Representative Firm

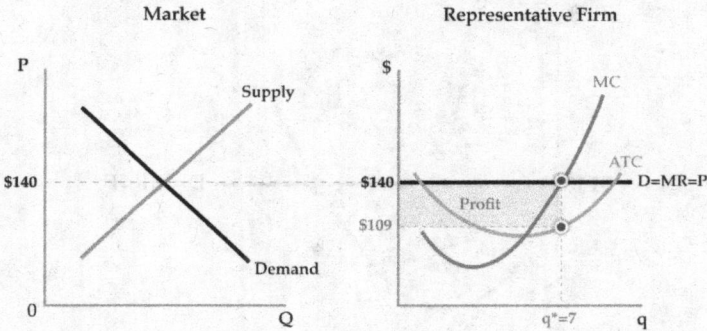

The profit-maximizing output is q* where MR=MC. Profit is also shaded on the graph. It's the difference between Total Revenue (TR) and Total Cost (TC). Where TR = P X q*= $140 X 7 and TC = ATC X q*= $109 X 7

You can calculate total revenue (7 rings × $140) and total cost (7 rings × $109). If you think in terms of geometry, the total revenue is the area of the price × quantity box. And the total cost box is ATC × quantity. In this case, the total revenue box is bigger than the total cost box, so Simone is making a profit.

Total Revenue > Total Cost

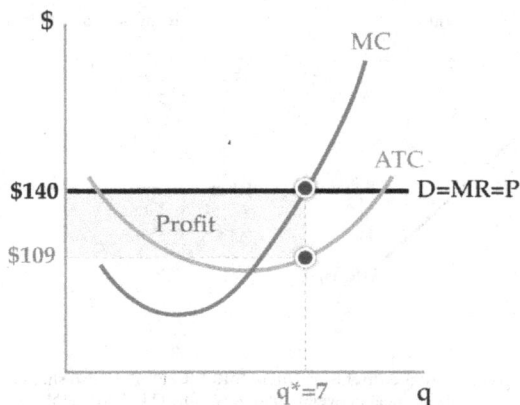

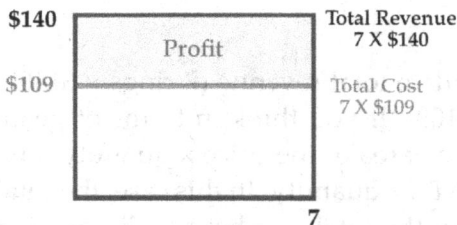

The Supply Curve Is the Marginal Cost Curve

The firm in the PC market responds to changing prices. When the price rises, suddenly the MR is higher than MC at the previous level of q, so the firm increases production. The new profit-maximizing quantity is greater (again where MR=MC). Because the marginal cost curve determines the quantity the firm is willing to supply at that price, the MC curve is the firm's supply curve. In Simone's case, the price in the market would have to rise to $220 for her to willingly supply that eighth ring since the marginal cost of that ring is $220. As the price in the market rises, it makes it more likely the firm can cover the additional cost of the extra units. And here's the big "aha!" moment.

In Chapter 1, we quickly glossed over the reason why the supply curve is upward-sloping; we said firms are more willing to supply at higher prices. Now we've also shown why the supply curve is upward-sloping using marginal analysis. That is, facing rising marginal costs, the firm needs a higher price to cover those rising costs in order to supply more.

The Break-Even Point

So, we've determined how the firm decides its profit-maximizing level of production, but what would happen if the market price fell significantly? Let's consider the case when supply and demand in the ring market set the price at $100.

Simone does the same calculation as before: she first determines where MR = MC. In this case, she asks, "Where does MC = $100?" This time, there's not a quantity where MR exactly equals MC. So, she finds the highest q where MR > MC. In this case, it's at five rings, and she produces at that level.

Table 6 is similar to Table 5, except the price has dropped to $100. This changes the total revenue ($100 X rings), the marginal revenue, and the profit, but Simone's costs are the same.

Table 6

Number of Rings	Total Revenue ($)	Total Cost ($)	Average Total Cost ($)	Profit ($)	Marginal Revenue (Price) ($)	Marginal Cost ($)
0	0	100	--	-100	--	--
1	100	200	200	-100	100	100
2	200	280	140	-80	100	80
3	300	340	113	-40	100	60
4	400	410	103	-10	100	70
5	500	500	100	0	100	90
6	600	620	103	-20	100	120
7	700	760	109	-60	100	140
8	800	980	123	-180	100	220
9	900	1,300	144	-400	100	320

When the price is $100, the profit-maximizing level is now five rings. Look at the profit now: it's $0. The total cost is $500, and the total revenue is $500. Also, notice the Average Total Cost (ATC) column. At five rings, the ATC is at its minimum.

- If total revenue is greater than total cost at q*, then the firm is generating a profit.
- If total revenue is less than total cost at q*, then the firm is generating a loss.
- If total revenue is exactly equal to total cost, then profit is zero.[79]

This should make sense intuitively: if the price is higher in the market, there's a greater chance the firm can make a profit.

We can restate these profit rules in relation to the ATC:

- If price is greater than the ATC minimum, the firm will make a profit.
- If price is below ATC minimum, the firm will incur a loss.
- If price is exactly equal to the ATC minimum, the firm will make zero profit.[80]

The figure below shows graphically the generic firm operating at the break-even point (when profit is zero). Now three curves intersect at the profit-maximizing level of output. In other words, MR = MC where ATC intersects the MC. There, P = MR = MC = ATC. The perfect competition equilibrium quantity produced is where price, marginal revenue, marginal cost, and average total cost are all the same.

**Profit Maximization for the Representative Firm
When Profit = 0**

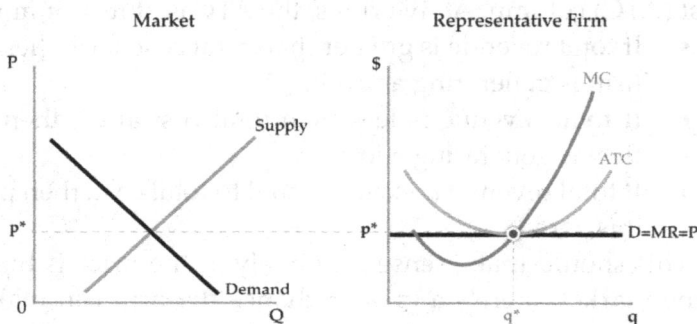

The profit-maximizing output is q* where MR=MC. Profit is zero.
Total Revenue (TR) = Total Cost (TC)
Price = ATC minimum

At q*, the total revenue exactly equals the total cost. That's because the price is exactly equal to the ATC minimum. There's not a profit box like before because the profit is zero. In this case, the total cost box (q* × ATC) is the same as the total revenue box (q* × P*).

Total Revenue = Total Cost Profit = 0

Representative Firm

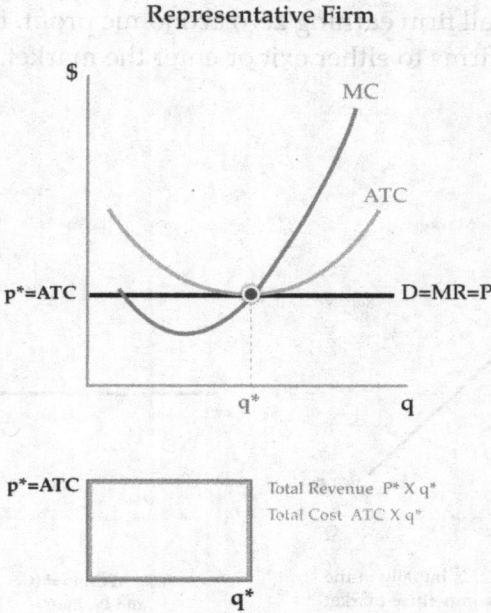

The Long Run Perfectly Competitive
Market Equilibrium

Adam Smith described how the market allocates prices and
quantities, and how competitive markets will result in the
creation of goods that society wants at the prices society is
willing to pay. We've come to understand the cost structure
of our ideal firm operating in our ideal world of perfect
competition. Now, we're finally in a position to prove what
Adam Smith was saying about competition using this model. To do this, we now move from the short run to the long
run, which importantly means we now allow firms to enter
and exit the market in our theoretical model.

Suppose the market for burritos starts with a scenario where each burrito firm is making zero economic profit. So, the price of $5 per burrito equals the minimum of the ATC. With each small firm earning zero economic profit, there's no incentive for firms to either exit or enter the market.

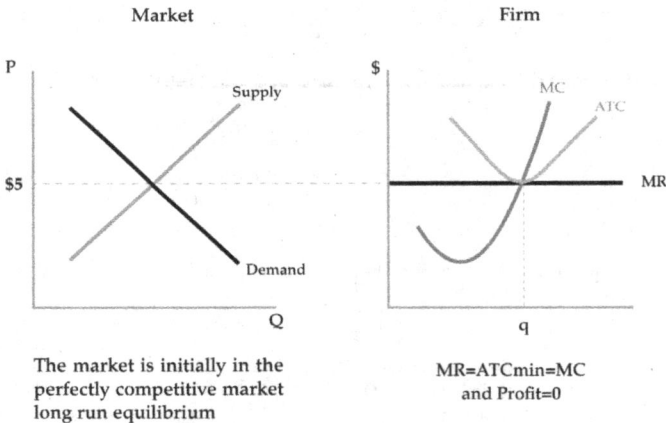

Market   Firm

The market is initially in the perfectly competitive market long run equilibrium

MR=ATCmin=MC and Profit=0

Now suppose there is a sudden E. Coli breakout in the ingredients that go into burritos. The E. Coli flare-up would cause fewer consumers to desire burritos. The demand curve for burritos would shift to the left as fewer customers want burritos.

Graphically, this will be a leftward shift in demand. Demand falls to Demand 2 in the figure below. As demand falls, the price in the market for burritos also falls. Now, instead of an equilibrium price of $5, the new price is at $4. That new price is below the representative firm's ATC minimum, which means some of the burrito firms can't make a profit at P = $4.

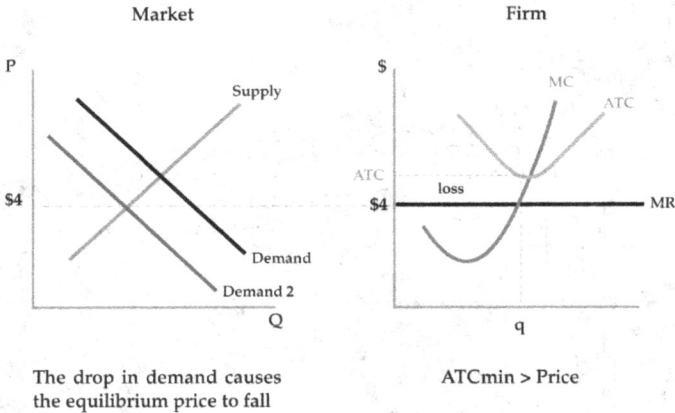

The drop in demand causes the equilibrium price to fall

ATCmin > Price

As the price falls below the "break-even point" (ATC minimum), some firms will have a loss in the short run. In response, some of those firms will decide to exit the market. As firms leave the market for burritos, this will cause another shift in the market, this time the supply curve will decrease (leftward shift). The next figure shows this scenario. Look at what happens when enough firms exit the market. The decrease in supply pushes up the equilibrium price for burritos. Enough firms will exit the market to move price back up.

Market

Firm

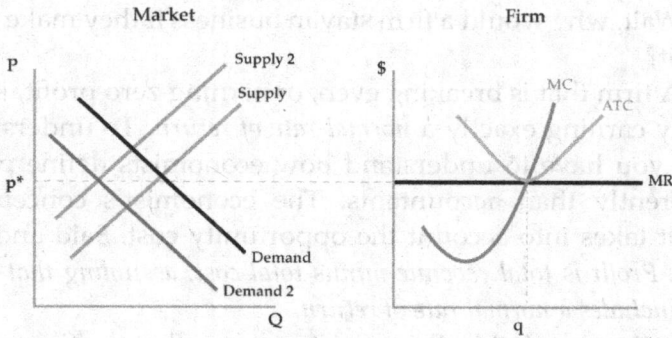

As some firms leave, supply
falls causing the equilibrium
price to rise

MR=ATCmin=MC
and Profit=0 (again)

In this case, the initial short-run loss was eliminated in the long run as enough firms exited the market. As long as firms can enter when there is profit and exit when there are losses, the market will tend toward the long-run equilibrium. And that long-run equilibrium will be where Price = ATC minimum and Profit = 0.

The mechanics work the same way, although in the opposite direction when there is initially a short-run profit. If word gets out there's profit to be made in the burrito market, it will cause a supply response. The market supply of burritos will shift to the right as new firms will enter the market. As more firms enter the market trying to capture that profit, the supply of burritos will increase (shift right) and drive down the price of burritos. If price is above average total cost, it encourages new firms to enter the market. If enough new burrito firms enter, that supply will shift until profit is eliminated.

As long as firms can freely and easily enter and exit the market, profit and losses will be eliminated in the long run.

Wait, why would a firm stay in business if they make zero profit?

A firm that is breaking even, or earning zero profit, is actually earning exactly a *normal rate of return*. To understand this, you have to understand how economists define profit differently than accountants. The economist's concept of profit takes into account the opportunity cost. Said another way, *Profit is total revenue minus total cost, assuming that total cost includes a normal rate of return.*

Let's unpack this. Economists assume that the firm's revenue must compensate the owner for the time and money she spends keeping the doors open. For example, assume Simone invested $300,000 to start up her jewelry business. If she instead invested that $300,000 in stocks or bonds, she could earn about $20,000 in investment income. In addition, she gave up another job that was paying her $55,000 a year. Simone's opportunity cost of running her jewelry business includes the investment income she could have earned and her foregone wages at her other job, a total of $75,000.

In our theoretical firm model, even if Simone's profit is driven to zero, the fact that she chooses to continue to operate her business shows that her revenue covers her opportunity costs. In other words, Simone is doing as well as she could elsewhere because she is getting the normal rate of return on the money she invests in her jewelry business. If that were not the case, she would shut down her business.

Under perfect competition, there are many buyers and sellers, and prices reflect the market supply and demand. Firms earn just enough profit to stay in business. If those businesses earned excess profits, other companies would enter the market and drive profits down.

Why the Perfectly Competitive Market is Efficient.

We built a model for a firm operating in the unique bubble of perfect competition and showed how price equals marginal cost, under these simplifying and ideal assumptions. There's a lot of information in the equation P=MC. What does it mean that the perfectly competitive firm will produce where the price of its output is equal to the marginal cost of its production? It means that the right things and the right quantity of things are produced. It also means buyers value the last unit of output by the same amount that it costs to make it.

Let's first remember the consumer's role in the price. The price reflects the consumer's willingness to pay. By buying that burrito at $5, the consumer is revealing that the worth of the burrito is at least as much as the other goods they could buy with the same money. In that way, the price reflects the value the consumer places on it. Rational consumers buy something as long as the marginal benefits are greater than the marginal costs. This is just cost vs. benefits thinking at the margin.

If buyers value that last unit more than the marginal cost, then resources aren't being used efficiently. In this scenario, making more of that good would boost society's gains. If buyers value that last unit by less than the marginal cost, then resources also aren't being used efficiently, because the resources to make that good could be better used somewhere else in the economy. The sweet spot is found when buyers value that last unit exactly as much as it costs to make it. (This will make more sense when we see what happens to efficiency when the markets aren't under the P=MC condition).

Next, we turned to the long run and allowed firms to enter. We showed how a frictionless market like this allows firms to enter and exit and drive economic profit to zero. At the same time, price also gets driven down to the minimum of the average total cost curve. A firm in the PC market producing at the minimum point of the average total cost curve (ATC minimum) is producing using the "least cost method." This means the minimum value of resources is being used to produce those goods. To clarify what that means, consider a quick mathematical example of when a firm isn't producing at the ATC minimum.

In scenario A, one firm makes all 20 units. But for that one firm to make 20 units, it must produce past the ATC minimum. In this case, each unit on average costs $7. To make 20 units requires $140 of cost.

Scenario A: 1 firm

Firm 1

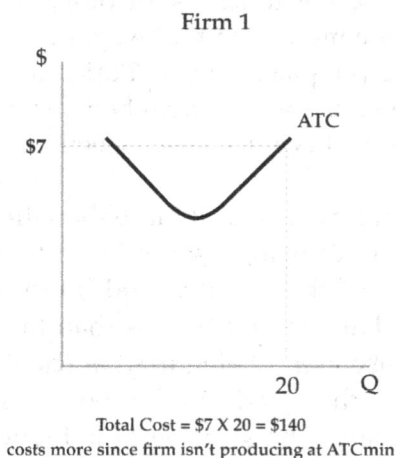

Total Cost = $7 X 20 = $140
costs more since firm isn't producing at ATCmin

Compare this to Scenario B, when two firms each make 10 units and operate at their ATC minimums. Each unit on average costs $5. So, 20 units only require $100 of cost. That's the "least cost method."

Scenario B: 2 firms each at ATCmin

Firm 1   Firm 2

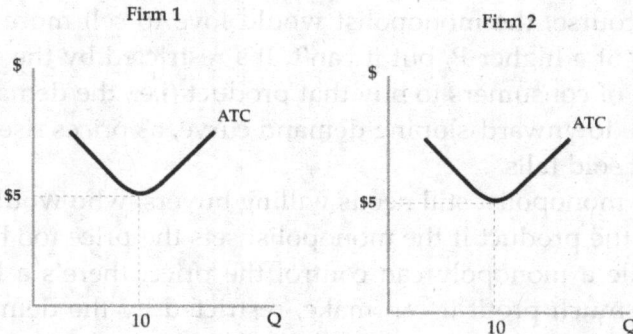

Total Cost = ($5 X 10) + ($5 X 10) = $100
Makes those 20 units at a lower cost than when only 1 firm makes all of them

The equilibrium condition in the long run is for each firm in the PC market to produce at the output level that minimizes the average total cost. When each firm is earning zero economic profit, there is no incentive for new firms to enter the market, and the existing firms have no incentive to leave. The perfectly competitive market is efficient.

Monopoly vs. Perfectly Competitive Market

The theoretical model of the firm in a competition embodies what Adam Smith said about self-interested buyers and sellers: they are led by the invisible hand to promote economic well-being. But a monopoly is unchecked by competition. As you might have guessed, this means the outcome in a market dominated by a monopoly is often not the best for society.

Monopoly is at the opposite end of the market structure spectrum from perfect competition. A true monopoly is a market with only a single seller. Unlike the small firm in the PC market that had no control over price (*price taker*), the monopolist has total control over price (*price maker*).

Of course, the monopolist would love to sell more and more Q at a higher P, but it can't. It's restricted by the willingness of consumers to buy that product (i.e., the demand). Given a downward-sloping demand curve, as prices rise, the amount sold falls.

The monopolist still needs willing buyers, who wouldn't all buy the product if the monopolist sets the price too high. So, while a monopoly can control the price, there's a limit to how much profit it can make, restricted by the demand. Therefore, the monopoly model starts from the demand curve.

The Monopoly Model

To illustrate the monopolist's profit-maximizing decision, let's consider a simple example. Table 7 shows the demand curve for the monopolist's product (i.e., how many buyers there are at different price levels). From the demand curve, the monopolist can calculate the total revenue curve (TR=Price × Quantity) and then the marginal revenue curve (MR=ΔTR/ΔQ).

For example, if the monopolist sets the price at $60, they will only get one willing buyer. So total revenue will be 1 x 60 = $60. If the monopolist sets the price at $50, then two customers would buy the product, and total revenue would be $100 ($50 x 2).

Table 7 Price ($)	Quantity	Total Revenue ($)	Marginal Revenue ($)
60	1	60	60
50	2	100	40
40	3	120	20
30	4	120	0
20	5	100	-20
10	6	60	-40
0	7	0	-60

To induce a third customer to buy, the monopolist must lower the price to $40. But if the monopolist does this, it loses $10 on each unit sold because it must sell all its units at $40. And, the marginal revenue of selling that third item is less than price, so the monopolist sells that third item for $40 but loses $20 in total revenue since the first two customers are each paying $10 less. Mathematically, it means marginal revenue for that third unit sold is only $20 ($40-$10-$10).

Said another way, as the monopolist cuts the price to attract new buyers, the old customers also benefit from a lower price, since all units are sold at the same price. The monopolist receives more revenue from the extra unit(s) sold, but less revenue on all the units sold previously. Thus, the marginal revenue curve for the monopolist lies below the demand curve faced by the monopolist, and a monopolist's MR is always less than the price of the good. The following figure shows the information from Table 7 graphically.

Demand and Marginal Revenue for Monopolist

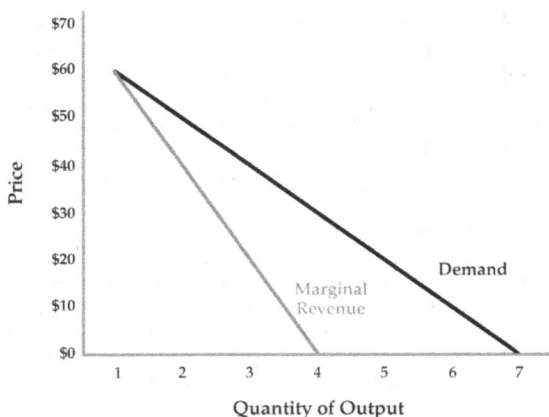

This is a significant difference from the marginal revenue curve faced by the firm in a perfectly competitive market. The firm in the PC market could sell all it wants at the market price, although it must "take" the market price, and that price was equal to marginal revenue.

The next figure compares the demand curve for the monopolist with the demand curve for the firm under perfect competition.

- In the PC market, that firm can sell as much as it likes without lowering the price, and so
    - the marginal revenue of selling each unit is equal to price, and
    - the PC market firm has a horizontal demand curve.
- In a monopoly market, the monopolist must lower the price to sell another unit, and so

142

o   the marginal revenue curve is less than price and
o   the monopoly market has a negatively sloped de-
    mand curve.

In the figure below, the monopolist lowers the price from $4 to $3.90 to attract the sixth buyer. But the monopolist doesn't make the full $3.90 at the margin because they have lowered the price on the previous five units sold. So, marginal revenue is only $3.40 and not $3.90, since it was lowered by 10 cents on the previous five units sold ($3.90-$0.10-$0.10-$0.10-$0.10-$0.10= $3.40).

Monopolist's Demand Curve

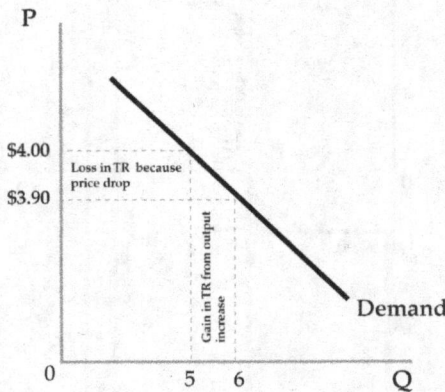

To sell the 6th unit, the monopoly must
lower price to $3.90 on all units

In contrast, the firm under perfect competition can sell as much as it wants at $4. If it sells the sixth unit, it gains the full $4 in revenue. MR=P for the firm in the PC market, but MR<P for the monopolist.

PC-Market Firm's Demand Curve

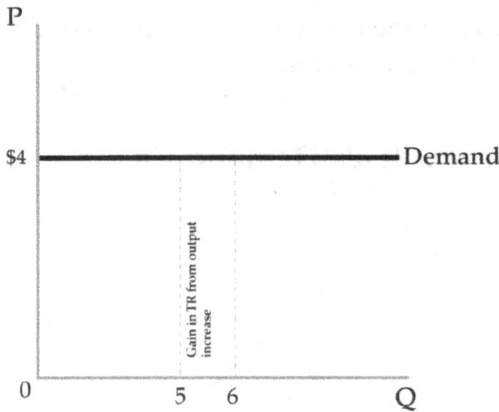

The firm in PC-Market can sell as much as it wants at $4.

A Monopolist's Profit Maximizing Output Level

The monopolist has control over both price and quantity. How does the monopolist decide what price or what quantity to sell? The information is embedded in the demand curve since it relates the quantity buyers are willing to buy at different prices. The monopolist still finds the profit-maximizing level of output where MR=MC. In that aspect, competitive firms and monopolies are alike. For readers who think in equation form, another way to view it is:

$$\text{For a firm under perfect competition: } P = MR = MC$$
$$\text{For a monopolist: } P > MR = MC$$

This also means that in competitive markets, price equals marginal cost, but with monopolies, price is greater than marginal cost. This is an important distinction in understanding the cost to society of the monopoly compared to a market under perfect competition.

The next figure shows the monopolist's profit-maximization decisions.

- First, find the profit-maximizing output level where MR=MC (point A).
- Then use the demand curve to find the price that will draw in that number of buyers.

Graphically, this means finding where the MR curve intersects the MC curve, then tracing that level of q up until you hit the demand curve to find the price the monopolist can charge (point B).

Price and Output for Monopolist

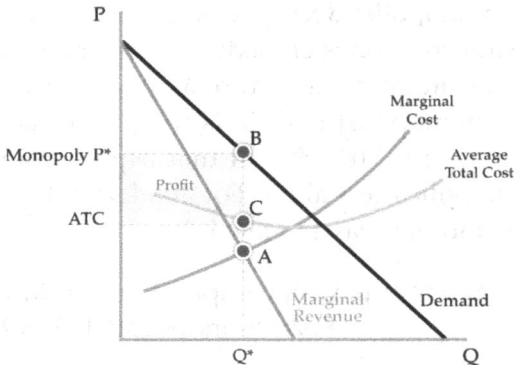

The monopolist sets MR=MC to find the profit-maximizing level of output. The monopolist prices from the demand curve. It uses the ATC at the level of output to find total cost.

Unlike the PC market, where entering firms drive profit to zero in the long run, the monopoly will make a profit in the long run.[81] (Shown in the gray box in the previous figure). The monopolist's total revenue is price X quantity, and their total cost is shown graphically by where the q intersects the average total cost curve (point C). Profit for a monopolist can only last if other firms can't enter this industry and whittle it away. For a monopoly to persist, there must be factors that prevent other firms from entering the market or *barriers to entry*. Otherwise, new firms would drive down profit as in a competitive market.

Perfect Competition Compared to the Monopoly

Since we can think of the marginal cost curve as the supply curve, we can compare the market outcomes, as shown in the next figure. Point A would be the equilibrium reached in a competitive market, at the intersection of Marginal Cost and

Demand. But the monopolist doesn't produce at that point. The monopolist sets MR=MC (at point B) and produces at a lower quantity. The monopolist also prices off the demand curve, at point C.

Monopolist Charges Higher Price and Produces Less than a Competitive Market

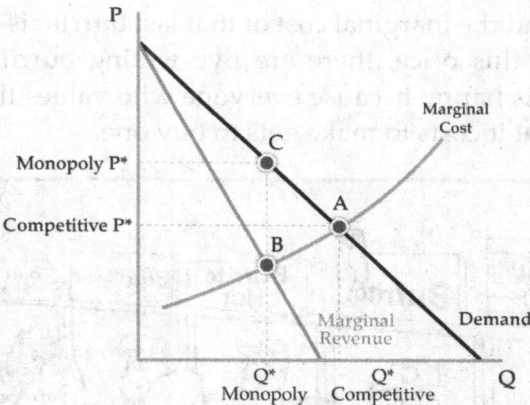

Here's the big crescendo of the chapter:

Monopoly P* > Competitive P*
Monopoly Q* < Competitive Q*

Dead Weight Loss: How Monopolies Create a Loss for Society

A monopoly produces less output and charges a higher price than a competitive market. Producing less and charging more isn't in the best interest of buyers. And those higher prices also create a social loss.

To understand how, we have to go back to what it means when P=MC. The price tells us what buyers are willing to pay for that burrito and the marginal cost tells us the opportunity cost of making that burrito. When they come together and price equals marginal cost, then consumers are paying the opportunity cost of making that burrito and no more. Every burrito can be made for equal or less than its value to buyers.

Let's consider an efficient market where the price of burritos is $7 and the marginal cost of that last burrito is $7, where P=MC. At this price, there are five willing burrito buyers. Everyone is happy because everyone who values the burrito above what it costs to make gets to buy one.

Now suppose, instead of a competitive burrito market, the burritos were produced by a monopolist charging $10. Only burrito buyers who valued the burrito above $10 would buy them now. All buyers who valued them at more than $7 but less than $10 now forego the burrito. Those lost consumers valued the burrito at more than its marginal cost, and yet they don't get to buy it from the market because a monopoly exists.

In other words, when the monopolist charges a price above marginal cost, there's a range of customers that value that good more than its cost, but less than the monopoly price. Some customers end up not getting the good that they would have gotten if the market was competitive. And, some resources that could be used to make burritos are not used. The monopolist's ability to raise price above marginal cost means the monopoly prevents mutually beneficial transactions from taking place. Economists call these lost transactions *dead weight loss*.

Suddenly, two buyers no longer get a burrito that they value above its marginal cost to make. Those two represent *dead weight loss*.

The figure below shows this graphically. The gray triangle represents the dead weight loss.

Dead Weight Loss from Monopoly

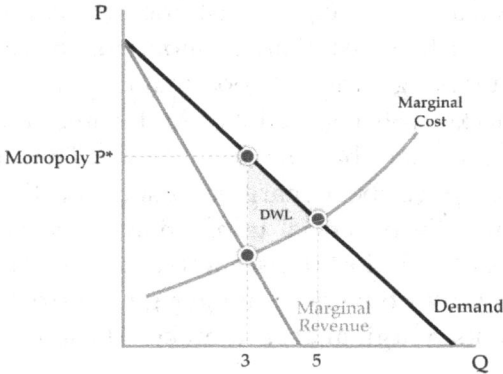

The monopolist sets MR=MC to find the profit-maximizing level of output at 3 units. The monopolist sets price from the demand curve. But a competitive firm would produce 5 and charge a price equal to marginal cost.

I think the easiest way to show why the monopoly is inefficient is to look at the fourth unit in the previous figure. Consumers value that fourth unit above the cost it takes to produce it. This is like saying it only costs $5 to make and someone values it at $8, so producing this would boost a consumer's happiness.

Lost Transactions

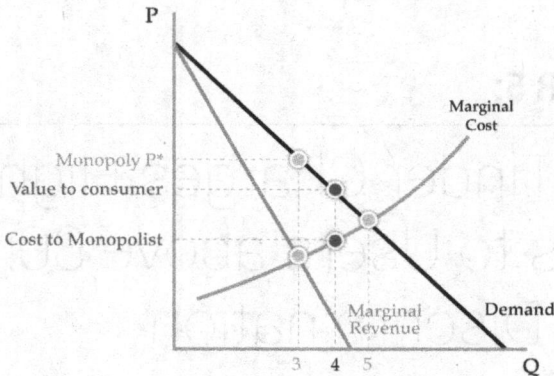

The monopolist produces 3 units and prices at the Monopoly P* The socially efficient level would be S units, that is, consumers value the 4th and 5th unit above the cost to produce it.

But that fourth unit doesn't get made. The monopolist profit maximizes by producing only three units. The monopolist would make less profit if they would sell that fourth unit since they would have to lower the price on all the previous units to attract that fourth buyer. So while the rational, profit-seeking monopoly benefits, those lost units (the fourth and fifth) are lost value to society.

We have looked deep into the economic theory of the firm to prove theoretically what you probably already intuitively knew: that monopolies charge higher prices than a market under competition and produce less. Next, we leave this world of pure theory and introduce some more real-world examples that will help answer more important questions. like: "How does economics explain why Tinder charges more to 30-year-old users for their premium subscription than users under 30?"

CHAPTER 5:

Why Tinder Charges Higher Prices to Users above 30: Price Discrimination

I have a good friend Shane who lives in Pittsburgh Pennsylvania. Shane has been in a long-distance relationship with a woman who lives in Orlando Florida. To see each other in person, they each take turns flying to visit each other. One month he heads to Orlando for a few days, the next time she flies up to Pittsburgh. On one visit the girlfriend mentioned how much she paid for her round-trip flight, $360. Shane told her that he paid $100 less for a round-trip flight to visit her in Orlando. Curious, they jumped online to see the price difference in flights. Flying from Pittsburgh to Orlando and back was a lot cheaper than from Orlando to Pittsburgh and back. But it's the same trip, just in the opposite direction.

Why would airlines charge you more to get to Pittsburgh than to Orlando?

If you're going to Orlando, there's a good chance you're planning to ride the Space Mountain rollercoaster and get a picture with Mickey Mouse at Disney World. Or maybe you'll see the whales perform at SeaWorld. Or maybe you'll go to Hogwarts at the Universal Orlando Resort or take the kids to Legoland.

There's so much to do in Orlando. It's a destination city and a place you've chosen to travel to over other vacation destinations you could've chosen. That is, most people flying into the city don't have to go to Orlando; they elected to go.

On the other hand, what's in Pittsburgh? As a vacation destination, it is considerably less glamorous.

If you're a Steelers fan, you can tour Heinz Field. Speaking of Heinz, you can tour the Senator John Heinz History Center, where there's an entire exhibit on ketchup. If you're looking for local cuisine, you can have a "sammich," which is basically a sandwich with French fries and coleslaw added. Sure, there's an aquarium, but it's no SeaWorld, and it's definitely not always sunny in Pittsburgh. There's an Andy Warhol museum in Pittsburgh. Do you think the kids would like that more than Space Mountain?

Obviously, people headed to Pittsburgh are more likely to be visiting family or to be business travelers. If you're flying in for Thanksgiving or a wedding, you've probably been planning the trip, and you're less likely to be price sensitive. The airlines know this.

Ever travel on your business's dime? The costs are covered by someone else, and you usually have a reason to be in certain town on a certain date, which means business travelers tend to be less price-sensitive; they have more inelastic demand than vacation travelers. This means business travelers are willing to pay more. Airlines know this too, so they design their pricing structures to boost profits.

This is a classic example of *price discrimination*, charging different customers different prices for the same product. (Remember, the flight between Orlando and Pittsburgh is the same distance either way; the only thing different is which direction you're going.)

In this chapter, we will see how price discrimination works, the different types of price discrimination, when it is illegal to charge different prices to different customers, and how price discrimination (from an economist's view) can improve the market.

But first a quick note about terminology. The economist's use of the term *discrimination* in the term *price discrimination* differs from today's common use of the term, which typically describes unjust treatment of a particular group, often accompanied by social and racial equity considerations. This book uses a less complex definition and the same terminology used 100 years ago by Arthur Pigou when his textbook *The Economics of Welfare* first discussed what he called the "discriminating monopolist."

One-Price vs Price-Discriminating Monopolist

In Chapter 4, we showed why a market dominated by a monopolist has a worse economic outcome than a perfectly competitive market. The monopolist charges a price higher than producers in a market with perfect competition do, so some people are priced out of purchasing the good, even though they are willing to pay more than it costs to produce. And the monopolist produces less than is economically efficient, so some resources sit idle. This is the idea of *dead weight loss*.

The monopolist ultimately doesn't produce those items because that monopolist must make a trade-off between price and quantity. The monopolist, who can only choose one price, is facing that downward-sloping demand curve. To gain more sales, the monopolist must lower the price. And, per our assumptions so far, the monopolist can only charge the same price to all customers.

But what if the monopolist didn't have to pick just one price?

What would it look like if the monopolist could charge different prices to different customers? In fact, what if a business could charge exactly what each customer is willing to pay? (You don't have to be a monopolist to apply price discrimination, but we start by looking at price discrimination in the monopoly model because it's much simpler than models with multiple firms in the same market).

Suppose there was an ice cream vendor who could magically determine each customer's willingness to pay for an ice cream cone.

Every customer standing in line to buy ice cream could have, say, a price tag floating over their heads revealing the exact maximum amount they're willing to pay for the treat. The first person in line would gladly pay $3 for a cone, and so the salesman would charge him $3. The next customer, a woman who's less price sensitive and a bigger ice cream fan, would pay $5.50 for a cone and gets charged that. Meanwhile, the last person in line, a teenage kid, is only willing to only 99 cents, so that's what the salesman charges him.

Would this system boost profit for the ice cream salesman? Of course, and here's how. Let's assume again each ice cream cone costs 50 cents to make. If the ice cream salesman has to select one price, he has a trade-off to make. If he prices at $2, he loses the kid only willing to pay 99 cents. If he prices at 99 cents, he forgoes the extra revenue he could make on customers who'd gladly pay $5.50 and $3.00. Suppose he chooses to price a cone at $3. His total revenue will be $6, and his total cost would be $1, for a $5 profit.

Profit: One-Price Monopolist = Total Revenue – Total Cost =
(2 × $3.00) - (2 × $0.50) = $5.00
Profit: Perfectly Price Discrimination = ($3.00 + $5.50 + $0.99)
- 3($0.50) = $7.99

It should not come as a surprise that a price-discriminating monopolist will boost profits by charging each customer's *reservation price*, the maximum price each person is willing to pay.

Not only would this boost profit for the monopolist, but it would also improve *economic efficiency*. The price-discriminating monopolist produces more than the one-price monopolist. Let's first see how that works before we get into the conceptual explanation.

We saw this example in the last chapter. The monopolist produces less than the perfectly competitive market and charges a higher price. The monopolist also creates dead weight loss. In the example below, the monopolist doesn't produce the 4th and 5th unit even though consumers value those units above the cost it would take to make them.

Dead Weight Loss from Single-Price Monopoly

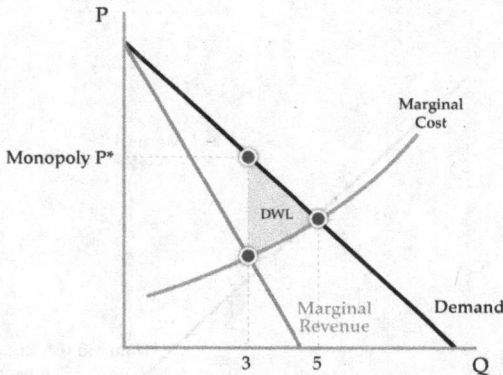

The monopolist sets MR=MC to find the profit-maximizing level of output at 3 units. The monopolist sets price from the demand curve. But a competitive firm would produce 5 and charge a price equal to marginal cost. The 4th customer doesn't get one.

Look at what happens if the monopolist can perfectly price discriminate. If this monopolist charges every customer their reservation price (or maximum willingess to pay), the marginal revenue curve won't be any different than the demand curve. The perfectly price-discriminating monopolist produces the exact amount that society wants. This eliminates the deadweight loss of the one-price monopolist because the marginal revenue curve of the perfectly price-discriminating monopolist is the same as the market demand curve. And so, the profit-maximizing monopolist sets MR=MC at the output level society wants. In this case, at 5 units.

The 4th and 5th customer are able to buy the item with price discrimination, but under the market with a one-price monopolist, those units aren't produced. Notice also there is no market price on the graph below since every customer paid a different price.

No Dead Weight Loss with Perfectly Price Discriminating Monopolist

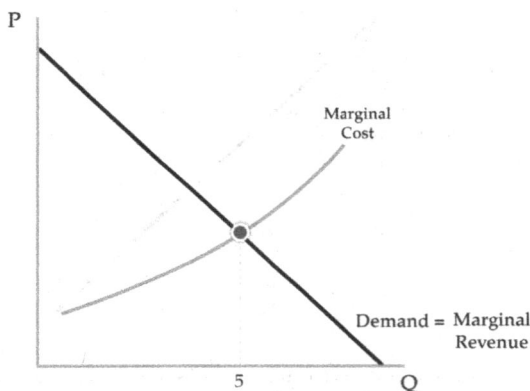

The perfectly price discriminating monopolist sets MR=MC but now the Demand Curve matches the MR curve since the monopolist charges everyone their reservation price. The perfectly price discriminating monopolist produces the same q as the PC market.

So, we've seen the two book-end examples, the monopolist who charges everybody the same price and the monopolist who charges everybody a different price. Price discrimination turns consumer surplus into the monopolist's profit while also producing the output level that would be reached in the competitive market.

Perfect price discrimination is extremely difficult to pull off, however: how often would customers walk into a store and easily reveal the maximum price they'd be willing to pay? Partial price discrimination on the other hand, is very doable. With partial price discrimination, the business doesn't charge each individual a different price, instead it charges different groups various prices.

Let's go back to our ice cream vendor. Now, instead of knowing what each customer is willing to pay, the vendor can only identify his customers as being in one of two unique customer groups. So instead the customer's reservation price, let's say that the tag tells the ice cream salesmen which customers are willing to pay a lot (those who are price insensitive) versus those who will only pay a little (who are price sensitive).

Partial Price Discriminating Ice Cream Salesman

If the ice cream salesman charges $3 to the cheap customers and $5 to the loaded customers.

$$Profit = Total\ Revenue - Total\ Cost = (Pcheap \times Qcheap)$$
$$+ (Ploaded \times Qloaded) - Cost =$$
$$\$3.00(1) + \$5.00(1) - \$0.50(2) = \$7.00$$

The partially price-discriminating monopolist will make a higher profit than the one-price monopolist but not as much as the perfectly price-discriminating monopolist.

In economics, price sensitivity is defined by how *elastic* or *inelastic* a buyer's demand is. While we consumers don't really have signs above our heads revealing our level of demand elasticity, we do have many "tells" that reveal to businesses what type of customer we are and how much we're willing to pay. We saw the first example earlier in the chapter, as the destination of your flight reveals your demand elasticity.

Economists call this a *segregating* or *separating* mechanism. To use price discrimination, a business:

1. Must have market or pricing power
2. Must have the ability to segment the market between customers with different demand elasticities
3. Must be able to prevent resale

The first criterion is straightforward. In order to charge different prices, a firm must have some control over price. In other words, it can't be a *price taker*. To charge multiple prices, the firm must command a share of the market large enough to have sufficient power to set prices.

The second criterion describes the ability of the company to determine who is more willing to pay and who is less willing to pay. If the company can't find clever ways to segment or segregate between customers with different price elasticities, then it can't successfully target prices to them.

The third criterion is preventing resale. If this doesn't happen, customers charged lower prices can turn around and sell what they've purchased to customers willing to pay a higher price. The economic term for this procedure is called *arbitrage*, or in more technical terms, "the purchase and sale of a good or asset to profit from an imbalance in price."

Arthur Pigou's 1920 textbook *The Economics of Welfare* was the first to describe three types of price discrimination:[82]

First-Degree: A seller charges a different price to each individual consumer; ideally, each price is based on the consumer's reservation price. It's sometimes called "perfect price discrimination."

Second-Degree: A seller offers quantity discounts or the opportunity to buy in bulk for a lower price.

Third-Degree: A seller can segment the market into unique groups based on demand elasticities and then offer a different price to each group.

How Do Sellers Segment Consumers and How Do Consumers Signal to Sellers?

If a business sells each item at the same price, the firm will leave money on the table no matter what price it picks as long as the customers have different demand elasticities between the customers. So, the strategy for sellers is to figure out how to get customers to "tip their hand" to reveal their willingness to pay. For instance, vacation travelers tend to book flights that include weekends in their itinerary and to book their flights further in advance.

And ski bums tend to sit at the bar.

One of my favorite ski towns is Crested Butte, Colorado. People from around the country and the world travel to this ski area. And along with their ski goggles and snow pants, tourists bring with them unique price sensitivities.

To keep it simple, let's say there are two unique types of people in a ski town. There's the local ski bum who lives on a modest income and the upper-income vacation traveler from Texas. The vacation traveler has a higher willingness to pay than the local ski bum. Economists would say the ski bum is more price sensitive, or has a more elastic demand, for tacos and beer than the vacation traveler.

If you go into the local Mexican restaurant in Crested Butte and look very closely behind the bar in between the myriad of tequila bottles on the wall, you'll notice a small sign that says, "Poor Boy Special." This sign inconspicuously advertises a shot of cheap tequila, a can of cheap beer, and a steak taco, all for $5. Meanwhile, if you look at the menu at a table in the dining area, two steak tacos cost $10, or $5 a taco. You'll also notice the "Poor Boy Special" isn't on the menu. You can only order the special at the bar.

Where you sit in the restaurant is a separating mechanism. Vacation travelers are most likely with their families and will sit in the dining room, since kids aren't allowed at the bar. Local ski bums don't mind sitting at the bar, particularly if they get a free shot and a beer for the same price the rich tourist is paying for the same steak taco alone. Patrons at the restaurant don't wear tags on their heads revealing how much to charge them, but where they sit in the restaurant is almost as good.

You see price discrimination and segmenting mechanisms in many other businesses. Popular segmenting mechanisms are time of day, day of the week, or consumer's age ("senior discounts" or "kids tickets"). All of these can be used to "read" your relative reservation price and/or demand elasticity.

One of my favorite examples of price discrimination was told to me by a student from Sweden, where people tend to have winter tires and summer tires for their cars. There are businesses that store drivers' tires during each season. But the monthly storage fee isn't based on the size of the tire---though it would make sense if larger tires were charged more because they take up more space and are therefore more costly to store.

No, that wasn't the case. The monthly fee to store the tires was based on the make and model of the car.

Even though the student's mother's tires were the same size as her father's, the mother was charged less because her tires came off a Cooper Mini, while her dad's came off an Audi. Expensive car owners are likely more willing to pay for tire storage.

Consumers are often unaware of the segmenting mechanism being used and can inadvertently signal their demand elasticity (which is why you should always be careful about the information you reveal). My brother works as an event planner for a luxury hotel, and many of the events he coordinates there are weddings. In addition to his base salary, he earns a commission: the more expensive the wedding, the bigger his paycheck. So it's in his interest to book the most expensive weddings possible, particularly since there are a limited number of Saturdays in a year.

When you call my brother up to start planning a wedding event, he'll get you chatting. "Oh, October is a wonderful month for a wedding," he'll say. "Why is October special to the wedding couple?" While he's got you gushing about how the couple met and why October is important to them, my brother is entering your zip code into real estate websites and determining the price of housing in your neighborhood: million-dollar houses mean more expensive weddings, so he's trying to gather data on how expensive a wedding he may be able to sell.

Customers can also actively try to signal less demand elasticity and more price sensitivity. I have friend, Jimbo, who recently got married. For the reception, he rented a large outdoor tent to accommodate 200 guests. The bride got the initial bid from the tent rental company after revealing the tent would be used for a wedding. Shocked by the sticker price, the groom called the same company and tried to book the tent for the same day, but said it was for a 10-year class reunion. His quote for the same tent was 35 percent cheaper than the one his fiancée got. Apparently, attendees at class reunions have much more elastic demand than wedding couples. In this case, my friend was able to figure out the business's separating mechanism and signal his price sensitivity.

A seller may create a way for customers to signal price elasticity, often using a "hurdle." Collecting coupons on groceries is one of the best examples. Everyone can use the coupons stuffed in their mailbox. But many people don't spend the time to collect, save, and use those coupons, and so they pay full price. The people who have more elastic demand for groceries will take the time to collect the coupons (jump the hurdle) and get the discount. And the grocery makes 75 cents extra revenue on the less price-sensitive customers.

Or in some cases, the signal may be a customer's offer to negotiate the price. The local pizza parlor doesn't overtly advertise each day's specials, but when I call to order a pizza, I always ask what type of specials they're running that day. The act of asking about discounts signals that I am a price-sensitive customer. This usually saves me a dollar or so. The next person who places the same order I did—and who doesn't ask about discounts—pays a little more.

At my local climbing gym in Denver, I overheard the climbing instructor giving an hour-long beginner class on rock climbing. The beginner class was at 2 p.m. and was advertised for those who were just getting started rock climbing. At the end of the hour-long class, the instructor offered the beginners a chance to get 50 percent off the monthly gym membership.

Finding 50 percent off the monthly gym fee a great bargain, I signed up for the 3 p.m. intermediate climber's class. After an hour of instruction, I had, in my mind, successfully jumped over the business's segmenting hurdle. After the class, I was poised to take advantage of the 50 percent off discount. But it never came. The instructor didn't extend the same discount given to the beginners. I was simultaneously disappointed as a rock climber and intrigued as an economist.

The climbing gym had devised a clever way for climbers to reveal their willingness to pay. Beginners, unsure whether they would enjoy climbing and could stand ripping the skin off their fingers, were more price-sensitive and so were offered the discount. Climbers in the intermediate class were already into climbing, so they were less price-sensitive and thus not offered the discount.

This only makes sense: Those intermediate climbers were likely already paying for a membership. Selecting between the intermediate and the beginner class was the segmenting mechanism that divided the more elastic from the less elastic. And spending an hour at the beginner class was the hurdle that separated anybody off the street from accessing the discount opportunity.

Sometimes the separating mechanism is age. The dating app Tinder has different premium monthly fees. Users under 30 are charged $9.99 a month while anyone 30 or older faces a $19.99 per month charge.[83]

A seller may also create different versions of the good and price them differently, allowing consumers to buy based on their elasticities. This explains why book publishers initially release a hardback cover version of the book at a higher price and then weeks later release the lower-priced paperback version. The readers who wish to read the book as soon as it comes out are more willing to pay the higher price for the hardcover, while those who are willing to wait will get the paperback version at a discount.

Preventing Resale

When you are dealing with tangible items, there is always the possibility of resale, which is a problem with price discrimination. Customers charged a lower price could turn around and then sell the items to individuals with a greater willingness to pay a higher price. There are all sorts of intriguing ways price-discriminating businesses prevent resale.

Sometimes the segmenting mechanism prevents resale: a teenager won't be accepted into the theater with a "senior discount" ticket. Sometimes transaction costs such as shipping prevent resale. Sometimes it's social pressure that prevents resale---it's hard to resell a taco at a restaurant to a stranger.

Is Price Discrimination Illegal?

The phrase "price discrimination" conjures a feeling of something illegal. Is it right that some people pay more and some less? I often get this question, particularly in the Friday morning lecture. "How is Ladies' Night legal? How is it fair I had to pay a $5 cover charge but women don't?"[84]

It turns out that federal law is more concerned with price discrimination between businesses to prevent monopolies and to encourage competition. In addition, courts at the federal level leave the price discrimination issue to states largely because the Equal Protection Clause of the Fourteenth Amendment speaks to state actions. In other words, gender-based discriminatory pricing allegations tend to arise from actions of private businesses and aren't subject to "state action."[85] Therefore, more discriminatory claims are brought under states' public accommodation statutes. Some states have prohibited gender-based pricing strategies, and some states have ruled in favor of them. California barred businesses from offering car wash discounts to women[86] Florida ruled that discounted drinks for ladies violated local anti-discrimination ordinances.[87] On the other hand, Illinois, for example, ruled in favor of discounts for women, holding that anti-discrimination provisions only disallowed actions that prohibited patronage, and discounts to women encouraged female patronage and didn't discourage male patronage.

Can We Avoid Price Discrimination as Consumers?

The prevalence of online shopping and big data have made price discrimination very sophisticated, as your computer history has tons of data that reveals your demand elasticity for various products. Even your choice of computer might also reveal your price elasticity: It turns out Mac users tend to be offered more expensive hotel rooms than PC users.[88]

So, as consumers aware of price discrimination, should we be more cognizant about not revealing our willingness to pay? Here are a few tips to help you avoid paying higher prices. For one, try disguising yourself online:

- Look for flights online at the library computer or internet café instead of your own computer at your home.
- Wipe your browser history and your computer cookies. Search for items online in different web browsers.

Another tip: Signal your greater demand elasticity. For example, put items in your online shopping cart and leave them there until a coupon comes in your email for that site.[89] Or, buy generic. Don't be afraid of generic tires or generic brand cereal; they are likely the same product but with a cheaper-looking label to attract more price-sensitive buyers while simultaneously discouraging shoppers influenced by name-brand items from taking advantage of the discount.

The best advice is simply to be more aware of the ubiquity of price discrimination in everyday life. Remember, the customer 20 feet away at the bar may be getting a free tequila shot with their cheaper tacos.

CHAPTER 6:

Game Theory and the Prisoner's Dilemma

I n 1970, the U.S. Congress passed the Public Health Cigarette Smoking Act that required cigarette packages be labeled with a "dangerous to your health" warning. It also banned cigarette companies from advertising on American TV and radio. What most people don't know is that regulations against advertising were actually supported by the tobacco industry.

Why would the tobacco industry ban its own ability to advertise on TV and radio?

The answer: to escape the even worse equilibrium the tobacco companies were already in.

To capture more market share, cigarette manufacturers competed aggressively with each other, requiring costly investments in advertising; it turns out the Marlboro Man was pretty expensive. With competing cigarette companies all running ads, each effort to steal market share was being canceled out by all the others.

So, the cigarette companies decided it would be better if no one advertised — since cigarette companies were all worse off when they advertised. But no one company would cut it's advertising on itself since a rival firm could advertise and grab more business. But when all the cigarette manufacturers do it, no one gets an advantage. Banning advertising eliminated that option, allowing for a drop in spending on advertising and an increase in profits.[90] And it worked: the tobacco companies' advertising budgets were 20-30% lower and profits were 30% larger in 1971.[91]

So far, we've assumed the consumers and producers in our models were playing golf: competitors are simply trying to achieve their individual personal best in a competition where everyone else is doing the same thing, independent of what anyone else was doing.

With strategic interactions, we are now playing tennis. What your opponent does changes what you do. If they're at the net, you need to play a lob. If they're deep on the court, then it's time to play a short shot. How you hit your tennis ball depends on your opponent's position and actions. In the same way, your pricing strategy depends upon what your competitor is doing with their prices.

Your advertising budget can be adjusted to respond to a competitor. In the perfectly competitive market, the interaction is very clear: if you price your product $0.01 above the equilibrium price, you'll sell no output. A monopoly firm is the only firm in a market, so there is no competition. But when a market is dominated by a few firms, then each firm must respond and react to the others. These types of strategic interactions necessitated a new branch of economics known as Game Theory.

Game Theory Thinking

On Tuesday mornings, I usually spend an hour at the local coffee shop. And during NFL football season, the discussion among the coffee shop crew is always answering the same question, "What would you have done differently if you were the Broncos' head coach?"

Here's the problem with Monday morning quarterback calls: they assume that the other team's strategy would stay unchanged. But if you change your strategy and zone cover the opponent's tight end, the quarterback would call an audible and change the strategy. Your change in strategy will prompt your opponent to also shift tactics.

This type of static-strategy thinking is different from Game Theory thinking. Static-strategy thinking says: hit the eight-ball at a 34-degree angle with a little speed, and it will go into the corner pocket. Game Theory thinking says: the eight-ball is going to see it coming and move out of the way.

We can distinguish Game Theory thinking from probability by the way poker players actually act at the table. A player adhering to probability theory alone to guide strategy would look at the probability that her hand is better than others', and she'd make bets in proportion to the strength of her hand. After many hands, the other poker players would pick up on this and know that this probability player has a good hand when she bets high.

The reaction of the other players would be to then fold when the probability player bet high, and that probability player wouldn't win big pots on good hands. That's why in the real world, good poker players don't only play the odds but instead also factor in the other players' conclusions drawn from their betting style. Poker requires sometimes deceiving your opponent: that is, to occasionally bet big when you have a bad hand and to bet small when you have a great hand, which is what Game Theory prescribes. (In poker, it's just called bluffing.)

Game Theory is a social science that studies strategical decision making. It teaches you to put yourself in the other players' shoes by predicting what the other players are doing and responding accordingly. It helps to find ways to cooperate even when people are motivated by self-interest. Game Theory teaches strategies to use in situations of competition, cooperation, and conflict, which is why a broad range of groups from the military to businesses have used Game Theory as a guide since its invention in the late 1940s.

Some Early History of the Field of Game Theory

Before Game Theory was invented, there were two big branches of economics: the theory of supply and demand in competitive markets, developed by Alfred Marshall and others, and Keynesian Economics, which described how the whole economy worked (Chapter 10). But answering questions such as how bidders decide how to bid in an auction or how businesses respond to regulation were areas where economists hadn't made as much progress.[92]

This is where John von Neumann comes into to the story. Von Neumann (1903-1957) often gets credit for being the father of Game Theory, and among his long list of accomplishments, which include pioneering the electronic digital computer, helping with the design the atomic bomb, and dabbling in quantum mechanics, von Neumann also teamed up with economist Oskar Morgenstern to write *Theory of Games and Economic Behavior* (1944). The 648-page monster of a book was hardly read and heavily laden with mathematics. But cut the pair a little slack; they were practically inventing a new discipline with its own unique language.

Part of Game Theory's language includes the terms *dominant strategy* (which gives you the best outcome no matter what your other choices are and what other people are doing) and *dominated strategy* (which gives a worse outcome than all other strategies, regardless of what the opponent does, leading to a worse payoff).

Von Neumann was blessed with a photographic memory. He read Greek and Latin in his childhood and impressed his family's houseguests with his ability to quickly memorize pages in a phone book.[93] Von Neumann drew inspiration from poker in studying deception, bluffing, and strategy, which he then applied to politics, economics, and foreign policy.

Much of the early history and development of Game Theory involved a mathematical proof of the "Minimax Theorem." The minimax principle involves analyzing a situation to see how much you might lose and then calibrating your strategy so as to *mini*mize your *max*imum possible loss. Or in other words, make the worst scenario the least painful.

The easiest way to grasp the minimax strategy is by considering the problem of two kids deciding how to divide a piece of cake between themselves. Often referred to as the "I cut, you choose" procedure, one child cuts the cake, and the other gets to decide which piece they get. It works because the cutter has every incentive to divide the cake equally in order to lose as little as possible: the minimax outcome.

In zero-sum games, the gains of one player come from the loss of another player, so when you add up total gains and losses at the end of the game, they sum to zero. The term "zero-sum game" is a popular phrase in everyday English that came from Game Theory.

Rock, Paper, Scissors" is an example of a zero-sum game. Each of my wins comes from my opponent's losses and vice versa. This also means that the best strategy can be worked out using the Minimax principle.

The best strategy when playing rock, paper, scissors over and over is to mix up your rocks and your papers and your scissors — throwing each one-third of the time. Just think: if you play rock two-thirds of the time, your opponent will catch on and play paper two-thirds of the time, and you'll lose. In Game Theory parlance, this is known as a "mixed strategy." The idea also explains how baseball pitchers mix up their pitches between fastballs, curve balls and change-ups to confuse batters.

In the early days of Game Theory, zero-sum games were the only situations that the nascent discipline envisioned. Von Neumann looked at two-party, zero-sum games which, when one player's gain is another's loss, involve no coalition strategies because your opponent's gain always comes at your loss. But zero-sum games couldn't account for economic interactions that create positive economic surplus to divvy up. That leads us to John Nash (1928-2015), who followed von Neumann as the next major contributor to Game Theory by studying "noncooperative" games.

Nash started by defining a particular solution to a game, a Nash Equilibrium, in which each player is making the best decision given the strategies that others are using. To say it another way, those solutions are where players have no regrets in their strategy.

Think of a Nash Equilibrium as, to quote William Poundstone, "an outcome in which no one, playing Monday-morning quarterback, regrets choosing the strategy he did given the other player's choice."[94] A Nash Equilibrium is a situation in which no player can improve their payout given what others are doing. Nash used the term "equilibrium" because the sense of a point of balance in a situation—in other words, the interaction of supply and demand like the Nash Equilibrium—is the place things end up. No side can gain from changing, which keeps them where they are. Nash showed that equilibrium solutions also existed for non-zero-sum, two-player games.

Nash's struggle with mental illness and his recovery led to Sylvia Nasar's biography, "A Beautiful Mind," which was adapted into the Best Picture Oscar-winning movie featuring Russell Crowe. In fact, the question "Who is John Nash?" was the answer to a Final Jeopardy question from a 2016 episode that asked, "The only Nobel Prize winner to be the title subject of a Best Picture Oscar winner is this man."

The concept of Nash Equilibrium is central to the most famous game in Game Theory: the Prisoner's Dilemma, in which certain incentive schemes encourage self-destructive behavior.

The mathematical set-up to the prisoner's dilemma (yet to be coined at this point in history) came from an experiment by RAND Corporation colleagues Melvin Dresher and Merrill Flood in January 1950. The RAND Corporation, a think tank founded shortly after World War II, was created to study strategies on nuclear war.

Dresher and Flood put two of their friends in a game where they either chose "cooperate" or "defect." Depending upon the combination of choices, each player won or lost between zero and two pennies (paid from the experimenter). The payout for "defect" was greater than the payout for cooperation. But when both played "defect," the outcome was worse than if they both had just cooperated. They played the game 100 times and kept track of the dialogue between players. Unique to their payout design was that both players found that one strategy was more profitable no matter what the other player did, yet when both of the players played their "better" strategy, both did worse. Their payouts would have been higher if both played the "worse" strategy, but only if both did so.

Dresher showed their experiment to a RAND consultant, Albert Tucker, a Princeton mathematician, who added the anecdote we know today. In May 1950 (a few months after the original Flood-Dresher Experiment), Albert Tucker was giving a lecture on Game Theory to the Stanford University psychology department. To appeal to the psychologist in the room who had little background in the mathematics of Game Theory, Tucker decided to present the dilemma as part of a story. In that story, he coined the term "prisoner's dilemma" (a testament to the power of teaching with stories).

In one of Tucker's letters, he includes a description of the prisoner's dilemma[95]:

> Two men, charged with a joint violation of law, are held separately by the police. Each is told that (1) if one confesses and the other does not, the former will be given a reward....and the latter will be fined...(2) if both confess, each will be fined .....at the same time, each has good reason to believe that (3) if neither confesses, both will go clear.

The story has gotten better over the years with various retellings, but the gist remains the same. Many of those versions include prison terms. A typical version in an Economics 101 class goes like this:

> Two members of a criminal gang are arrested with a substantial amount of illegal drugs in their possession. The prisoners are taken to two separate jail cells with no means of speaking to or exchanging messages with one another. Given that they are caught red-handed on drug possession, both are facing two years in jail. The police also have a suspicion that the same two criminals were responsible for a bank robbery the week before, but there is no evidence that ties the criminals to the robbery. The only way the police can get a conviction for the bank robbery is to get one of the criminals to confess. Prosecutors offer each

criminal a deal: "If you confess to the bank robbery, your partner gets five years in jail and you get one year in jail."

The police go on further to say, "If both of you confess to the bank robbery, then both of you will get three years in jail, and if neither of you confess, then you are still facing two years on the drug possession charge." The two gang members are informed that the other prisoner is being offered the very same deal. Each is concerned with his own welfare — minimizing his own prison sentence length. The prisoners must make their decision without learning what the other prisoner has chosen.

Both prisoners have two choices: to confess or to deny. So, each prisoner has two separate strategies, which means there are four different outcomes. The decision can be framed as a matrix (shown below), illustrating the players' payoffs. For instance, if both prisoners deny, then each gets two years in jail. (See the upper left quadrant of the matrix). If both confess, then they get to the bottom right square of three years for each.

A payout matrix is a quick way to show each players' incentives and strategies. In matrix form below, the payouts on the left side of each box correspond to the row-player's (prisoner 1) payouts, while the second number (right side of the box) gives the payouts for the column player (prisoner 2). This will make more sense as we work through this scenario.

Prisoner's Dilemma Payoff Matrix

		Prisoner 2		
		DENY	CONFESS	
Prisoner 1	DENY	2 years 2 years	5 years 1 year
	CONFESS	1 year 5 years	3 years 3 years

Here's the logic of the dilemma in each prisoner's mind: "If I confess and my partner doesn't, then I only get one year in jail rather than spending two years in prison for the drug charge. I should confess in this case." Look at this situation from prisoner 2's position. If prisoner 1 decided to confess, then prisoner 2's choices are between five years if he denies and three years if he confesses.

Prisoner 2's Payoffs if Confess

Prisoner 2

		DENY		CONFESS	
	DENY	2 years	2 years	5 years	1 year
Prisoner 1					
	CONFESS	1 year	**5 years**	3 years	(**3 years**)

If prisoner 1 confesses, the best pick for prisoner 2 is to confess.

Prisoner 1's Payoffs if Deny

Prisoner 2

		DENY		CONFESS	
	DENY	2 years	**2 years**	5 years	(**1 year**)
Prisoner 1					
	CONFESS	1 year	5 years	3 years	3 years

If prisoner 1 denies, the best pick for prisoner 2 is to confess.

Also, "suppose I confess, and my partner also confesses, then I get three years in jail instead of five. Either way, I'm better off confessing. To look at it another way, confessing reduces my sentence no matter what the other guy does!"

The trouble is that both prisoners come to the same conclusion. It's in their best interest to confess. But as both players choose to confess, both get three years in jail. If they both would've stayed quiet, they could've each received only a two-year sentence.

No matter which strategy prisoner 2 selects, it is always in prisoner 1's best interest to confess. If prisoner 2 denies, then prisoner 1's options are between two years in jail if denying, and only one year in jail if confessing. Since one year in prison is better than two, the best strategy for prisoner 1 is to confess in this instance.

Prisoner 2's Payoffs if Deny

		Prisoner 2	
		DENY	CONFESS
Prisoner 1	DENY	2 years **2 years**	5 years (1 year)
	CONFESS	1 year 5 years	3 years 3 years

If prisoner 1 denies, the best pick for
prisoner 2 is to confess.

If prisoner 2 confesses, then prisoner 1's options are between five years in jail if denying, and three years in jail if confessing. Since three years in prison is better than five, the best strategy for prisoner 1 is to confess in this instance.

Prisoner 1's Payoffs if Confess

		Prisoner 2			
		DENY		CONFESS	
	DENY	2 years	2 years	**5 years**	1 year
Prisoner 1					
	CONFESS	1 year	5 years	(3 years)	3 years

If prisoner 2 confesses, the best pick for
prisoner 1 is to confess.

What strategy works best for you when your partner is also looking out for his own interest? The answer is confess. But there is a seemingly odd contradiction: if both stayed quiet, both would get two years instead of three.

Finding the Nash Equilibrium

Prisoner 2

		DENY	CONFESS
	DENY	2 years 2 years	5 years (1 year)
Prisoner 1	CONFESS	(1 year) 5 years	(3 years) 3 years)

Nash Equilibrium

If both prisoners stay quiet, they'd get to a better outcome, but by playing their best response (dominant strategy) they end up in a worse outcome. The prisoner's dilemma is used to embody those situations when players, who think about their individual interest, get into a Nash Equilibrium that is worse for each in the group. The prisoner's dilemma can be used to describe a variety of situations in business and in everyday life. The prisoner's dilemma is not always about reducing losses. Sometimes it can be about pursuing gains, like our tobacco company example. The key facet to a prisoner's dilemma is when two entities pursue their own self-interest, they arrive at a worse collective outcome than if they had coordinated with each other.

Prisoner's Dilemmas in Everyday Life

Unlike many airlines that allow you to choose your seat when buying the ticket, Southwest Airlines has an open boarding policy. You aren't assigned seats on this airline, and instead you can select any available seat as you board the aircraft. The first ones to board have better options, like taking the emergency exit rows that contain extra leg room or snagging the window seats. Having a boarding position in the C group generally relegates you to a middle seat. The order in which passengers board is important.

Southwest knows this and offers extras for priority boarding. Let's say there are 10 emergency exit seats available with extra leg room. The first 10 adults on the plane will select those seats. For an extra $25, you can buy a $25 priority seating upgrade and guarantee yourself an A group boarding position. It's all about relative order.

I had a student who was traveling with his family on a Southwest flight out of Denver when he overheard another family talking near the gate about paying for the $25 priority boarding upgrade to snag the emergency row seats. My student had an early A boarding position but didn't pay for the upgrade. Once they saw the other family pay the extra $25, it was just like someone jumping the line right in front of you. His family was losing their advantage in real time. To get it back, they also approached the desk and shelled out an extra $25 to leap in front of the family that just did the same. This sent the boarding order back to where it originally was before any family upgraded. Everyone would have been better not upgrading, but once one family did, it forced the others to respond.

The boarding gate at an airport isn't the only place where you can find a prisoner's dilemma. It happens at baggage claim too. When's the last time you were at the luggage carousel at an airport waiting for your bags and everybody was politely standing back five feet from the carousel so everybody else could see bags arriving? Exactly. Never.

Instead, everyone crowds right next to the carousel forcing the other travelers to crowd around and strain their necks across everyone else crowding around the carousel—a slightly different version of everyone ending up standing at a concert.

If everyone would just stand back from the baggage carousel, all travelers would be better off. But once one passenger stands right at the baggage chute, it obstructs everyone else, forcing them to respond with the same strategy (the

Nash Equilibrium), straining their necks down the row to see if their bags are coming out.

The Prisoner's Dilemma helps explain why hockey players normally vote unanimously to require full face guards to protect their face and teeth but left to their own choices, no single player decides to wear a full face mask.

Why?

If you are the only hockey player who wears a full face mask, you lose a slight competitive advantage. You might have a little of your vision impaired or you might appear weak compared to the rest of the players in the league who don't wear the masks. The end result is many more hockey players with front teeth damage than would otherwise be the case. (The same dynamic played out in the 1950s and 1960s when NHL players didn't even wear helmets to cover the tops of their heads.)

The same logic explains why you rarely see NFL football players wearing full sleeves under their jerseys to stay warm, even when they are playing at the Green Bay Packers' Lambeau Field in 24-degree weather. All players would be more comfortable if they all wore long sleeves, but sleeves cover up your muscles, and you lose the intimidation factor. Rarely is there a sole lineman who wants to be the only one with sleeves because they might fear the ridicule of opponents.

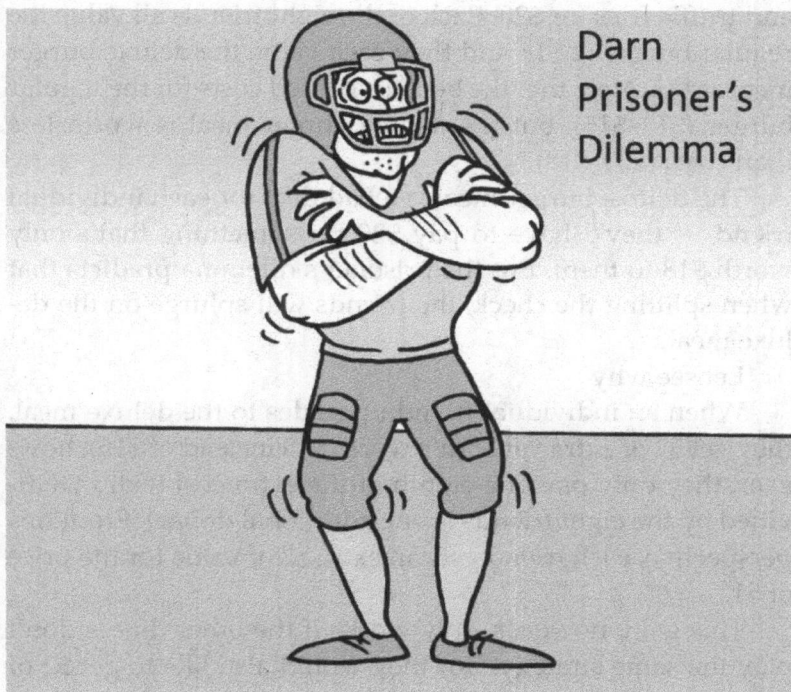

Darn Prisoner's Dilemma

The same bad equilibrium can occur when you decide to split the bill with fellow diners at a restaurant.

Imagine you go out to eat with seven other people and you decide to split the check evenly. Knowing this, do you order the modest dish and water to drink or do you splurge on extra appetizers and costly drinks?

Let's simplify the check-splitting game to see why everyone ends up paying more for items they don't even value above the actual cost and to see how this results in the bad equilibrium of a prisoner's dilemma.

Suppose there are eight friends splitting the bill at a restaurant. There are two items on the menu: a $12 burger and fries and a deluxe burger with bacon and blue cheese and truffle fries for $20. Each of the eight friends all value the regular burger at $16 and they each value the deluxe burger meal at $18. Note that the benefits exceed costs for the regular burger ($12<$16), but the deluxe burger meal is worth less than costs ($20>$18).

The deluxe burger meal is a bad deal for each individual friend — they'd have to pay $20 for something that's only worth $18 to them. But the prisoner's dilemma predicts that when splitting the check, the friends will splurge on the deluxe meal.

Let see why.

When an individual friend upgrades to the deluxe meal, they get $2 of extra value (it's worth $18 instead of $16), however, they only pay one-eighth of the extra cost (extra $8 divided by the eight friends is one additional dollar). From this perspective, each friend gets an extra $2 of value for the price of $1.

This gain, however, only works if the other diners don't play the same strategy. But they would also like to get $2 of value for the cost of $1. And so every diner sees their best strategy is to splurge.

The math example also helps explain why it is a losing strategy to order the regular burger when everyone else is ordering the deluxe. If one friend ordered the regular burger meal, the total bill would fall from $160 to $152 causing everyone's bill to drop from $20 each to $19 each. So the person ordering the regular burger is now paying $19 for a burger they only value at $16 — a $3 dollar loss between value and cost. That's even worse than paying $20 for something they only value at $18.

The outcome has everyone paying $20 for a meal they only value at $18. Each has a dominant strategy to order the deluxe burger meal, and it throws the check-splitters into a prisoner's dilemma.

When a Few Liars Force Everyone into a Prisoner's Dilemma

Let's say you have a small ski resort in the Colorado Rockies that needs to attract skiers to buy your single-day lift tickets. Your potential customers decide which resort to ski based on which resort gets the most snow overnight. You also know that the owner of the rival ski resort 30 miles away always lies about the resort's snow totals. Both your mountain and your rival's mountain only got one inch of fresh Colorado powder snow last night, but your unscrupulous rival lies and reports to the public four inches. The embellished snow total will allow your rival to capture many more skiers who would have otherwise skied at your place.

What do you do? Do you lie in response to the liar?

Since fresh snow is a big driver of a skier's enjoyment of skiing, there are incentives for resorts to over-report snow totals. So, do ski resorts lie? Jonathan Zinman and Eric Zitzewitz set out to answer that exact question in "Wintertime for Deceptive Advertising."[96] The authors looked at over 56,000 single-day snow reports from ski resorts in the U.S. and Canada between 2004 and 2008. They also had a great control group in the National Weather Service: since it has no incentive to lie, it provides reliable snowfall totals compared to those resorts might report.

The pair found that ski reports announced new snow totals that were around 15-20% greater than nearby snowfall totals reported by the National Weather Service system. They also found that overreporting occurred more often on weekends when there was more ski traffic and thus a greater reward to lie.

It also turned out that ski resorts that had better cellphone service were less likely to overreport their snow totals because of the monitoring impact of skiers posting their own snow totals from their smart phones. *Monitoring* can be one solution to escape this prisoner's dilemma.

Just like ski resorts had to embellish their snow totals in response to other resorts fudging the figures, users of online dating sites have to embellish their attributes in response to other lying online dating site users. This dynamic plays out in online dating (there are just way too many men claiming to be six feet tall making $100,000). The prisoner's dilemma helps explain how we get stuck in situations of bad equilibria.

Think of it another way, if you are 5 foot 10 inches, and you know that everybody else in the online dating world (your competitors) are skewing their profile answers, it forces you to claim that you are six feet tall. Particularly since being above the six-foot mark gets you more potential dates. You must assume that the people looking at your profile are going to discount what you say. To be in the running, you are forced to exaggerate your features too, so it's no wonder that dating profiles report that men are taller, make more money, and stretch the definition of "athletically fit."[97] If everyone is doing it, it puts the truthful profile at a disadvantage. But so long as everyone is stretching the truth, it does you no good to be the only one telling the complete truth — that's a *dominated* strategy.

One solution would be *verification*. But how are online dating apps supposed to double check your height, weight, income and whether that featured picture is actually from 10 years ago? People discount what people say knowing they are lying. If everybody is lying, it puts the truthful person in a bad position. The ones who are actually telling the truth lose here. It's a prisoner's dilemma.

I see the same Catch-22 logic trap of the prisoner's dilemma when I'm looking for lodging every March for a weekend getaway in Leadville, Colo. Every year, Leadville (elevation 10,151') hosts an annual ski joring festival. Ski joring is a sport where a horse and rider race down a snow-packed main street pulling a skier who's holding on to a rope. As the horse gallops, the skier flies over jumps and grabs rings set up along parts of the course. The event is an excellent spectator sport.

Every year, I make it a weekend trip to watch the event. This requires me to find lodging for Friday and Saturday night, which usually means me trying to find a place on Airbnb about two months in advance.

I jump on the website and see an advertisement for the Miner's Shack apartment in Leadville for $61 a night! That seems like great deal. But then I realize that the $61 price doesn't include the $40 cleaning fee, the $14 service fee, and the $9 in occupancy fees and taxes. The total is actually $124 a night.

OK, $124 is a little more than I want to spend per night, so I keep looking. I see a condo that says "Pets OK" for $85 a night. Seems like a great deal! I won't have to find a sitter for my dog. Then I see that the cost doesn't include the $40 cleaning fee, the $18 service fee or the $11 occupancy taxes. What seems like a place to stay for under $100 a night turns out to be $154 all in.

Hmm....

I keep searching until I see a private room with a hot tub just a block from historic downtown Leadville that's only $94 a night! After a quick inspection, I learn that, with the cleaning and service fees and the occupancy fees, the total cost is actually $151 a night. Close to $60 more than the originally advertised price. I see a tiny house is listed for $166 a night, but $246 once all those fees are included.

Why don't Airbnb listers just tell you the total price to begin with?

Consider what happens when the owner of one Airbnb decides to advertise its total price. The listing that plays it straight puts itself at a disadvantage with its competitors because it seems to be charging the highest price when customers do a comparison Airbnb search. The all-in price gets a lot less clicks and views from potential Airbnb renters. Even worse, since renters are accustomed to having extra fees and taxes applied at checkout, the all-in price will look even worse. In other words, the problem could be solved if everyone advertised the full price, but the first one to do so loses and therefore it doesn't happen. This is known in Game Theory as a "first mover" problem.

The problem here is that the whole situation is stuck in a bad equilibrium. The prisoner's dilemma illuminates the logical conundrum that explains why we often stay in bad equilibria. Customers assume there will be a lot of added hidden fees at the end. It makes it hard for the honest listing to cut through the clutter. A better outcome for Airbnb customers would be to legislate a change in the convention: require that only the total price be shown (fees and taxes included) to all listings.

Or think of how we originally got to this equilibrium. If Airbnb listers originally advertised the all-in price (fees and taxes included), there would be a tempting incentive for one lister to switch to the hidden fee method and capture more renters. Just like one person standing up at a concert forces all others to stand, the one lister grabbing the relative advantage would force all others to do the same. Again, it's back to the "relative advantage," that only works to your advantage if the rest of the competitors don't do it. The problem with the prisoner's dilemma is that all the competitors *do* do it!

We can see that play out when competitors are setting their prices.

For our example, consider two competing ice cream stands along a popular beach boardwalk: Ed's Ice Cream Stand and Andrew's Ice Cream Stand. Both Ed and Andrew sell ice cream cones that cost $1 to make. Each stand knows that if they charge $4 for the cone, each will sell 100 cones a day for a profit of $300 (total revenue - total cost: ($4 × 100) − ($1 × 100) = $300.

Ed and Andrew also know that if they lower their cone price by $1 while the other holds his price unchanged, then the lower-priced ice cream stand will gain an additional 60 cone sales, 40 of whom shift to it from the other stand and 20 customers who are new.

Each ice cream stand therefore has the temptation to undercut the other and gain more customers. The purpose of this example is to show how these temptations play themselves into a prisoner's dilemma. For simplicity, let's suppose that each firm chooses between two prices: $4 or $3 per cone.

If one cuts his price to $3 while the other remains at $4, that seller gains an additional 60 customers, while the other loses 40 customers. The profits are ($3 × 160) − ($1 × 160) = $320 for the price cutter and only $4(100 - 40) - $1(100 - 40)= $180 for the other stand.

If both ice cream stands cut their price to $3 at the same time, the existing customers all stay put, and each gain an additional 20 customers. Under this scenario, each makes ($3 × 120) − ($1 × 120) = $240.

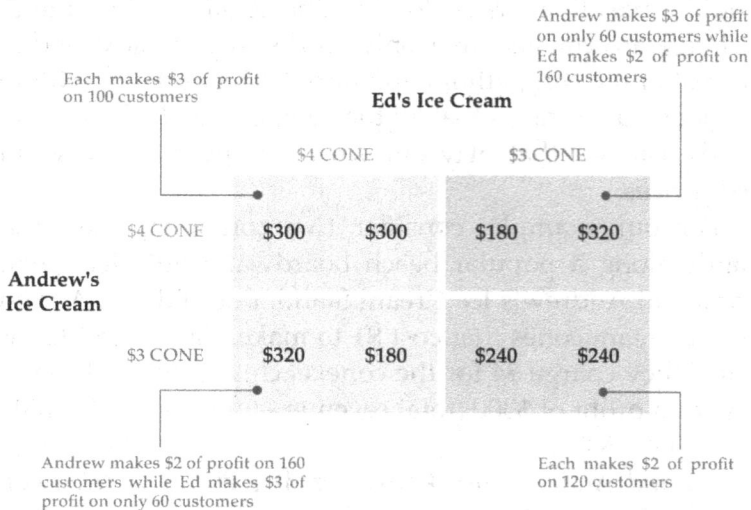

Andrew makes $3 of profit on only 60 customers while Ed makes $2 of profit on 160 customers

Each makes $3 of profit on 100 customers

Ed's Ice Cream

		$4 CONE		$3 CONE	
Andrew's Ice Cream	$4 CONE	$300	$300	$180	$320
	$3 CONE	$320	$180	$240	$240

Andrew makes $2 of profit on 160 customers while Ed makes $3 of profit on only 60 customers

Each makes $2 of profit on 120 customers

We also assume that each ice cream stand acts simultaneously, so each must think about what the other ice cream seller is thinking. Let's see how each, using the same reasoning, gets themselves into the prisoner's dilemma.

Starting with Andrew, if Ed prices at $4, Andrew can get $320 instead of $300 if he lowers his cone price to $3, so pricing $3 is the best option here. We identify that by circling $320 in the matrix below.

Ed's Ice Cream

		$4 CONE		$3 CONE	
	$4 CONE	**$300**	$300	$180	$320
Andrew's Ice Cream					
	$3 CONE	(**$320**)	$180	$240	$240

If Ed prices at $3, Andrew can get $180 if he prices at $4 or $240 if he prices at $3 — again, pricing at $3 is the best option. Circle $240 below. In both cases, pricing at $3 is better than pricing at $4.

Ed's Ice Cream

		$4 CONE		$3 CONE	
Andrew's Ice Cream	$4 CONE	$300	$300	**$180**	$320
	$3 CONE	$320	$180	**$240**	$240

Ed's reasoning is the same as Andrew's analysis. Each has a dominant strategy to price at $3. The result of the "game" is shown below where both charge $3.

Ed's Ice Cream

		$4 CONE		$3 CONE	
Andrew's Ice Cream	$4 CONE	**$300**	**$300**	**$180**	**$320**
	$3 CONE	**$320**	**$180**	**$240**	**$240**

Nash Equilibrium

When both players use their dominant strategy, both do worse than if they could somehow come together and agree to keep cone prices at $4. Note that customers do better from lower prices from competition; the prisoner's dilemma described occurs between the interests of the two competing firms.

What can Ed and Andrew do to escape the prisoner's dilemma and get to the $300 payout?

Ed and Andrew could agree to keep prices high. This type of explicit agreement is known as collusion and allows two competitors to act like a monopoly. (We learned chapter 4 how monopolies charge higher prices and produce less than a competitive market). Ed and Andrew's Ice Cream acting as a cartel produces the same monopolist outcome.

Collusion might work if both sellers can trust each other. But then again, there's always the problem of each ice cream seller reneging on their promise. And that's the catch of the prisoner's dilemma: the temptation to cheat on the agreement since each has an incentive to do better (at least for a little while) by cheating on that agreement.

One factor that tempers that temptation is *repeated interactions*. In the case of Ed and Andrew's ice cream shop, each ice cream seller will be in business every day for the next four summer months. Knowing that they will continue to play the same "game" each day would change their strategy. Consider, for example, if each ice cream seller only had one day to sell ice cream (a one-time game). Then each would play their dominant strategy, and we'd expect each to price low at $3.

If collusion won't work, businesses instead sometimes turn to a policy that appears to promote competition, but it's actually a method to keep prices high.

We see this in businesses that have "price match" promotions. This occurs when companies commit to charging no more than their rival firms. "If you find the same product sold for less," they say, "we will match that price."

Consider Firm A, which is selling an item at $50 that costs only $40 to make. The firm is making a $10 profit. With profit available, there's room for a competing firm to jump in and sell that item for $45, thereby undercutting the competition and gaining customers. But the "price match" mechanism prevents this from happening. The Game Theorist would call this *credible commitment*.

Here's why: Firm B reasons that if it does cut its price, the rival Firm A already announced it will match that lower price, so firm B won't gain any customers. Firm A's declaration that it will match a rival's price actually looks more like collusion. At first glance, you would think that the winner of a "price match" policy would be the consumer. But a little Game Theory analysis shows just the opposite: it helps prices stay high.

Escaping the Prisoner's Dilemma

The notion that players can take action to "change the game" was added by Thomas Schelling in his articles in the late 1950s and early 1960s that were collected into his books.[98] Schelling added to Game Theory the formulations of the concepts of commitment, threat, and promise.

One solution to the prisoner's dilemma is to avoid the prisoner's dilemma in the first place. This is what we try to do with regulations, laws, ethics, disclosures, and other coop-eration-promoting mechanisms.

One such threat is known as the "code" in hockey that helps explain why the gloves coming off during hockey games in a violent fight might curtail violence in hockey. The enforcement mechanism is typically the fist-fighting ability of the team's "enforcer." In hockey, skilled players measure success in goals and assists while the enforcers measure it in penalty minutes. Fighting is often a form of retaliation after an opposing player endangers another opponent and can be a strategic tactic.

The National Hockey League is the only major professional sports league that allows fighting. The game governs itself. The objective is to prevent cheap shots and dirty play, because if one team is relying on a strategy of cheap shots and dirty play, it forces the other team to do the same. Fights serve as a deterrent, keeping both teams out of the prisoner's dilemma where every team would have to play dirty.

Game Theorists describe two categories of threats: *credible* and *noncredible*. For a threat to work and encourage good behavior, there has to be follow up — making it credible. And it's best described by an anecdote in Ross Berstein's 2006 book "The Code: the Unwritten Rules of Fighting and Retaliation in the NHL" when the St. Louis Blues' team doctor, J.G. Probstein, described an incident from the late 1960's in which defenseman Noel Picard came into the locker room with a cut over his eye that would eventually need 11 stitches. Picard then asked the doctor, shared by both teams, how long he would be down there.

"Till the end of the game," the doctor said.

"Good," said Picard, "because the guy that did this to me will be down to see you in 10 minutes!"[99]

That's following through.

Once that reputation about fighting was established, fighting wasn't needed as much since the threat of fighting helped encourage good behavior. NHL player and enforcer Tony Twist described a compliment he once received about his role as a feared enforcer: "I had become so good at my job that after a while they didn't even need me anymore . . . that they just needed to put a cardboard cutout of me down on the end of the bench like a scarecrow. That was enough for the opposition to behave."[100]

Retaliation also helps explain why Major League Baseball batters in the American League get hit by more pitches than batters in the National League.

Why?

In the U.S., there are two separate leagues with slightly different rules. Because the American League has the designated hitter; the pitcher doesn't bat in the American League. That's unlike the National League, where a pitcher who plunked an opponent an inning earlier might be looking at a 95-mph fastball to his shoulders when he steps to the plate.

National League   American League

In addition to retaliation, sometimes communication and negotiation (like that of the ice cream stands above) are methods to break out of the prisoner's dilemma. Solving the problem of cooperation requires finding an agreement and finding ways to ensure people stick to that agreement.

Those dynamics are illustrated with a delicious prisoner's dilemma in the end segment of the British TV game show called "Golden Balls." In the ending segment of the show, two contestants play a game called "Split or Steal." Say the contestants have won $100,000. That prize money is divided depending on how each of the two players chooses to "split" or "steal" the money. If both choose the "split" ball, then they both share the prize money evenly. But if one chooses "split" and the other picks "steal," then the person who chose "steal" gets all the money (all $100,000) and the other player gets zero. And if they both pick the "steal" ball, then both players get zero.

In a payout matrix form, the game looks like this with the payouts representing what portion of the total purse each player receives.

Split or Steal Payoff Matrix

		Player 2			
		SPLIT		STEAL	
	SPLIT	50%	50%	0%	100%
Player 1					
	STEAL	100%	0%	0%	0%

Each player has a dominant strategy to "steal," but as each plays that strategy, it gets both to a worse outcome. It's the prisoner's dilemma in game show form. You should be able to understand why the lower right quadrant of the above payout matrix is the Nash Equilibrium.

The TV show adds a twist for the audience and allows the players to talk to each other before choosing their "split" or "steal" ball. The extra communication usually sees the players trying to convince the other to not play the dominant strategy. This usually means that each player promises they will play "split" and also tries to persuade the other player to do the same.

But if we apply the logic of Game Theory, we can see why promising to split doesn't work. Let's look at the payout matrix when Player 2 promises to "split." By vowing to split, Player 2 is telling Player 1 to look at the game with the assumption of Player 2 splitting.[101]

Player 1's Payoffs if Player 2 Splits

		Player 2	
		SPLIT	
Player 1	SPLIT	50%	50%
	STEAL	100%	0%

If Player 1 knows Player 2 already chose "split," the choice is between winning 50 or 100 % of the prize money. It makes it very tempting to steal because Player 2 is saying, "Don't worry about the mutual steal outcome because I'm going to split."

This seems like a paradox, but what if Player 2 tells them that they are going to steal?

That's what happened with a player named Nick. At the start of the "Split or Steal" segment, Nick quickly announces to the other player, "I want you to choose split, and I promise you that I will split the money with you (after the show)." Nick promises that he is going to steal.

The next few minutes of the show was a funny and intense exchange between Nick and the other player, Ibrahim. Nick kept promising that he was going to steal, and Ibrahim didn't seem to know what to do with Nick's threat. If Nick was going to steal, then split later after the show, why not just both choose "split" originally?

Let's go back to our Game Theory analysis to see why Nick's strategy was very clever. Nick changed the game into the payout matrix below by explaining he was going to steal.

Player 2

		STEAL	
SPLIT		0%	100% ●
STEAL		0%	0%

Player 1

Guarantees a 50% 50% split when show is over

The other player, Ibrahim, could still steal, but he now knows that stealing will surely result in zero for both. The other option is for Ibrahim to split and hope Nick kept his word to split the money after the show. Game Theory would describe what Nick did as transforming the game so that the dominant strategy was no longer to steal.

In the end, Ibrahim played split and Nick also played split (Nick didn't steal like he said he was going to). They each won half of the prize money. Nick's lie to Ibrahim about playing steal help beat the Prisoner's Dilemma. Nick's tactics also helped my students escape the prisoner's dilemma.

On my final exam, I present my students with a similar prisoner's dilemma scenario when I give them a chance to earn bonus points. I found out that my students used a similar strategy to what Nick used in the "Split or Steal" segment of "Golden Balls." The last question of their final exam says:

Bonus: Circle how many bonus points you want on this final exam (there's a catch: if more than 10% of students circle 4 points, then nobody gets any bonus points)
1 bonus points   4 bonus points

I allowed the students 30 seconds to communicate before the exam started in order to discuss their strategy. A student named Ethan, popped up from his second-row seat and asked to borrow a whiteboard marker. He drew two columns on the board, one he titled "1 point" and the other he titled "4 points." Then he signed his name under the "4 points" column. The last thing he said to the class was, "there are 40 students in the course. This means four students can go for four points as long as the other 36 go for 1, we can all get bonus points." As Ethan walked back to his seat, a gal in the very back row of an elevated lecture hall sent an evil dagger-eyes look at him and mouthed something that looked like "forget you" (or close to that).

Then a light bulb went off in her head. Instead of sitting there irritated, she stood up and ran down the lecture hall steps, grabbed the white-board marker and wrote her name under the "4 points" column. Right after that, two other students did the same. With four names claiming to be going for the four points, it eliminated options for the remaining players in the game. If the remaining students went for four, everybody would get zero. There was no way to pick four and get those four bonus points. This eliminated a potential strategy. Game Theory lingo would describe Ethan's move as "restricting a freedom of action." Put differently, it eliminated the option to go for four points and bust the game for everyone. He changed the game.

Did it work? Was this the first class in 14 previous classes to beat the prisoner's dilemma I had set up?

Well, it turns out there was a fifth student who also went for the four points. And this should have busted the game for the entire class. But it didn't because of an even more clever strategic move by Ethan, who had been thinking an extra step ahead. Ethan, who originally took the initiative to write the columns on the board and put his name under the "4 points" column, actually lied. He went for one point and told the rest of the class he went for four.

He did what Nick did in "Golden Balls." His lie eliminated the strategies of his fellow students, but by lying and only going for one, he gave the class a cushion in case another student went for one just to bust the game intentionally.

Recap: Strategies to Escape the Prisoner's Dilemma

Game Theory offers some strategies to tip the scale between cooperation and conflict: regulation, reputation, relationships, repeated games, retaliation, removing choices, and cartel.

Regulation: The idea behind regulation is to change the player's payoffs and create incentives to avoid the bad equilibrium.

Example: Rules on overfishing mitigate the problem that fishermen each have a dominant strategy to catch as many fish as possible but when everyone does it, the fish stock collapses and doesn't repopulate (sometimes referred to as the Tragedy of the Commons - more on this in chapter 8)

Reputation: You can promote cooperation if a cheating player's reputation is damaged when they don't cooperate. A blemished reputation can be an important incentive to promote cooperation and good behavior.

Example: Reviews on Etsy, Ebay, and Uber for revenue-generating outcomes.

Relationships: People are more likely to trust and cooperate with those who are closer to them.

Example: Repeat customers at a mechanic shop or restaurant are more likely to get a better deal.

Repeated Games: Promotes cooperation because the outcome of current game is linked to the outcome of future games.

Example: Pricing ice cream cones each day during summer.

Counter-example: Why you should beware of quality of goods sold from stores going out of business. Or why a once diligent dish-washing roommate slacks on cleaning up as the end of the lease approaches.

Retaliation: The ability to punish "cheaters" can promote cooperation.

Example: The threat of the "enforcer's" fists promotes clean hockey.

Removing Choices: Create a mechanism that removes a subset of the other player's actions such that a different equilibrium could be deduced.

Example: Declaring that you will steal in the game-show "Golden Balls."

Cartel: Collusion allows players to act as single unit to promote collective interest. Sometimes referred to as 'coordination'.

Example: Andrew and Ed's ice cream stand getting together and promising to keep prices high.

Flipping the Prisoner's Dilemma to Your Advantage

Game Theory helps you recognize strategic interactions and transforms them to your benefit. If you can find ways for others to play a prisoner's dilemma, you can end up the winner.

Etsy, the online marketplace for handmade goods, throws its sellers into a prisoner's dilemma through its advertising scheme.

When I started an Etsy page to sell my Colorado Vintage posters, I kept getting emails titled "Bring buyers straight to your new listings." In those emails, Etsy was trying to get me to pay for ads for my poster page. Etsy displays a seller's listings more prominently on the website and mobile app if the seller pays for ads than it does for sellers who don't buy ads.

But prominence on a website is all relative. If none of my competing posters sellers paid for ads, we'd all be on the same playing field. But there's a temptation to gain the upper hand if you advertise and your competitor doesn't. Just as in the prisoner's dilemma, the dominant strategy is to always advertise. Ultimately my page earns less and all the other mountain poster sellers earn less while Etsy makes more from advertising revenue. This is why tobacco companies legislated themselves out of advertising.

Or you can use your celebrity status to get companies to give you free products to wear and advertise. In most cases, a popular celebrity wearing your product is a good thing and should translate into more sales. It's normally a win-win: the celebrity gets paid and company increases the number of eyes on its product. (Think of the Dwayne "the Rock" Johnson wearing Under Armour gear in his Instagram photos.) But what happens when the "celebrity" who is showcasing your product isn't the type of person you want showcasing your product? What happens when the "celebrity" championing your brand in public is doing so while getting arrested for drunkenly and disorderly conduct?

You do what Gucci and Coach did to the "Jersey Shore" star Snooki.[102]

The expensive handbags makers like Gucci and Coach were sending designer bags for free to Snooki. But Gucci wasn't sending her Gucci bags. Gucci was sending its competitor's bags, that is Coach bags, to Snooki, Coach was sending her Gucci bags causing an "unbranding" war.

It was the same dynamic that occurs when one seller lowers their price — the competition has to follow suit. "Better she puke into a competitor's handbag than our bag," is Coach's logic. In this case, if Coach is sending Snooki Gucci bags to wear in public then Gucci has to respond with a similar strategy and send her Coach bags. The "Jersey Shore" celebrity makes out with free handbags from Gucci and Coach's prisoner's dilemma.[103] Too bad there wasn't a big pugilistic hockey enforcer to punch them all.

CHAPTER 7:

Babies on a Plane: The Economics of Externalities

I have a skiing buddy who is notorious for skiing too fast and too aggressively and consuming too many alcoholic beverages on the chair lifts. His skiing tends to irritate me and the fellow skiers around him on the slopes. Most of the time it's just aggravation he imposes on other skiers, but on a few occasions, he has actually caused crashes, making him a clear nuisance for fellow skiers.

I think his skiing is causing a negative externality on the rest of us.

How does economics deal with situations like this? Up to this point, we focused on the *voluntary* exchange between buyers and sellers. And in our economic models, we've focused on measuring costs against benefits. If the benefits exceed the costs, the purchase of that good will boost the buyer's happiness. If the marginal revenue exceeds or equals the marginal cost, then the seller will voluntarily sell that item. Voluntary exchanges occur because it benefits both parties. The perfectly competitive market models how buyers and sellers produce efficient outcomes.

But what happens when the deal between buyer and seller impacts a third party? What happens when a transaction harms someone nearby who is neither the buyer nor the seller? What happens when the costs are not born solely by the party that receives all the benefit?

With my drunken skiing buddy, his alcohol consumption and skiing tactics create *spillover effects* on other skiers. The active party (my friend) is doing fine, but the crashed-into-bystander-skier is not. The cost of his ski pass and alcohol doesn't consider the related costs for other people on the slopes.

The Pigouvian Tradition

An economist observing the private cost and social cost of my drunken skiing buddy would use an analytical framework pioneered by British economist Arthur Pigou in the 1920s. Economists now call this an *externality*. An *externality* occurs when the actions of one person or group impose a cost or convey a benefit on a second or third party that isn't accounted for. Externalities can be positive or negative. Although originally Pigou and others didn't refer to them as such, other words were used at the time such as "spillover," "nuisance," "neighborhood effects," or "social costs" to describe these externalities.

Pigou's teacher, British economist Alfred Marshall, was one of the first to articulate the concept of externalities, and Pigou further elaborated on the idea. Both Marshall and Pigou helped launch the notion that economic analysis was needed to address external costs. Marshall portrayed the nascent concept of externalities mostly in terms of industrial policy (firm and industry) by describing how a firm entering an industry would "externally" raise or lower the costs of the existing firms already in that industry, while Pigou saw externalities in terms of social issues, such as the costs of smoke pouring out of a factory or a train whose sparks caused damage to farmers' crops next to the train tracks. Both thought that taxes or bounties would be used as solutions.

Pigou also wrote about the spillover impacts of producers and sellers of "intoxicants," arguing that beer sellers didn't have to pay for the law enforcement costs associated with the rowdiness those "intoxicants" caused. Pigou's solution: tax beer kegs.

Although economic textbooks give most of the credit to Pigou, there were economists in the 1950s and 1960s who really honed today's idea of externalities. The classic and oft-repeated example by British economist James Edward Meade, involved beekeepers and apple farmers.[104]

The story begins with a farmer growing apples in an orchard next to a beekeeper raising bees to make honey. Because the bees need the apple nectar to produce honey, the level of honey production is dependent on the apples. More apples make more nectar available for the bees which in turn creates more honey. But the apple grower doesn't get compensated for this positive spillover that the apple blossoms have on honey production.

The result is a less-than-optimal number of apple trees. Meade's solution, which is in line with Pigou's reasoning, is that the apple grower should be subsidized to produce more apples. Meade's bee example in 1952 re-energized the movement for corrective government action in the face of externalities.

To interpret Pigou's ideas graphically, the standard economics textbook utilizes the same supply and demand model, except we interpret the upward sloping supply curve as the marginal cost and the downward sloping demand curve as the marginal benefit.

In the case of a positive externality, there's going to be an extra marginal benefit curve (demand curve). Let's say the apple producer, looking at her private costs and benefits, decides to produce only 100 apples per week. The benefit to the honey maker from those apple blossoms is illustrated by the second demand curve, which includes the private benefit to the apple grower but also includes the benefit to the honey maker. (The Marginal Social Benefit curve includes the benefits to both the apple grower *and* honey maker while the Marginal Private Benefit curve only captures the benefits to the apple grower). If we find the intersection of private costs and social benefit, the ideal number of apples is 130.

Positive Externality

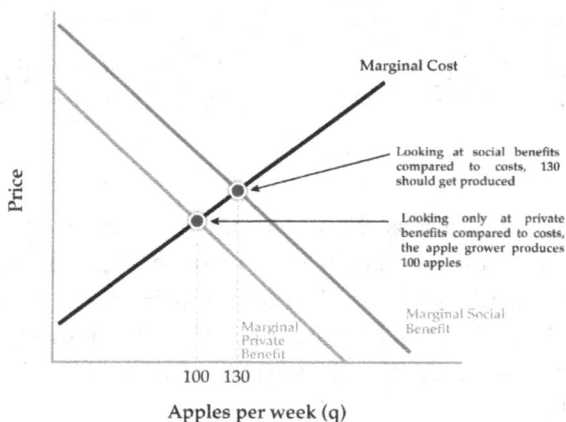

The problem with positive externalities is that the private market underproduces them. In other words, there are goods and services that are not efficient for the market to produce but that still have a social benefit that exceeds the cost of producing them. To see this, consider the 115th apple. The marginal cost of that 115th apple, let's say, is 30 cents. And we'll say the marginal benefit to the farmer (private benefit) of that apple is only 20 cents. From that perspective, that 115th apple shouldn't be produced. But the marginal benefit of the apple farmer and the bee keeper (social benefit) of that 115th apple is 40 cents, which is greater than the cost. From the perspective of both (society's perspective), it should be produced.

Positive Externality

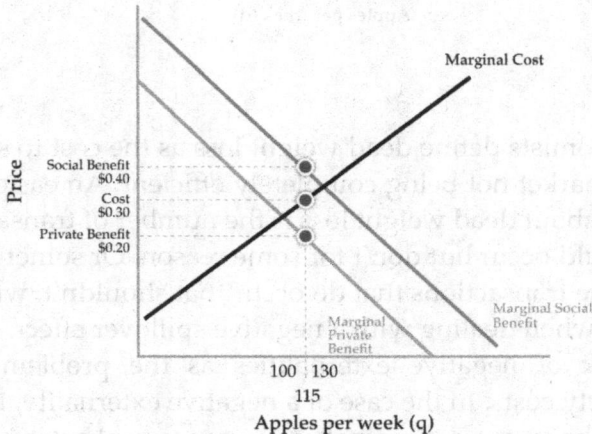

The 101-130 apples should get produced from a social perspective, but only 100 get produced from a private perspective. Economists call those 30 lost apples the *dead weight loss.*

Positive Externality

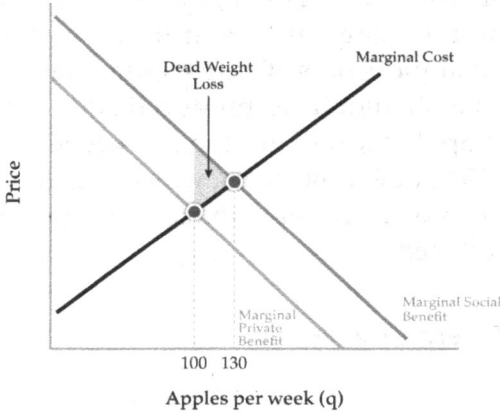

Apples per week (q)

Economists define dead weight loss as the cost to society from a market not being completely efficient. An easier way to think about dead weight loss is the number of transactions that should occur but don't for some reason. Or sometimes it can be the transactions that do occur that shouldn't, which is the case when dealing with a negative spillover effect.

Think of negative externalities as the problem from third-party costs. In the case of a negative externality, there's going to be an extra marginal cost curve (supply curve).

Consider the market for plastic shopping bags. There is the private cost of making the bags and a private benefit for plastic shopping bags. But there is also a third-party cost from having them: they become litter, they blow on the side of highways, and they cause environmental damage. This third-party cost is captured by the marginal social cost curve, which is the curve that is higher than the marginal private cost curve since it includes the marginal private cost plus the external cost.

Negative Externality

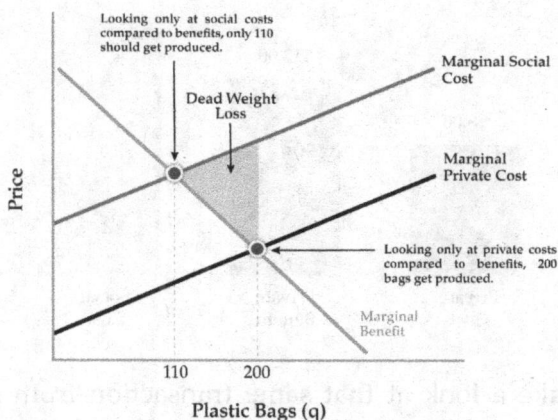

Looking only at social costs compared to benefits, only 110 should get produced.

Dead Weight Loss

Marginal Social Cost

Marginal Private Cost

Looking only at private costs compared to benefits, 200 bags get produced.

Marginal Benefit

Price

110   200

Plastic Bags (q)

The difference between the marginal social cost curve and the marginal private cost curve is society's cost per bag. If the private bag producer only looks at its private costs compared to the marginal benefits, 200 bags will be made. But if the social costs are factored in, only 110 bags are socially optimal.

The 111th-200th bags shouldn't be made from the social perspective. The area of the dead weight loss represents the loss of efficiency from overproduction. The root of the problem is that the individual or group can look at only the individual benefit or cost and can ignore the costs and benefits imposed on the rest of the world.

For instance:

From the individual perspective, in a case where $12 of benefit exceeds $8 of cost, that transaction should occur.

Benefit > Cost (from private perspective)

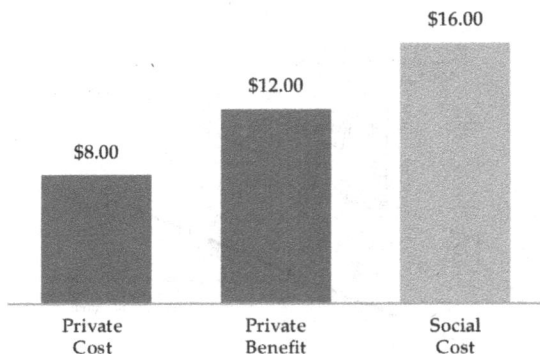

But take a look at that same transaction from society's view. The social cost is $16, and the private benefit is only $12. Now costs are greater than benefits. This transaction should not occur from society's perspective.

Cost > Benefit (from social perspective)

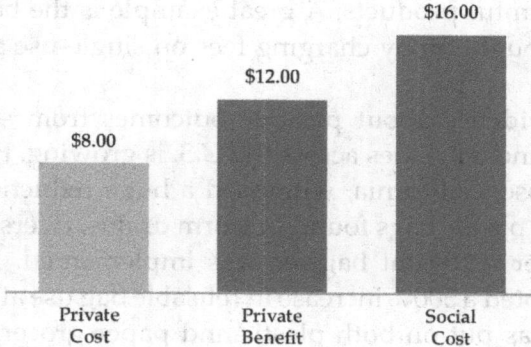

This can cause a misalignment between what society or a third party wants and what the individual wants. An externality could also be defined as the gap between private costs and social costs.

The problem with externalities, according to the Pigouvian tradition, is that the market left alone won't fix them. Externalities create situations where goods and services aren't allocated efficiently by the free market, leading to a social loss of welfare. Economic textbooks call those situations *market failures*.

Of course, Pigou didn't use that term either. It wasn't until 1958 that we got the term *market failure* from the pen of Francis Bator, who gave economic students the four reasons for market failures: monopoly power (we saw the dead weight loss created by monopolies in chapter 4), externalities, public goods, and imperfect information.[105]

Pigou thought negative externalities were pervasive in the world and that the best solution was for the government to regulate or tax those firms or individuals who imposed costs on others. Pigouvian taxes also create a double benefit. First, the taxes generate revenue governments can use. Second, they are meant to alter behavioral by raising the cost of harmful products. A great example is the behavioral change brought on by charging fees on single-use shopping bags.

The evidence about positive outcomes from single-use bag ordinances in cities across the U.S. is growing. For example, San Jose, California, witnessed a huge reduction in the number of plastic bags found in storm drains, rivers, and city streets after a 10-cent bag fee was implemented. Portland, Oregon, noted a 300% increase in reusable bag use after a five-cent fee was put on both plastic and paper grocery bags.[106] The bag-fee-trend, unlike grunge music, didn't start in the Pacific Northwest or even in the United States. Ireland was one of the first countries to limit single-use shopping bags in 2002. After the Irish levied the bag fee, annual bag consumption dropped from 328 to 21 bags per capita.[107]

In May 2012, the city of Aspen, Colorado, banned plastic grocery bags and installed a 20-cent fee for every paper bag distributed at grocery-store checkouts.

Unfortunately for researchers, data on bag consumption in Aspen prior to the installation of the fee was not available for comparison. The next best method to determine whether the fee was changing behavior was to compare the bag consumption in Aspen to the bag consumption in a neighboring town without a bag fee. That turned out to be the town of El Jebel, Colorado, 22 miles northwest of Aspen. Researchers found that 76 percent of El Jebel shoppers left their grocery store with a single-use bag, while only 15 percent of shoppers in Aspen, with the bag fee, did during the winter of 2017.[108]

The "double benefit" in Aspen's case was (1) the change in behavior by raising costs to shoppers so they would use fewer bags, reducing litter and harm to wildlife, and (2) the revenue generated from those bags would be used to fund programs in the Aspen community to reduce waste and encourage recycling.

Pigou suggested that the government use subsidies and taxes to alter the cost-benefit calculations of individuals to get them to change behavior. It's this same question of the role of government to encourage or discourage certain behaviors that was central to a debate in 17th century France.

In 1845, the French parliament received an open letter petitioning members to support the candle makers of France. The letter asserted that candle makers were suffering unfair competition "of a foreign rival who works under conditions so far superior to our own for production of light that he is flooding the domestic market with it at an incredibly low price." Who was the foreign rival the petition referred to? Turns out it was the sun. So, the letter proposed a mandatory shutting of all windows, shutters, curtains and blinds during the day in order to support the candle-making industry.[109] More darkness means more candles.

The author of this letter was the French economist, author and statesman Frederic Bastiat (1801-1850), who founded a weekly newspaper called the *Le Libre Échange*. He wrote numerous papers and essays promoting his ideas. Some call him an economist and others, a bit disparagingly, refer to him as a fantastic "communicator of economic truths," because many of his pamphlets used hyperbolic and humorous examples to illustrate a confusing economics concept more clearly.

In the spirit of Bastiat's silly, yet economically relevant examples, I have my students try to brainstorm hyperbolic and senseless solutions to overcoming common externality conflicts seen in their daily lives.

One of the recurring discussions during this lecture involves screaming infants at 30,000 feet.

Imagine this scenario: you are boarding an airplane for a flight. You settle in with a crossword puzzle and your concentration is immediately interrupted by a screaming infant several seats away. Think about the external costs a crying baby with an ear-piercing pitch imposes on all the travelers within screaming distance. Normally it's only the caregiver who deals with the costs of those baby cries but on a tightly packed metal tube in the air, everyone must bear some of the costs: a classic example of a "nuisance" or "negative externality."

One solution to a negative externality is to tax the firm or person to make it more expensive and help align with the level of production society wants. Allowing a baby on an airplane for free is a subsidy. That's subsidizing a polluter!

What type of hyperbolic solution might Frederic Bastiat have suggested to solve this dilemma?

The solution to overcoming the market failure of negative externalities is to either mitigate the costs or boost the benefits others receive for bearing those costs. What if the people with the baby were forced to compensate their annoyed fellow passengers? What if we required people flying with a baby to pack chocolate-covered pretzels along with their diaper bag? And when they board the plane and see the eyerolls of the travelers who are going to bear the costs of the bawling offspring, they must say, "I'm sorry dude, my child might cause some external costs to you during the flight. So, to compensate you for bearing those costs, I'd like to give you a pretzel." This would help align society's benefit with society's cost.

Another hyperbolic example that would make Bastiat proud is compelling my neighbors to pay for the cost of my flowers.

Each spring I plant petunias, marigolds, columbines, and pansies in wine barrel planters in my yard. The barrels are right on the property line with my neighbor's house. In fact, the flower barrels are closer to my neighbor's driveway, so it's easy to think those beautiful petunias are the work of my neighbors. And indeed, I've witnessed my neighbor actually take credit for those beautiful flowers from a passersby complimenting them. From an economist's lens, my neighbor enjoys the benefit of those flowers (and sometimes enjoys the credit for those flowers), but my neighbor didn't bear any of the costs of those flowers.

My cost/benefit calculation has me buying about 20 petunias and columbines each spring. If I could somehow also consider the benefit my neighbor gets from each petunia, the ideal number of petunias would be more than 20. But since I'm the one bearing all the cost, I underproduce compared to the level that society (the neighborhood and I) wants.

And that's again the problem with positive externalities. They get underproduced.

I've tried to explain this to my neighbor to no avail. She wouldn't agree to pay for some of my flowers, i.e., she wouldn't bear any of the costs, even though she receives a benefit from my colorful Colorado columbines. If she pitched in for some flowers, we could solve the market failure. I have, at least, convinced the neighbor to stop taking credit for my flowers. My neighbor is content enjoying the benefit of my flowers without paying for them. My attempt at bargaining didn't work, but that doesn't mean bargaining can't work to deal with spillovers.

Solving Externalities through Bargaining
Pigou and others thought government intervention was the solution to limiting the activities that produce negative

spillover effects, but that might not always be the best solution. The existence of an externality shouldn't lead to the presumption that a policy intervention is necessary; that is, government isn't always needed. Sometimes there are private solutions to externalities, and I learned this firsthand from my noisy neighbor.

Another one of my neighbors works long hours, which means he's hardly ever back home before the sun goes down. Since he's never home in the daytime, he doesn't have many opportunities to mow his lawn. He also travels frequently on the weekends, so no time to mow then. Given these circumstances, my neighbor decided the only time he could get his lawn cut was in the early morning, usually Wednesday mornings at 6:30 a.m. Now this would be fine if my neighbor were the only one hearing his lawnmower early in the morning, but he isn't. My bedroom window is right next to his yard, and the result is that I get one less hour of sleep than normal on Wednesday mornings.

After being frustrated with an early morning wake-up call on Wednesday, with Pigou's nuisance terminology spinning through my sleep-deprived brain, I had a conversation with my neighbor about the costs he was imposing upon me with his crack-of-dawn mowing. I suggested he pay the local high school kid who cuts lawns to do it in the afternoon when I wasn't sleeping. But my neighbor didn't want to pay $80 a month to have someone else cut his grass.

Since my neighborhood ordinance forbids using machinery before 8 a.m., I could easily force an end to the situation. There was a regulation in place that forbade this scenario, but that wasn't the best solution.

If I had the neighborhood association forbid my neighbor from mowing his grass in the early morning, he would have to pay the local kid to cut his lawn, costing $80 a month.

I endured some irritation from the sound pollution, but it wasn't $80 worth of irritation. I figured I experienced about $10 worth of utility loss, disutility, or grief from the early wake-up call each month.

Since the benefit of my neighbor's mowing saved him $80 a month, and I only experienced $10 worth of cost, there was room for negotiation and a mutually beneficial solution.

The solution: my neighbor offered to buy me a $12 Colorado microbrew six-pack each month to make up for the cost of his lawnmower noise. That was a win for me, since I traded $12 of benefit for $10 of cost. It was also a win for my neighbor, since $12 of cost was way less than the $80 he would have had to pay to hire someone else to cut his yard. We bargained our way to a private solution to a negative externality dilemma.

This is exactly what economist and Nobel Prize Winner Ronald Coase wrote about in 1960, except he described wandering cattle and a neighbor's trampled crops instead of beers, sleep, and lawn mowers.

The plot begins with two adjoining landowners, one using the land to grow wheat and the other using the land for grazing cattle. Because there is no fence between the plots of land, the cattle can wander into the wheat farm and destroy some of the crop, imposing a cost on the wheat farmer.

The Pigouvian tradition would quickly look at that situation and profess the need for government intervention to keep the cattle from damaging the neighbor's wheat. But Coase turned that argument on its head. Coase's analysis of the problem suggests there was no need for government intervention. Under Pigou's logic, where negative externalities are ubiquitous, it's easy to see and to blame the cattle for doing harm to the wheat farmer. It's harder to see that the wheat farmer could be blamed for limiting the number of cattle by using land to grow wheat; and this is the key point Coase illuminated as the flip side of the conflict. In his example, the increase in cattle production could only be obtained by a decrease in the supply of wheat.

Let's say that patch of trampled crop is worth $300 a month in wheat production. If the cattle rancher is excluded, say by some legal intervention, from having the cattle use that patch of land, he'll have to raise one less cow. That lost cow is worth $800 in value. Given this numerical example, there's room to bargain. The rancher could add that additional cow and then pay the wheat farmer $400 for the destroyed crop and still make a $400 profit. The wheat farmer would benefit, since the bargain turned $300 of wheat production into $400. The cattle rancher would win, too, compared to the scenario where his cattle were banned altogether from the area.

Even if the assignment of rights is flipped and the wheat farmer has no right to keep the cattle out, the two parties can still trade and bargain their resources so the land on both properties will jointly produce the maximum amount of total output.

Coase argued that the party that is the most productive should be able to use the space. Coase further argued that it didn't matter who legally has the right to use the property, because as long as bargaining can occur, the best outcome will be found. Bargaining forces each party involved to take a global view of the situation instead of solely focusing on their own individual production value.

Ronald Coase was the champion of allowing the pricing system to produce the best outcome. And in "The Problem of Social Cost" (1960), one of the most frequently cited articles in economics and legal scholarship, Coase did just that, while also criticizing the spillover framework established by Pigou.

One of his insights was that if transaction costs were low, legal rules wouldn't matter to the maximization of production: just let people bargain with one another to produce the best distribution of resources and solve externality problems. Coase wanted to focus less on the externality and more on maximizing production, writing, "The economic problem in all cases of harmful effects is how to maximize the value of production."

Coase suggested that the lessons of several centuries of common law were being overlooked — that years of legal decisions about property rights and liabilities were already correcting externality problems. Coase's article first dealt with the economic problem of externalities by scrutinizing a few of those legal cases.

Coase used a legal case from 1879 about a doctor's office next to a candymaker or "confectioner" in the parlance of the time. The candymaker's noisy machinery disturbed the doctor working next door. Specifically, the vibrations and noise from the candy machinery made "auscultation " (listening to organs through a stethoscope) very difficult. So, the doctor brought legal action against the candymaker to stop the machinery's use.

But Coase argued that the government shouldn't prohibit the candymaker from operating machinery just because it causes damage to the doctor. He argued that the Pigouvian method of dealing with externalities ignored the choice between whose actions are most valuable.

"To avoid harming the doctor would inflict harm on the confectioner. The problem posed by this case was essentially whether it was worthwhile, as a result of restricting the methods of production which could be used by the confectioner, to secure more doctoring at the cost of a reduced supply of confectionery products...."

Coase called this the "reciprocal nature" of externalities. In other words, if the law assigned the right for the candymaker to continue using the machinery, the doctor could always pay the candymaker to be quiet. Bargaining would allow the person whose production is most valuable to prevail.

It's this reasoning that forms the foundation for the Coase Theorem: when there are well-defined property rights and low transaction costs, externalities can be "internalized." Coase himself didn't call it the "Coase Theorem" in the article---that'd be weird and braggy, like giving yourself a nickname. The term "Coase Theorem" was coined later by George Stigler in a 1966 economics textbook.

These ideas helped Coase win the Nobel Prize in Economics in 1991. In an earlier work published in 1959, Coase developed his ideas while examining the regulation of radio frequencies and how rival radio stations in the 1950s could use the same frequencies to transmit and therefore interfere with another station's broadcast. Instead of regulation, Coase suggested that (in what initially seems paradoxical), it didn't matter whether competing broadcasters jumped on the same frequency as long as they were allowed to bargain.

After bargaining between radio broadcasts, the right to broadcast on that frequency would go to the station that could put that frequency to the most highly valued use. So, Coase's suggestion was to trade and bargain to the best outcome: the one that uses resources to maximize production.

In this context, the extra costs of negotiation and executing a deal are transaction costs: the extra costs of making the deal beyond what the actual good or service costs. If transaction costs are high, Coase's bargaining won't work.

For example, if my neighbor's mowing bothered an apartment complex with 200 people living it, the cost of getting them together to agree on an acceptable solution would be prohibitively high: the transaction costs are too great. It is also difficult to know the exact value of reducing an externality. If either side lacks information about the costs or the benefits of the externality, it would be hard to get to a compromise.

It would be this similar method that Coase would use to resolve the issue of the crying baby on a plane. And, in fact, some airlines have responded with a solution that would make Coase smile. There's no need for the government to ban kids from flying even if they do produce negative externalities. These airlines offer flyers "quiet" spots for additional fees. Usually, this means several rows of the plane are "child-free." And the travelers who want the peace-of-mind that their slumber on a redeye flight won't be disrupted by a squealing baby can pay for the quiet zone.

Other Critiques of the Pigouvian Tradition

Two of the biggest criticisms of the Pigouvian Tradition are that it overprescribes government intervention and that Pigou and his externality disciples are too confident in the government's ability to determine the actual cost of the externality. And indeed, the standard textbook treatment of Pigou's state intervention assumes the government's action will also produce a better outcome. But we can't assume this is always the case. Government's tools at correcting externalities involve price-based measures (either taxes or subsidies) or quantity-based measures (regulation or quotas).

But policymakers are at best guessing what that subsidy or tax should be. Coase suggested another strategy, one that allowed the market to determine that price by allowing participants to reveal their private information instead of relying on the policymaker's best guess on the cost of the externality.[110]

This logic forms the basis for "cap-and-trade" environmental policies, in which a government sells emissions permits allowing the bearer the ability to emit up to a certain level of a particular pollutant. The companies that can more quickly reduce their pollution can sell their pollution permits to the companies that pollute more. Tradable permits allow the private bidding to reveal the permits' worth and help eliminate uncertainty around pollution abatement costs. Once private rights are established, parties get to bargain, leading to the party that values the permit most highly being the one who ends up owning it. The auctioning of and bargaining for permits allows the market to solve the externality.

Bargaining between polluters helps solve the issue of the government not knowing the exact tax amount to charge to mitigate the externality. By allowing the polluters the ability to buy and trade pollution permits, the market determines the price of pollution instead of the government guessing at it.

Coase said it this way: "The main advantage of a pricing system is that it leads to the employment of factors in places where the value of the product yielded is greatest and does so at less cost than alternative systems."

Another criticism of Pigou comes from those who concede that externalities exist, but argue that if government intervention is more expensive than the cost of the externality, then the current situation, although less than ideal, is still best. For example, if a polluter causes a negative externality of $100, but it costs $101 of government resources to correct that negative externality, then it shouldn't be done. Put differently, this critique acknowledges that externalities are real but may not be worth the cost of eliminating them.

Another critique of the Pigouvian tradition is that it doesn't adequately account for expectations. To say it another way: if anticipated consequences are considered, the externality is already "priced in."

For example, if you rent an apartment above a bowling alley, the (relatively low) rental cost will already reflect the expectation that you'll have to deal with noise. With all things being equal, an identical apartment that is not above a bowling alley will rent for a higher price. The racket of strikes and gutter balls shouldn't be viewed as an externality problem since the cheaper rental payments have already accounted for it.

The same type of logic could be applied to our earlier example of the screaming baby on a plane and would argue the baby's cries aren't truly a negative externality since they are already accounted for in the cheaper price of the ticket. The alternative to flying with 180 other passengers is to fly on a private plane, which is much more expensive. The cheaper plane ticket on the public flight includes the expectation there will be a crying infant on your flight. In other words, you're already getting a benefit from a cheaper flight, since babies fly, too.

All About "Internalizing" the Externality

Whether economists agree or disagree with Pigou's or Coase's treatment of externalities, they all seem to agree those externalities should be considered or internalized in some way. Coase says the ability to bargain is enough to internalize the externality. Others argue that expectations already internalized it.

Pigou says the government should tax or subsidize to internalize the externality. For some positive externalities, Pigou suggested that those goods should be fully provided by the government. And one of those goods, which has been debated in economic theory for more than a century, is the lighthouse.

It was a Henry Sidgwick, an English philosopher and economist, who in 1883 used the lighthouse as an insight into the importance of what our current economic textbooks call a positive externality. All ships can benefit from the light (a positive spillover), but it's hard to get them to pay for that benefit. The impossibility of getting payment from the ships that benefit from the existence of the lighthouse implies that a private firm would find it unprofitable to build and operate a lighthouse.

"There are some utilities which, from their nature, are practically incapable of being appropriated by those who produce them or would otherwise be willing to purchase them. For instance, it may easily happen that the benefits of a well-placed lighthouse must be largely enjoyed by ships on which no toll could be conveniently imposed."[111]

So, the school of thought favored by Sidgwick and Pigou suggests that the government should build and maintain lighthouses since the ships that enjoy the light can't be forced to pay for it. You can't adjust a lighthouse's beacon so that it's only seen by ships that have paid a fee. The inability to collect payment meant that the private market would underproduce lighthouses or not produce them at all.

Sidgwick and Pigou didn't make a clear distinction between positive externalities and goods such as lighthouses. That credit goes to Francis Balor. Along with creating the widely accepted list of externalities, Balor was the first to clearly distinguish between externalities and public goods. An inability to charge the people using the product ultimately causes a market failure like the underproduction problem of a positive externality, and that is the topic of the next chapter: public goods.

CHAPTER 8:

Mamihlapinatapai: Free-Riders and Public Goods

I n an archipelago between Chile and Argentina, at the southern tip of South America known as Tierra del Fuego, there lives an indigenous tribe of the Yaghans whose language contains one of the most succinct words in the world. The Guinness Book of World Records has even acknowledged this word for its conciseness. That word is *mamihlapinatapai*. Thanks to linguist and missionary Thomas Bridges, who spent years living with the Yaghans in the late 1800s and who later compiled a Yaghan-English dictionary, we know the word *ihlapi—a portion of mamihlapinatapai*—translates to "awkward."

But the entire word *mamihlapinatapai* means "to look at each other, hoping that either will offer to do something, which both parties much desire done but are unwilling to do."[112] In one word, the indigenous community of the Yaghan sum up the economic conundrum economists call the *volunteer's dilemma*.

The *volunteer's dilemma* is a concept used to describe a situation in which an individual can either make a small sacrifice that benefits the entire group, or instead wait in hopes that someone else will make the sacrifice from which they can benefit. The problem occurs when everyone decides to wait for someone else to volunteer, and then the task never gets completed.

In other words, "I want this to happen, but I'd rather you make the sacrifice and bear the cost, and I'll wait around to enjoy the benefit of your sacrifice; I'll be the free-rider." Another way to illustrate the volunteer's dilemma is a situation where the person making the first move loses out while the rest of the group gains; that is, others benefit from the actions of one bearing all the cost. One of the most famous examples in nature comes from the African Serengeti — during the annual migration of wildebeests across Tanzania and Kenya.

Each year, nearly 1.5 million wildebeests follow a clockwise loop covering about 1,000 miles from Tanzania's

Serengeti to Kenya's Maasai Mara National Reserve seeking grazing grounds and following water throughout the year. Around December, wildebeests, following the rains, make their way to graze on the short-grass plains of the Serengeti. After giving birth in February, the herd starts its great migration in April following the rains.

September sees the wildebeest migration presented with the largest obstacle, the crossing of the Mara River, which flows through the northern Serengeti from the Maasai Mara Game Reserve. The animals congregate there until a large group of grazers forms before moving across the crocodile-infested waters.

This treacherous river crossing presents another natural example of the volunteer's dilemma. The skittish animals pace back and forth, crowding and congregating as more and more wildebeests cram along the far side of the bank. If no wildebeest *volunteers* to go first, the entire herd is cut off from grazing lands. Finally, one wildebeest takes the plunge, inciting the rest to follow.

The wildebeests who go into the water first have a greater risk of dying than the ones who wait and cross the river later, while the crocodiles are distracted chewing on the bolder volunteers.

The ultimate volunteer's dilemma was taught to soldiers during World War II. In the U.S. infantry manual, a soldier was instructed that, if a grenade fell into a trench where the soldier and others were sitting, he was to jump on the grenade to sacrifice himself to save others.[113] If the grenade went off in the trench, all the soldiers in the vicinity died. But if one soldier threw his body on the grenade, he could save the others. That would make for some lightning-fast *mamihlapinatapai*.

Anybody who has shared an apartment with roommates can relate to a little *mamihlapinatapai*. One of the most relatable examples of the volunteer's dilemma involves a kitchen space shared by four college roommates. Invariably, there is at least one roommate who doesn't clean. And the usual excuse is, "Uh, the pan has to soak awhile before I can clean it."

The common kitchen means each roommate will benefit from having clean counters, clean pots and pans, and sanitized utensils, so the roommates who don't clean up can still benefit from a clean kitchen produced by another roommate. In order words, the roommate who incurred the cost of cleaning can't prevent the roommate(s) who didn't from enjoying the benefits of that work.

THAT PAN LEFT TO SOAK IS FROM *LAST* SEMESTER.

Let's simplify this example to illustrate in economic terms why it is efficient for some goods to get produced when there is not a great enough incentive for any one individual to produce them. All four roommates get some level of benefit from having a clean kitchen. Let's say each roommate places $5 worth of value on having a clean kitchen for the week. But, for the sake of argument, we'll say the cost of cleaning the kitchen requires $8 of cost or "disutility" per week.

Someone must bear the cost of scrubbing the melted cheese off the pan or taking out the trash and cleaning out the refrigerator infested with month-old leftovers and mold colonies.

From an individual perspective, the $8 of cost exceeds the $5 of individual benefit. You wouldn't pay $8 for a five-dollar bill, would you? So, it's not rational to incur $8 of cost to only get $5 of benefit.

Individual Perspective: Costs > Benefits

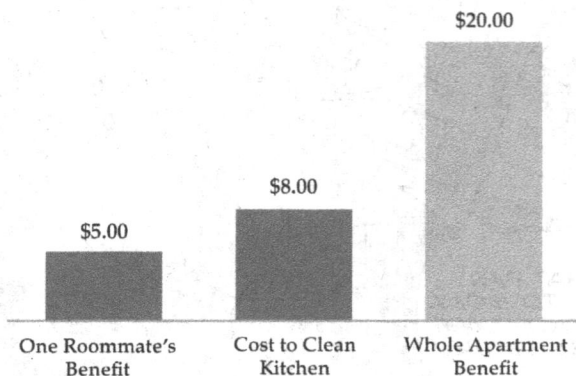

But, in addition to the individual benefit, there is a collective or *societal benefit*. Each of the four roommates gets $5 of happiness from a clean kitchen. Add each individual roommate's benefit up, and society values that clean kitchen at $20.

Group Perspective: Benefits > Costs

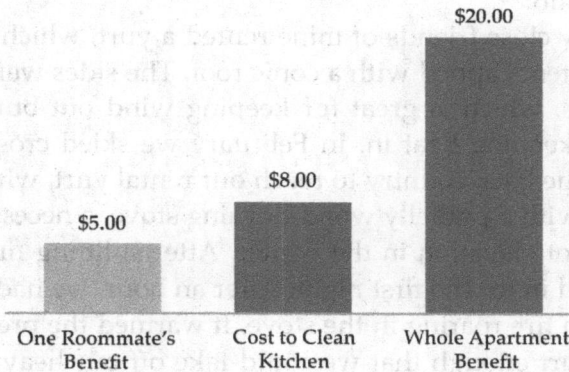

To get a rational individual to want to volunteer, you'd have to get their individual benefit to exceed the cost. One way to do that is to pay off the good actors. In other words, boost the payout/benefit of the people who provide and make the sacrifice from which we all benefit. Economists call this a *subsidy*.

One way to overcome the volunteer's dilemma in a messy communal kitchen would be to have the roommates who don't clean the kitchen each give $1.50 to the roommate who does the cleaning. That would increase the volunteer's benefit to $9.50 (= 5.00 + (3 x 1.50)) and would tip the scales so that the benefit exceeds the $8 cost of cleaning for that individual's view.

Sometimes it takes a few failed attempts before you can find a solution. I recently found this out during a camping trip wherein everybody in the group initially decided to "free ride," and the public good was never provided. And the public good that wasn't provided happened to be heat during a minus 20-degree February night in the San Juan Mountains of Colorado.

A few close friends of mine rented a yurt, which is a cylindrical tent capped with a conic roof. The sides were made of canvas, which is great for keeping wind out but not so great at keeping heat in. In February we skied cross-country into the back country to reach our rental yurt, which was stocked with a potbelly wood-burning stove, a necessity at a 10,000-foot elevation in the winter. After splitting firewood, we settled in for the first night. After an hour, we had a blazing warm fire roaring in the stove. It warmed the previously frozen yurt enough that we could take off our heavy down jackets and fade off to sleep in our cots.

Then, at around 1 a.m., we all woke up right about the same time to the sight of our frozen breath. No one had gotten up to put additional logs on the fire and it had gone out. And it didn't take long for the canvas tent's heat to escape.

In this case, the public good wasn't provided, and all four of us suffered a chilly hour before we got the fire roaring again, heating the yurt back up to the point we could sleep. If one of us has woken up and gotten out of our sleeping bags to put more fuel on the fire, everybody would have benefitted. But that required some costs on the individual volunteer. We each tried to free ride, and everyone incurred the cost.

The next night we decided upon the subsidy solution. The three individuals who would stay in their sleeping bags paid for the dinner of the volunteer that offered to set his alarm at 2 a.m. and feed the fire.

Another Market Failure

Goods such as heat from a fire in a communal yurt and a distracted crocodile preoccupied with the first wildebeest diving into the Mara River have two properties that distinguish them from the private goods we've been discussing so far in this book. These goods are:

1) **Non-excludable,** meaning that people who don't pay can still access the good, and

2) **Non-rivalrous,** meaning the goods can be consumed by one person without preventing consumption by another.

If a product meets those two qualifications, economists call it a *public good.* To better grasp the two defining characteristics of public goods, it's helpful to think about a regular good such as burrito.

A burrito is easy to separate and sell to a single buyer. If you don't pay for the burrito, the cook won't serve it to you because a burrito is *excludable.* But if I clean the kitchen and take out the trash, I can't prevent you from enjoying that clean space. I also can't easily prevent you from entering a public park. These goods are *non-excludable.*

Once a burrito is consumed, it can't also be consumed by another person. If I buy a burrito and eat it, you can't also eat it. A burrito is a *rival* good. But heat in a shared space doesn't work that way. If I'm providing the heat from a fire, you can also benefit from the heat without interfering with my enjoyment of the heat. If I'm playing volleyball in the park, you can also be in the park jogging. These are *non-rival* goods.

Unlike private goods, which businesses can easily charge for and thus have an incentive to produce, public goods benefit many people, whether they pay for them or not. This means that public goods can't be efficiently produced by the private market. If you can't keep the people who don't pay for your good from enjoying the benefits of the good, then you'll run into the free rider problem.

When this occurs, it's hard for the private market to get to the efficient level of production. A quick numerical example can best illustrate what it means that public goods get "underproduced."

Consider two individuals' demand for hiking trails on a mountain. Assume hiking trails are nonexcludable and non-rivalrous; so, they are public goods. Think of each hiker's demand curve as reflecting how much they value each trail. Each hiker's marginal benefit for each trail is shown in the table below, along with the marginal cost of each trail.

Number of Trails	Rich's Marginal Benefit ($)	Shawn's Marginal Benefit ($)	Marginal Cost ($)
1	$8	$18	$10
2	$7	$15	$12
3	$6	$10	$15
4	$2	$7	$20

From an individual perspective, we can see Rich isn't willing to pay for any of the trails because the costs exceed his benefit. For example, the first trail costs $10 but Rich only gets $8 of benefit. Shawn, however, would gladly pay for two trails since he gets more personal benefit than the trail costs.

Because the hiking trails are nonexcludable, we can't keep Rich out even if he doesn't pay. He won't pay for a trail, but if the trail gets constructed, he'll enjoy the benefit of it. The individual outcome is that Shawn pays for the two trails, and Rich pays for none.

The inefficiency arises when we look at the collective benefit. Because each hiking trail is non-rivalrous, both Rich and Shawn can both simultaneously hike them. This means we can add up the benefit they get from each trail. For example, Rich values the first trail at $8, and Shawn values it at $18, so they collectively receive $26 of value from that first trail, $22 for the second, $16 for the third, and $9 of collective marginal benefit for the fourth.

Number of Trails	Rich's Marginal Benefit ($)	Shawn's Marginal Benefit ($)	Rich's Marginal Benefit + Shawn's Marginal Benefit ($)	Marginal Cost ($)
1	$8	$18	$26	$10
2	$7	$15	$22	$12
3	$6	$10	$16	$15
4	$2	$7	$9	$20

The analysis is different from a collective perspective than from an individual's perspective. The third trail costs $15 to build, but neither Shawn nor Rich values that third trail above $15. So, no individual would pay for the third trail. However, from the collective perspective, adding Shawn's $10 value with Rich's $6 value means the collective benefit from that third trail is $16. This is greater than the $15 costs, so the third trail should be produced. Underproduction occurs because although society values the third trail more than what it costs to make it, no individual would pay for it on his own.

To say it another way, a public good should be provided if the collective benefits to consumers from the good are equal to or greater than its cost. Economists call this the "Samuelson Rule."[114] When there is personal cost but common benefit, individuals tend to underinvest unless there is a way to overcome the free-rider problem.

What About Goods that Aren't Quite Private and Aren't Quite Public?

So, now we've looked at private goods that are both generally excludable and rivalrous and compared them to public goods that are non-excludable and non-rivalrous. Are there goods that are not quite private goods and not quite public goods? Can there be goods that are nonexcludable and rivalrous, or perhaps, excludable and non-rivalrous?

Goods that are excludable and non-rivalrous are called *club goods*. These are things that typically require a membership payment. Netflix, or any streaming service, is a classic example; it requires a monthly fee (making it excludable), but my viewing of movies doesn't interfere with someone else's ability to watch that same movie, so it's non-rivalrous.

Then there are non-excludable and rival goods. And a good way to understand them is to think about toilet paper in a shared bathroom.

I once had a student who cleverly, and somewhat reluctantly, shared with the class her experience with the shared resource problem in the bathroom. The student revealed that among the four roommates in their apartment, there was one woman who didn't want to spend money on toilet paper. Her strategy was to use the toilet paper that her roommates purchased and kept beside the toilet. Without paying for the toilet paper, she was still able to benefit from it being available because the toilet paper was nonexcludable: it sat beside the shared toilet and could be used by anybody. But the toilet paper is a rival good. Once one person uses a few squares, nobody else can use them.

	Rival	Non-Rival
Excludable	Private goods (burrito)	Club goods (streaming TV)
Non-excludable	Common Good (the ocean, toilet paper in shared bathroom)	Public Goods (heat in a yurt, public parks)

In this case, toilet paper is nonexcludable but also rivalrous. Fans of the 1990s sitcom Seinfeld will also remember that toilet paper is a rivalrous good. In a 1994 episode of the sitcom, a woman in the neighboring toilet stall wouldn't share her toilet paper with Elaine in the next stall over, telling Elaine that she "can't spare a square (of toilet paper)." The line "I can't spare a square" should be associated with the fact toilet paper is a rival good. If Elaine uses that square of toilet paper, no one else can. Because of these traits, common goods tend to be easily over-consumed, a situation economists call "The Tragedy of the Commons."

The term got its roots from an 1833 publication by William Forster Lloyd, a British professor of political economy looking at pastures in England in the early 1800s and wondering why cattle on the common grounds were smaller than cattle grown on private pastures.[115]

The term later gained popularity because of a 1968 article in *Science* magazine by ecologist Garrett Hardin. The article recalled Lloyd's work in describing the problem where benefits from an action are private, but the costs are borne by the group. A feature of the "commons" is that individuals can consume resources without restrictions. Using this parable of villagers adding too many cows to a communal pasture, Hardin illustrated how communal resources would suffer from overexploitation and other problems of noncooperation, since each farmer has an incentive to add an extra cow, i.e., to create more marginal revenue with no marginal cost. If all farmers thought that way, the pasture is quickly overgrazed and ruined for the whole group.

Another illustration is overfishing. If anybody is permit-ted to go fishing in the lake, then the lake becomes nonex-cludable, but if I catch a fish and take it out of the water, it means one less fish for others. This means that the fish in the lake are rivalrous. Up to a certain point, the common resource is abundant enough that anyone can use it without adverse impacts. A single fisherman cannot catch all the fish in a big pond. But there is a tipping point when the pond can only sustain a certain number of anglers.

And once every person fishing happens to be overfish-ing, there aren't enough fish to repopulate the lake for next year; the common resource is destroyed. The dilemma arises because fishermen don't have to consider the costs of their harvest on the other anglers. It's a problem created by the reasoning of "get it while you can."

The tragedy of the commons doesn't have to always in-volve people depleting or taking away too much of a com-mon resource. It could also involve individuals leaving too much of something behind in a common resource.

In 2017, Elk Meadow, an off-leash dog park 40 miles west of Denver, fell victim to the tragedy of the commons. This occurred because dog owners weren't picking up and dispos-ing of their dog poop.[116]

Because the park has steep slopes on both sides and a creek running through the middle, the high levels of dog waste were running off into the watershed below. When the creek tested with extremely high levels of E. coli, the park finally was shut down. Nature can absorb some dog waste, but once too many visitors abused the common space, it was ruined for everybody.

The same is happening in popular overnight backpacking and camping spots in Colorado's mountains, where human waste is ruining the commons. Again, a few can get away with it, but once everybody does it, the commons get destroyed.

It's a problem that rhymes with "hit and run."

In October 1984, the editors of *Science 84* Magazine concocted their own type of tragedy of the commons experiment. They invited their readers to send in a card either asking for $20 or $100 (although the magazine made it clear that no actual cash was to be handed out). There was, however, a small catch: everyone would win what they asked for as long as no more than 20 percent of the entries asked for $100. If more than 20 percent requested $100, then no one would get anything.

Under these stipulations, everybody entering could receive $20 easily and some could receive more since there is also some room for a portion of the readership to go for the $100. So long as too many people didn't ask for $100, they could still get it, while everybody else could get their $20.

What percent of readers went for $100? Of the 33,511 entries, 35% of them asked for $100, busting the contest for everybody. The editor would have been safe offering real money.

Game theorist William Poundstone described the individual's decision process:

In this experiment, the readers who went for $100 didn't have to feel too guilty about being greedy. Since there were thousands of participants, the chance that any one reader's choice to ask for $100 would be the one that puts the fraction over the 20% threshold is very small.

- If the portion going for $100 is well below the 20% mark, then going to $100 won't bust the contest for everybody.
- If the portion going for $100 is well above the 20% mark, then the contest is busted anyway so your greedy $100 request wouldn't make a difference.

The tragedy/dilemma occurs when everybody thinks the same way. And just like the prisoner's dilemma in Chapter 6, it's another situation when an individual's interest is at odds with the group's interest. And, it shows why the volunteer's dilemma and the tragedy of the commons are hard to overcome: as in this case, there is no social cost to appearing greedy.[117]

Not a New Dilemma

The problem of common resources isn't a recent dilemma. The problem of managing resources that don't belong to anyone was even addressed by the Greek philosophers.

In Plato's landmark political-philosophical work, *Republic*, he writes that Socrates suggests cities be unified and share private property. Later the fourth-century philosopher Aristotle, in his work *Politics*, pointed out a drawback to Socrates' notion of a city where everything is shared. Aristotle observed how people care for what is their own differently than what is common property.

"What belongs in common to the most people is accorded the least care: they take thought for their own things above all, and less about things common, or only so much as falls to each individually," Aristotle wrote.

We see the same problem of the free rider from the ancient Greek historian Thucydides. *The History of the Peloponnesian War* recounts the fifth-century war between the Peloponnesian League headed by Sparta and the Delian League led by Athens.

Unlike works such as Homer's Iliad to Herodotus' account of the Persian Wars, which occurs years before either of those authors' lifetimes, the battle between Greek city-states in the Peloponnesian War occurred within Thucydides' lifetime. This allowed Thucydides to write an authoritative version of the conflict in which he included speeches in his history.[118]

It's in one of these speeches where we read about the same collective action problem. In the first book, in which the Athenians are debating going to war with Sparta, Thucydides recounts a speech by the Athenian leader Pericles. The speech contrasts the democratic Athenian understanding of cooperative group action with Sparta's approach to community that is based on coercion and forced conformity. Pericles articulates how Sparta's version of community will suffer the same free rider problem in describing how Spartans lack the sense of cooperation and self-sacrifice for the *polis* the Athenians possess.[119]

> Slow in assembling, they devote a very small fraction of the time to the consideration of any public object, most of it to the prosecution of their own objects. Meanwhile each fancies that no harm will come of his neglect, that it is the business of somebody else to look after this or that for him; and so, by the same notion being entertained by all separately, the common cause imperceptibly decays.[120]
> -Thucydides, Peloponnesian War, Book 1, Chapter 5

Cooperation in the Commons

So how do you avoid the tragedy of the commons?

Getting back to ecologist Garrett Hardin's 1968 article for *Science*, Hardin called for "mutual coercion mutually agreed upon," basically a mechanism for preserving a common resource. Hardin's article carried a pessimism about avoiding the tragedy of the commons without regulation, saying things as dire as "freedom in the commons brings ruin to all." Hardin suggested two solutions: private property and top-down regulation.

The three roommates trying to overcome the "toilet paper depletion dilemma" attempted to use the private-property solution.

When confronted by annoyed roommates who asked her to pitch in for communal bathroom supplies, the previously free-riding roommate began providing the cheapest single-ply toilet paper she could find, which she had stolen from public bathrooms.

The other three roommates were not happy with this resolution. So, their next attempt in overcoming the "free rider problem" tried to make the toilet paper *excludable*, i.e., by turning it into a private good. To do this, each roommate decided to keep their own individual toilet paper hidden in her bedroom and not in the communal bathroom space.

My older brother, whose Netflix Account I use, employs the same solution to the free rider problem. Until I paid him $5 per month for the access to his Netflix account, my brother wouldn't share his password, which he changed monthly, effectively excluding me until I paid.

Economists would call this maneuver an attempt to define property rights. When property rights aren't defined, common resources tend to get overused quickly. (Think of this the next time you are in the last boarding zone of an airplane and can't find any overhead bin space to store your carry-on luggage.)

When establishing property rights doesn't work, regulation is another solution. Permits tend to be one of the most common forms of regulation. We commonly see this with hunting permits that only allow the permit-holder to hunt a certain amount of a given animal species during a defined period or season.

It turns out that there is a third solution, the development of which helped Elinor Ostrom become the first woman to win the Nobel Prize in Economics. Ostrom won the 2009 Nobel Prize for Economic Sciences for her work that demonstrated how ordinary people can create mechanisms to manage common resources. Ostrom helped disprove the notion that natural resources would be overused and destroyed in the long run. Studying worldwide common-pool resource groups such as villagers off the coast of India sharing fishing waters and Swiss cheese makers from the 1200s sharing pastures, Ostrom demonstrated groups can avoid the tragedy of the commons without top-down regulation and without completely privatizing the commons, as long as certain conditions were in place. Ostrom identified a series of factors helpful in overcoming the tragedy of the commons, such as having the ability to control membership and the capacity to define boundaries and define rules. And of course, the ability to monitor behavior and punish those who violate the rules of the commons.[121] Her work is filled with creative solutions to governing the commons across the world.[122]

An example of Ostrom's research looked at Swiss villages where farmers share communal pastures to graze their cows. The villagers solved the problem of overgrazing with a rule that dates back to 1517. That rule states that no one can graze more cows on the meadow than they can care for over the winter. Since it is very costly to winter a cow in the Alps and requires the farmer to have buildings to keep their cows, the rule rations the common grazing land by tying it to private property rights.

Fishing villages across the world use similar rules so the ocean isn't overharvested. Longstanding regulations include things such as limits on the size of fish, residency requirements, and seasonal restrictions. A size limit assures the fish reach maturity and can produce offspring before being harvested. Residency rules usually require the fisherman to live in the village to gain access to the commons. Seasonal rules forbid fishing during certain times of the year.

Rules are not the only ingredient in avoiding inefficient outcomes with common resources; there also must be a way to enforce the rules.

I saw a rule that prevented the depletion of a communal resource in a mountain town bar in Colorado. The bar offers free chips and salsa, a common good. The chips are offered buffet style where the customers serve themselves. To prevent customers from taking giant amounts of chips and salsa then wasting them, the bar has a unique rule. There's a sign directly above the non-excludable-yet-rival free chips and salsa that says, "You'll be charged for any chips that you take but don't eat." The chips are free, but if you overindulge and waste chips, then you're in trouble.

Enforcement might be an issue, and the establishment never specified what they charge customers for wasted chips, but that might not matter. I'm not 100% sure the bar really charges anyone for wasted chips, but the mere mention of the rule made me cognizant of taking too many chips in one pass. The mechanism served its purpose.

Sometimes public shame is the mechanism that regulates behavior. This is what the locals use in Himalayan villages to make sure their community forests don't fall victim to the tragedy of the commons. The community forests are called *panchayat,* and the local institutions that monitor them are called *van panchayats.* To prevent their forests from being overharvested, the villagers devised ways to manage the forests that require rules, monitoring, and punishment for rule breaking.

For example, to make sure they don't harvest more than grows back each year, one rule states that when cutting down leaves from trees, villagers much leave behind at least two-thirds of the leaf cover on the tree.[123] Other rules specify how many grass bundles each villager is permitted to extract. Punishment for the rule breakers that can involve fines, confiscation of equipment, and required public apologies.

What's especially interesting is the fact that the *van panchayat* has no legal authority to impose fines, yet many of the rule breakers end up paying the fines anyway. The fines get paid, because the alternative is for the rule breaker to make a public apology and endure the shame from the community members. The shame of a small village is often times much costlier than a small pecuniary punishment.

I was debating whether to contribute to a coworker's wedding gift. This occurred when we were asked to voluntarily contribute money for a gift card. Because the wedding card would say "from your coworkers," and not from each individual coworker that actually gave money, I could still get credit for the gift and not pay. It was the perfect chance to be a free rider, except I would have to endure the shame from my coworkers. And that cost was greater than the money I ended up contributing. The fear of public shaming kept me in line.

A similar instance involved Larry David and an unwritten rule, which relies on social pressure as a mechanism to keep from ruining the communal resource, about overeating hors d'oeuves at a party. In an episode of *Curb Your Enthusiasm*, Larry David castigates Christian Slater for eating too much communal caviar, saying that he isn't observing the "unwritten laws in our society . . . you take a little bit and then you step away for 20 minutes . . . if nobody's taking any, maybe take a little bit more . . . step away again."[124]

To wrap up the chapter, we'll conclude the story of the four apartment roommates fighting over communal toilet paper. Keeping their toilet paper in their own bedrooms, an attempt to make it excludable, was a huge inconvenience; especially after they realize how often they forgot to bring their toilet paper with them. Their final solution was to force each roommate to contribute $10 each month to collective items used around the apartment including: paper towels, dish soap, cleaning supplies, and toilet paper.

This final solution to the toilet paper dilemma is similar to what a government does to provide public goods to its citizens. It collects taxes and pays for things that are used by all of us, such as sidewalks, parks, police, traffic lights, and bike paths. Otherwise, we all might free ride.

CHAPTER 9:

Hidden Lemons, Jumping Gazelles, and Online Dating: Asymmetric Information

O ne of the assumptions about perfect competition is that there is perfect information among all parties. To allow the "invisible hand" to function requires all parties in a deal to have the same information about what they are buying and selling. For example, with perfect information, economists assume every customer and seller at a burrito stand knows exactly how much each burrito is worth (i.e., its quality).

But what if this weren't the case? What if the seller knew more than the buyer? What if the buyer knew more than the seller? What if the facts were what economists call *asymmetric information*?

Economists understand that if one person in a deal has more information than the other, the market won't work as well as it should, and the "invisible hand" cannot function perfectly. But this idea was made clearer when George Akerlof published a groundbreaking paper in 1970 that explained how dramatic and commonplace the problem can be.[125] And he did it with a very simple example involving used cars that he explained in just two pages; a paper that later won him a Nobel Prize in economics.

Akerlof proposed a simplified market for used cars in which there were high quality cars and there were low quality cars (referred to as "lemons"). His example went a little something like this:

Let's assume the good cars are each worth $10,000 to a buyer, but the lemons are each worth zero. Also, let's assume there are 50 good cars on the lot and 50 lemons on the lot. The last and crucial piece for this scenario is that the buyers of the used cars can't discern the quality of each car; they don't know whether they are looking at a lemon or a good car. They could buy the car only to find out it won't start the next day. Meanwhile, the used car salesmen know which cars are good and which are lemons.

There's asymmetric information here. One party in the transaction has more information than the other.

What the used car buyer sees

What the used car dealer sees

With an equal likelihood of buying a car worth nothing and a car worth $10,000, a buyer, who doesn't mind taking a fair gamble, would only offer the expected value of a car, which in this case is its average: $5,000 for any car on the lot.

While the buyer has a 50/50 chance of getting the lemon, the seller of each used car knows with 100% certainty whether the car being sold is worth zero dollars or $10,000. Since no seller of a good quality car worth $10,000 will sell it for $5,000, only the lemons are for sale at that price.

The market breaks down, creating a market where only the worthless lemons are for sale, and the good quality products will not be sold. The sellers with good cars want to hold out for a good price, but the problem is that they can't show that the car they are selling is a quality vehicle. So that seller doesn't sell.

Akerlof wasn't describing a market in which some buyers get a bad deal, he was describing a market that should exist but doesn't because of the problem of asymmetric information. There could be mutually beneficial transactions that create value for both buyer and seller, but they don't occur. The market breaks down.

The market also breaks down if there are varying levels of car quality on the lot instead of just good quality cars and lemons. For this situation, let's assume there are 100 cars on the lot. The first car is worth $100, the second is worth $200, the third is worth $300 all the way to the 100th car that is worth $10,000.

Since the buyers can't tell if they're looking at a $400 car or an $8,000 car or a $6,500 car, they aren't willing to pay more than what the average quality car is worth ($5,050). Let's say they again offer $5,050 for any car on the lot. With an offer of $5,050 for any car, the owners of the highest quality cars (those worth more than $5,050) won't sell and will exit the market.[126]

Market for Lemons

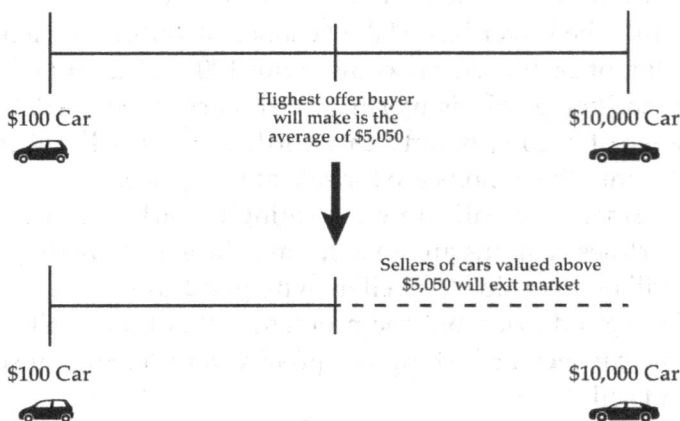

$100 Car

Highest offer buyer will make is the average of $5,050

$10,000 Car

Sellers of cars valued above $5,050 will exit market

$100 Car

$10,000 Car

When this happens, the average quality of cars falls. Now, only 50 cars are left on the market, ranging from $100 to $5,000. The buyer then would recalibrate the offer of the value of the average car on the lot. This time the buyer offers $2,550. The same process happens again: sellers of cars worth more than $2,550 won't sell.

Market for Lemons

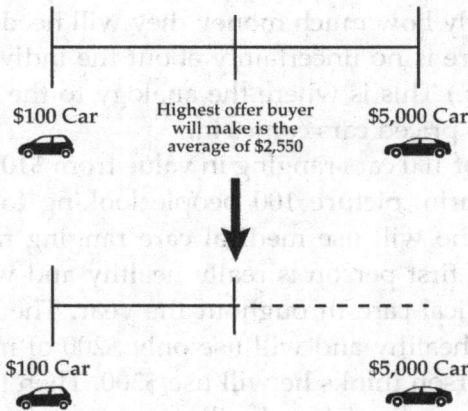

$100 Car Highest offer buyer will make is the average of $2,550 $5,000 Car

$100 Car $5,000 Car

This process will continue until only the $100 car gets sold, but none of the other cars get sold. The market unravels again.

The lemon market example has been used to illustrate the problem of asymmetric information in a lot of other markets, including the market for health insurance, and its risk of *adverse selection*.

Adverse Selection

When you buy insurance, you transfer the risk of a loss to the insurance company in exchange for a fee or premium. Insurance companies use probability to determine the cost of the insurance premiums it must charge its clients in order to generate a sufficient amount to pay the claims in the future, pay its expenses, and still make a reasonable profit.

The people buying health insurance have a wide range of costs for the potential cost of the medical services they will use that year. (For simplicity, assume everyone knows for certain exactly how much money they will need for medical services; there is no uncertainty about the individual's own health needs.) This is where the analogy to the used car lot with various priced cars comes in.

Instead of 100 cars ranging in value from $100 to $10,000, in this scenario, picture 100 people looking to buy health insurance who will use medical care ranging from $100 to $10,000. The first person is really healthy and will only use $100 of medical care throughout the year. The next person is also very healthy and will use only $200 of medical care. The third person thinks he will use $300. Then there are the ones who are really sick and will use a great deal of medical services. One person will use $9,800 of medical care, one person will use $9,900, and the sickest will use $10,000 worth of medical care.

How does an insurance company make money? It figures out what the average cost of medical treatment will be and then charges people annual premiums slightly above that average. Again, the crucial piece is that the buyers of health insurance know more about their health than the health insurers. Each individual buyer knows their health conditions, their risk of injury, and their medical needs.

What the health insurance buyer sees

Complications arise because the health insurers see a different view; in our scenarios they can't discern who is really healthy and who is really sick, who has a pre-existing condition, or who's at risk of breaking a leg while snowboarding. And so, the health insurance seller will offer health insurance for a price that is a little above the average of medical payouts.

What the health insurance seller sees

Let's assume health insurance is offered for $5,050 per year. The individuals who know the cost of buying insurance is greater than their expected health care costs won't buy health insurance. The person who believes they will only use $400 worth of medical care won't pay $5,050 for it. That's not a good deal for the healthy ones. So, when health insurance is offered for $5,050, half the people will drop out of the market--- but they are the healthy ones.

When this happens, it leaves the pool of health insurance buyers with a higher concentration of sick people. Now there's 50 people looking to buy health insurance with a range of expected care costs between $5,100 to $10,000 each. The health insurance seller now must readjust its offer to operate profitably. With a sicker pool of applicants, health insurance plans are offered for $7,550 a year. The process repeats itself and the spiral continues. Now, anybody who anticipates using less than $7,550 of medical care won't buy the insurance plan, decreasing the number in the remaining pool and making them the more likely to incur more costs. This process continues until only the sickest individuals can buy health insurance for exorbitantly high rates.

The key problem here is that the healthiest people don't buy insurance, but the insurance market works best when the healthier individuals are helping pay the costs of those who are less healthy in the same way that good drivers end up paying the costs of bad drivers' car accidents. If insurance is distributed over a wide range of buyers, the average cost of insurance can stay affordable. But if healthy people drop out of the insurance pool, the price of insurance must rise, and when that happens, even more people drop out, causing premiums to rise even further until the market breaks.

This illustrates a problem economists call adverse selection.

Adverse selection helps describe situations where hidden information is revealed by choices or actions, in particular, a choice reveals an estimate of value. You see comedians tapping into the concept of adverse selection with the hidden information certain actions reveal. For example, in 2016, Conan O'Brien tweeted, "If you can say Happy Valentine's Day in Klingon, you're probably not celebrating it." The joke here — or the hidden information that is revealed is that knowing how to communicate in a language from the humanoid warrior species from the Star Trek universe also correlates with a lower probability of having a date.

Meanwhile, Groucho Marx once said, "I don't want to belong to any club that would have me as a member." He's joking that, because he's a person of low quality, the hidden information he'd learn from being accepted by a club is that the club must also be of low quality.

One way to ensure healthy people stay in the pool is to require them to buy insurance, which explains why in 2010, when redesigning how Americans get health insurance, the

Affordable Care Act included an "individual mandate" to purchase health insurance. If you didn't have health insurance, you had to pay a tax penalty. Without the individual mandate, the health insurance market will break down because of the adverse selection problem. In contrast, where health insurance is provided as employee compensation, it sustains a broad-based pool of insured individuals, since it includes all employees both sick and healthy.

Economists analyze the many markets that have asymmetric information. These markets are characterized by actors on one side of the transaction having much better information than those on the other side. Borrowers know more than lenders about their ability to repay loans, managers know more than shareholders about a firm's profitability, drivers know more than insurance companies about their accident risk, health insurance buyers know more about their health than health insurance sellers, and auto mechanics know more about car engines than the typical driver does.

Solutions to Asymmetric Information: Signaling and Screening

Akerlof's lemon problem showed how asymmetric information can distort incentives, deter mutually beneficial transactions from happening, and lead to a suboptimal outcome. Akerlof also demonstrated how markets where sellers have more information than buyers result in an adverse selection of low-quality products. Thirty-one years later, those lemons became lemonade when Akerlof shared a Nobel Prize in Economics in 2001 with A. Michael Spence and Joseph E. Stiglitz. Akerlof proposed the problem of asymmetric information, and the other two economists proposed solutions.

In a 1973 article, Michael Spence identified ways to overcome the problems of adverse selection using *signaling*[127]: the better-informed party takes costly actions in an attempt to improve credibility with the less-informed parties. The first party sends a signal to reveal information to the other party, who interprets the signal and adjusts its behavior accordingly. Signaling Theory has helped shed light on various kinds of behavior, from how someone acts in a job interview to how animals respond to predators.

One of the best examples of signaling from evolutionary biology is the seemingly counterintuitive jumping by gazelles that sends signals to would-be predators. If you were to translate those signals into English, they would say something like, "Hey predator, I know you're watching us, but I'm faster than you, so you'd better not bother trying to chase me because you'll just waste your energy. You can't catch me." Such behavior typically involves an animal showing off feats of strength.

When a gazelle spots a cheetah, it starts jumping very high into the air in a movement called "stotting." Why would the gazelle make itself more visible to a predator? Why would it waste energy jumping instead of saving that energy for fleeing? Because it signals to the cheetah that the chase would be unfruitful. With such a signal, the predator might not even attempt the chase.

Because a gazelle has to be in good physical shape to jump high into the air, the signal works, since gazelles who *aren't* in good shape can't jump as high. What's more interesting is that both the cheetah and the gazelle benefit from the signal. The gazelle is happy to avoid having to outrun the cheetah, and the cheetah is happy to avoid wasting their energy on an unsuccessful chase.

Signaling theory can also explain why banks in the 19th century American West were built with expensive marble when the rest of buildings in town were made of cheap lumber or canvas tent material. In the days before the government insured banks, customers didn't truly know whether their money was safe in the bank. What if the unscrupulous banker took the money and then left town overnight? One way to signal to customers that the bank wasn't going anywhere was to invest in a marble building. A marble building was an effective signal of bank quality.

Signaling can also be used to separate high- and low-quality job applicants. Consider the information asymmetry in a typical job interview. The job applicant knows a lot about her own aptitude and ability for hard work, but the employer/interviewer does not. At one glance, the employer can't tell if the applicant is a high-productivity worker or someone who is going to watch professional wrestling videos on YouTube all day long. Of course, during the job interview, the good candidates will emphasize what a high-quality worker they are. But the low-quality workers, who have no intention of working hard, will also emphasize what high-quality workers they are. Talk isn't worth much; in fact, it's a weak signal.

For many employers, a degree in Latin has little obvious utility. But the fact that the job applicant has completed a degree, even if it's reading a dead language, tells the interviewer something. It indicates that the job applicant can get through four years of college without flunking out. Though the ability to read Latin might be just as functionally useless for the job as speaking Klingon is for getting dates, it signals to potential employers that the candidate has intellect and discipline.

A signal that works best may be very costly for some and relatively cheap for others. For example, signing a prenuptial agreement is very costly to the gold-digger but relatively cheap for the non-gold-digging spouse.

George Clooney's character in the movie Ocean's Eleven, a 2001 American heist film remake from the 1960 original film of the same name, uses signaling to overcome a problem of asymmetric information. Early in the film, Daniel Ocean (Clooney) is recruiting the 11th member of the group to rob a Vegas casino. He recruits Linus (Matt Damon), who we first see in the film, on a crowded subway train as he steals or pick-pockets a stockbroker's wallet. Ocean needs to approach Linus to join in his illegal activity, but Linus doesn't know who Ocean is. Linus faces a dilemma: he can't be sure if the person approaching him for an illegal job is actually an undercover cop. There is a problem of asymmetric information. Daniel Ocean knows this, so in order to "signal" to Linus that he's really a criminal and not a cop, he pick-pockets the same wallet from Linus that Linus had just stolen. An undercover cop wouldn't have the ability to pick-pocket like that. The act of pick-pocketing worked as a signal to distinguish Ocean from someone of low-quality in stealing. Effective signals separate certain groups and serve as a form of communication.

Signaling theory can also explain why sports agents spend more money on cars and clothing than do college professors with the same income level. Expensive cars and clothing serve as a signal for prospective baseball players and help them discern the talent level of agents. As a college baseball player trying to make it to the pros, you can't tell the difference between good agents and bad ones at first glance: there's asymmetric information. Talented agents earn more so they should spend more on clothes and cars, therefore attracting new clientele. Expensive cars and clothing serve as a signal for prospective baseball players and help them discern the talent level of agents. My twin, who does sports contracting law, dresses differently than I do.

In contrast, a professor's success is in writing books, publishing papers, getting grants funded, and giving entertaining lectures about gazelles. The people accepting papers for publication don't care nor do the students care about how a professor dresses or what car they drive. Professors don't have as much to gain with a signal of expensive clothes and cars. It's why I wear a corduroy blazer and jeans all the time and my twin wears custom suits and ties.

Signaling also helps explain why companies, particularly new companies who haven't had a chance to establish their reputation for producing high quality items, would offer guarantees or product warranties to customers. The company my brother uses for customized tailored clothing offers a 100% remake or refund guarantee. A low-quality clothing company wouldn't be able to offer such a refund guarantee because they would have to refund too many items and quickly go out of business. The signal works—effectively separating the high from the low quality.

The same is true with companies that offer warranties. Those warranties effectively say, "I know my product is a good product and so I can afford to offer a warranty." Poor-quality companies can't offer the same warranties.

Signaling theory also helps explain why fashion retailers care so much about preventing counterfeits of their products even though the people who buy the knockoffs wouldn't buy their expensive fashion items to begin with. If a lot of people buy knockoff Prada bags, then when we see someone with a Prada bag, we suspect there's a high chance it is a fake. If that is the case, the few who can afford Prada might not be willing to pay as much for it since the knockoffs dilute the potency of the "Prada" signal.

How much time, money, effort, or energy went into that signal? An effective signal works if it separates the people who can afford Prada from those who can't, the fast gazelles from the slow, the high-quality employees from the low-quality employees, and the shoddy clothing makers from the great clothing makers.

Low-quality signals don't separate the good from the bad. And this lesson is no more apparent than in the online dating world.

In the world of American online dating, male users outweigh the number of female users, with a roughly 60%-to-40% ratio. But this market is much more lopsided than that since men tend to be much more active (sending messages and likes) than women. Because men are almost twice as active, it's more like an 80% to 20% ratio.[128] As women are flooded with low-quality messages, checking their messages becomes tiresome, and drives many users away.

This scenario is similar to the tragedy of the commons we discussed in Chapter 8, wherein individuals acting in their own self-interest overuse a shared resource and hurt the common good. With online dating apps, the common resource is women users' attention. As they are inundated with boring, annoying, or unappealing messages, the women's patience and tolerance runs out.

The dating app Bumble found one solution to this tragedy of the commons with a unique feature that only lets women send the first message. A better market would see men sending fewer and higher-quality messages. This is why well-crafted and thoughtful first messages that show the sender has carefully read the recipient's profile have a better response rate than "hey," a totally uninformative first message.

To use the framework of Michael Spence, boring messages are a very weak signal. Messaging a dating app user with "hey" is extremely weak. And very weak signals don't distinguish the high-quality from the low-quality. A signal that is uninformative is called a *pooling* equilibrium. The kind of signal that successfully distinguishes the good from the bad is called a *separating* equilibrium.

Before online dating and text messaging, it was a lot more costly to reach out to potential partners: you actually had to call someone, requiring time and effort. With today's technology, you can now rapidly send out 10 texts or messages. With cost-free ways of contacting potential partners has come floods of weak-signal "heys."

Two economists, Soohyung Lee and Muriel Niederle, had an idea about how to fix that problem. The experimenters used college-educated Korean men and women in their twenties and thirties as test subjects to see whether signaling theory could improve online dating.[129]

To overcome the problem of users being inundated with low-quality messaging, the experiment allowed the users to send "virtual roses" to help signal their interest in another user they deemed special. Since each participant had a limited number of roses to attach to date requests, using up a rose becomes costly.

The participants could browse the profiles of other participants of the opposite sex and then send up to 10 date requests to potential partners, but only two of those date requests could be paired with one of those virtual roses. With the date requests sent out, some with roses and some without, recipients could say yes or no to any date request.

This allowed the experimenters a chance to see the acceptance rate of date requests that were paired with roses and one that had no rose attached.

It turned out that attaching a rose along with the date request increased the chances a date was accepted by 20% compared to the roseless requests. What's even more intriguing is that the participants, to help control for factors like looks and wealth, were divided into three tiers by the experimenters based on their desirability.

Participants in the top tier received more date requests, which wasn't a surprise. What was more interesting is that by attaching a rose to the date request increased the probability of having the date request accepted. Your chances of having a date accepted was increased by the same magnitude by sending a virtual rose as it was moving from the bottom desirability tier to the middle. Which means by sending the virtual rose, a bottom-tier participant was equally attractive as their counterpart in the middle desirability tier. The rose attachment effectively made them better looking!

The virtual roses acted as an successful signaling device that separated the "hey-senders" from the individuals who were truly interested, improving the online dating market.

Another way the matches are separated from the non-matches is by what information is in each user's dating profile. With a few clicks, many dating sites allow users to filter out other users based on several characteristics. Do they smoke? Are they six feet tall? What's their age? What's their religion? Do they speak Klingon? This is a practice economists call *screening*. And this is the same concept Joseph Stiglitz proposed as a solution to problems of adverse selection.

While Spence suggested signaling could be one solution to the problems of asymmetric information, the third person to share the Nobel Prize in Economics in 2001, Joseph Stiglitz, proposed another solution.

In this case, the poorly informed persons find ways to extract information from the better informed by screening.[130] Signaling requires the better-informed party to take actions to pass information to the less-informed party, while screening involves the less-informed party finding ways to get information from the more informed party. Another way to distinguish signaling from screening is by who moves first.

In signaling scenarios, the informed party moves first. In screening, the *un*informed party takes action and moves first.

For example, insurance companies will try to balance out some of that asymmetric information by getting information about the health insurance buyers. They screen applicants by asking them to submit information about indicators of expected health care costs: age, pre-existing medical conditions, alcohol or tobacco use, etc., or by requiring a physical exam by a doctor. The more that the information gap closes, the better the market can operate.

Offering a menu of purchasing options for something like health insurance can also be a screening mechanism: the health insurer can glean information about the insurance buyer from their choices. For example, some plans are cheaper up front but require large out-of-pocket payments when medical services are used. All else equal, customers who buy those plans would be those that expect better health and less use of medical services.

Another Risk of Asymmetric Information: Moral Hazard

Adverse selection is a risk of asymmetric information that affects a transaction, such as buying insurance. But asymmetric information can also have aftereffects, for example, what happens when people change their behavior once they purchase insurance? Once you're insured, someone else bears the risk or cost, and you may act differently than you would if you were uninsured. This concept is called *moral hazard.*

There isn't one single definition of moral hazard. Across economic textbooks, you will find this concept defined as "impact of insurance on the incentives to reduce risk."[131] Moral hazard predicts change in behavior following the buying of insurance. It also refers to situations where people make profit-maximizing but inefficient decisions because they don't have to personally bear the full costs of those decisions. Some economists define it in reference to a contract, as moral hazard occurs when one party to a contract changes his or her behavior when under the contract and thus passes on the risks/costs to another party. The basic sense is how people change their behavior is a situation where someone gets the benefits while someone else pays the costs.

Moral hazard can explain why once parents give their college kid a credit card to buy groceries, the college student overspends and buys items they'd never buy if they themselves were paying for them. The student receives the benefits, while the parents bear the cost of high-end grocery shopping. Moral hazard can explain why skiers might ski over rocks and tree roots in rental skis but won't do so with their own skis, which might get scraped up.

Moral hazard doesn't have to be intentional either. Of course, if you purposefully set fire to your property just to collect the insurance money, that would fall under moral hazard. Even being less diligent in checking your fire alarms and maintaining your sprinkler systems is a form of moral hazard. In this case, you are acting differently than you would without insurance.

It was moral hazard that the mother of one of my students was trying to prevent when purchasing Apple Insurance for her son's laptop. Before the semester, my student bought a new Apple computer and was deciding whether he should pay extra to buy the insurance on the laptop in case it got damaged.

He didn't buy the insurance. Thinking the laptop wasn't insured, the college freshman was much more careful with it — he avoided having drinks around his desk and was careful while transporting it in his backpack. But during finals week, someone ended up spilling a full coffee on his laptop at a cafe.

He called his mom to tell her the bad news and lamented not buying the insurance policy. His mother started laughing. It turned out that she had purchased the insurance plan but didn't tell her son because she knew if her son knew about the insurance, he wouldn't have been so careful. In this case, a signaling lie was the solution to prevent the perverse incentives caused by moral hazard.

A student of mine recognized the moral hazard with a unique contract he had with his dad. The student had an agreement with his father that if he paid for his car, his dad would cover the cost of gas. His father gave him a credit card during the college year to be used for paying for gas and nothing else.

But under this contact, the student's behavior changed. He quickly began taking more frequent trips into the mountains of Colorado. No matter how many miles he drove, he didn't bear the cost of gas. He was quickly labeled the designated driver every weekend by his friends. And the moral hazard didn't stop there.

The father monitored the credit card to ensure it was only being used at gas stations by looking at the monthly credit card statements. But the agreement was abused when the student realized gas stations didn't give itemized credit card charges. What the father didn't account for is that you can buy beer in gas stations as well as auto fuel, which is exactly what his son was doing. What looked to be a $40 fill-up on the credit card statement was actually a $12 six-pack and only $28 of gasoline. The student received the benefit, and the father dealt with the costs.

Even though the same six-pack was $2 cheaper at the grocery store, the contract he had made with his father encouraged the son to buy the beer at a more expensive spot; as long as the beer was purchased at a gas station, he could use his father's credit card, and paying 0% of $12 is much better than paying 100% of $10.

The father's solution was to make the son bear some costs by requiring a co-payment (or co-pay). Every month the son had to pay 20% of the credit card statement, adding some incentive to manage his purchases more carefully.

Insurance companies use co-pays and deductibles to help deal with moral hazard. A typical health insurance plan will only compensate you for a certain amount of a medical procedure, so coverage is less than 100%. Or car insurance policies will require drivers to pay a deductible before the insurance companies cover the rest of the costs of repairs. With a $500 deductible, the careless driver who backs into a pole in a parking lot pays for the first $500 of the repair even if they have insurance. The deductible provides some motivation to drive carefully and reduce the moral hazard.

A copayment works very similarly to a deductible. A copay usually requires the insured to pay a set portion of the expenses, such as under the father's revised gas station credit card arrangement. For example, a health insurance plan has a $500 deductible and a 20% co-pay. If an insured person breaks his arm skiing a double black diamond, goes to the hospital, and has surgery that costs $3,500, the injured but insured skier pays $500 right away (the deductible) and then 20% of the remaining costs (the copay) which would be an additional $600 (20% of $3,000, the difference between the deductible and surgery cost). In some cases, this may induce the insured to ski a bit more carefully.

Where Did the Term "Moral Hazard" Come From?

The field of economics didn't import the idiom "moral hazard" into the discipline until the 1960s. Yet the term had been around for about 100 years at that point, and the concept had been around even longer. The creation of the idiom followed a meandering path through disciplines ranging from theology, statistics, and insurance and was used a lot differently than how economists and social scientists use it today.

The first recorded use of the term "moral hazard" came in 1865 in a book titled "The Practice of Fire Underwriting."[132] In this fire insurance manual, moral hazard was defined as "the danger proceeding from motives to destroy property by fire or permit its destruction." The idiom was used to describe a correlation between the incidence of the insured event and the possession of insurance for that event. In other words, people with fire insurance were more likely to have their stuff burned than people without fire insurance.

While the first recorded use of the term came in 1865, the concept of moral hazard existed for centuries beforehand. Cases of fraud in the insurance industry have been documented since the 1600s.[133] The Great Fire of London in 1666, which provided momentum for the development of fire insurance, helped develope the initial concept of moral hazard.[134] Then came a deeper development of actuarial science, statistics, and probability that gave insurers empirical tools to predict numbers of insurance claims and the ability to quantify risk.

The probability literature of the 1600s and 1700s, while not directly referencing moral hazard, developed a theory of risk that contributed to the formulation of the term.

But you really have to trace the etymology of the term "moral" back to its Latin roots before you understand how probability literature contributed to the term. The Latin word *moralis* derives from the word *mos*, which was defined as "manner, custom, way, usage, practice... as determined not by laws, but by men's will and pleasure, humor, self-will, caprice."[135] It had a sense of "man's subjectivity or impulse."

It's the Latin meaning of "men's caprice" that best suits the term moral expectation. While working on a theory of probability in 1738, mathematician and physicist Daniel Bernoulli developed the term. Bernoulli contrasted *mathematical expectation* with *moral expectation* when dealing with situations of chance. And he did so with a thought experiment:

Imagine a poor individual came across a lottery ticket with a 50% chance of winning zero and a 50% chance of winning $20,000. To use a term from probability, the expected value is closely related to the weighted average. With an equal chance of winning $0 and $20,000, you'd expect to win on average $10,000 if you made the gamble over and over. The mathematical expectation (expected value) says the lottery ticket is worth $10,000.

But that value isn't the same for all people.

Bernoulli suggested that the poor individual would gladly accept $9,000 to sell that lottery ticket. On the other hand, a rich individual in the same situation wouldn't sell that lottery ticket for $9,000, since the rich person would evaluate the gamble differently.

Bernoulli's theory suggested that people don't consider only the monetary gain or numerical probability in a risky situation (mathematical expectation), but also act upon the subjective value of that risk (moral expectation). In this sense, "moral" had nothing to do with morality, rather, it was used to describe an individual's subjective expectation instead of an ethical judgment.[136]

That subjective moral value placed on the risky situation was a function of the risk-taker's total wealth. It also helped to show the difference between what people were willing to pay versus what people were mathematically expected to gain from the game. This was a huge contribution to the development of a theory of risk.

A translation of the Latin text in which Bernoulli wrote, "Specimen theoriae novae de mensura sortis," is necessary to understand where the term "moral expectation" came from. To better explain this concept, Bernoulli incorporated a copy of a letter by mathematician Gabriel Cramer written in French, in which the concept is called *valeur morale* for "moral value" and *esperance morale* for "moral expectation."

Now apply Bernoulli's "moral expectation" to evaluate the purchase of insurance. The person seeking insurance trades the risk of a bad outcome for the risk of a good outcome, based on subjective moral expectation and objective mathematical expectations. Likely some of this meaning flowed into the formulation of "moral hazard" in the insurance literature of the 1800s.

As the flavor of "moral" in the phrase has evolved overtime, so has the meaning of "hazard." The usage of "hazard" doesn't mean "risk or peril" like it does today. Rather, the term had a different meaning in the 1800s. The original meaning of "hazard" was a dice game that was similar to the modern game of craps. To the ear of someone in the 1800s, "hazard" would have had a flavor of chance.[137]

It was the insurance literature of the 1800s that brought morality into the idiom of "moral hazard." At this point, the flavor of "excellence of character" was applied to the word "moral," in part, as some scholars suggest, to help legitimize the insurance industry in the eyes of the church. And in doing so, it also helped to popularize the idiom's usage.

Before the insurance industry became mainstream, many theologians had argued that the insurer was selling something that was not theirs, since the safety of a particular venture came only from God's will. In fact, one 13th century pope issued a decree prohibiting insurance.[138]

Another objection to insurance was that it was a form of gambling. To grow the industry, the insurers had to differentiate gambling from insurance. The emphasis on moral hazard helped accomplish this.[139] By excluding the immoral and corrupt—the moral hazards—from being able to acquire insurance, it helped distinguish buying insurance from gambling. The logic was this: gambling is immoral, and people who gamble are immoral, but the insurance industry excludes the immoral from buying insurance. By excluding the immoral, the insurance industry becomes moral — therefore insurance isn't gambling!

During this period, moral hazard was also typically ascribed to the immoral and unscrupulous personal characteristics of the individual obtaining insurance. The manuals on fire insurance in the late 1800s and early 1900s distinguished between physical hazards of a property and moral hazards that stemmed from things such as carelessness, negligence, or even arson.

The Difference between Adverse Selection and Moral Hazard

The first usage of the term "adverse selection" appeared nearly 30 years after the appearance of moral hazard in a publication that pointed out that sick people were more likely to purchase health insurance than healthy people.[140]

- Adverse selection occurs *before* the purchase of insurance and describes how the ill are more likely to use the insurance.
- Moral hazard occurs *after* the insurance is purchased and describes how the insured is more likely to engage in undesirable activities, making them more likely to use the insurance.

Economic students as well as the writers in the late 1800s had difficulty distinguishing the two concepts. In fact, during a large portion of the 1800s, the term moral hazard encompassed both concepts.

Both moral hazard and adverse selection are outcomes of asymmetric information. And both terms describe an increased correlation between insurance and filing a claim for that insurance. The crucial distinction between the two is the direction of causation.

Moral hazard says people purchasing insurance change their behavior or invest in less preventive effort, that the purchase itself distorts incentives. Deciding to burn more candles in your home once you have fire insurance is a moral hazard.

On the other hand, adverse selection posits that high-risk people are the ones who buy more insurance. The person first in line to buy fire insurance is the one who knows he is already at high risk of burning his house down.

It wasn't until the 1960s that discussions of moral hazard began to appear in the field of economics. And it all started with Nobel-Prize-winning economist Kenneth Arrow's watershed article about uncertainty and moral hazard and the economics problems of medical care and health insurance.[141]

The economist's treatment of moral hazard harkened back to the original sense that had hardly anything to do with morality.[142] Economists after the 1960s began again to use "moral hazard" in a non-pejorative manner. They returned to the meanings that Bernoulli used with the term "moral expectation," stripping the expression of its morality and broadening it to describe situations where an individual gets the benefits while someone else bears the risks or costs.

Timeline of the Development of the Idiom "Moral Hazard"

Bernoulli introduces the concept of "moral expectation" to describe subjective evaluation of a gamble	"Moral Hazard" referred to people and situations in addition to covering "adverse selection" before life insurance industry made the distinction.	**First use of term "adverse selection" by McClintock**	Imports "moral hazard" into economics, stripping its pejorative undertones and broadening it to encompass the studying of decisions under uncertainty like the principal-agent problem.
1738	**1865**	**1892**	**1963**
Term "hazard" was name given to a dice game and carried a meaning of "chance" during this period.	**First use of term "moral hazard" which was found in fire insurance manual**	"Moral Hazard" maintained its derogatory connotation and was emphasized to assuage the concerns of the church of the immorality of the insurance industry as a form of gambling.	**Kenneth Arrow's "Uncertainty and Welfare Economics of Medical Care"**

Following Arrow's lead, economists have applied the concept to analyzing a wide range of public policy situations from unemployment insurance to corporate bailouts. Economists took the insurance industry's term and assimilated it within the economics discipline to consider the role that incentives play in a broad range of relationships. And one such example is the relationship between the ski resort owners and the employees who run the ski lifts and check ski passes.

Another Risk of Asymmetric Information: The Principal-Agent Problem

Many skiers and snowboarders in Colorado buy annual ski passes that allow unlimited number of visits to their favorite mountains. With that deal comes the incentive to "borrow" someone's pass and ski for the day. This is ski pass fraud. If you are caught using someone else's pass, the pass is confiscated, and the violator can face police charges.

Ski pass fraud typically spikes in March as Spring Break arrives. The penalty for losing the pass is also lower in March since it is toward the end of the ski season, and the future value of the ski pass isn't worth as much as it is in December. (Losing your pass in December means four good months of skiing gone, while losing it in March might only mean a few weeks of good skiing gone.)

At ski resorts in Breckenridge, Colorado, when someone is found committing ski pass fraud, the resort security at Breckenridge can call the police, who go to the slopes and issue a ticket. According to an official at the Breckenridge Municipal Court, the average fine for ski pass fraud is around $400.[143]

So, there is a risk with using someone else's ski pass. But how big is that risk? To be punished, you have to get caught. How vigilant are the workers who check your ski ticket? Or a better question to ask is "what's in it for them?" Do the pass-checkers have the appropriate incentives to confiscate and call out people who are using someone else's ski pass?

For pass-checkers making an hourly wage, their pay doesn't change whether they catch eight people committing ski pass fraud in a day or zero. There's no individual incentive mechanism to care. And with an incentive problem, the employee (agent) won't act the way the boss (principal) wants.

This is a situation called the principal-agent problem. It occurs when one person, the agent, acts on behalf of another person, the principal, often because there is an employment agreement between them, i.e., the agent works for the principal. The problem occurs because the agent is motivated by self-interest and acts in ways contrary to what the principal wants. This problem persists because the principal and the agent have asymmetric information, usually because the principal cannot monitor and/or control the agent's actual activities. The principal-agent problem is an example of moral hazard.

In this case, the ski pass checker (the agent) is hired by the resort owner (principal) to make sure everyone is buying lift tickets and isn't ripping off the resort by using someone else's pass. It is in the best interest of the resort owner to sell as many lift tickets as possible and so to catch as many violators as possible, and the principal pays the agent to do just that. But being vigilant, staying attentive, and dealing with confrontation has a cost to the ski pass checkers, and has no effect on their paychecks. It is less costly for them to just slack off.

One solution to overcome the principal-agent problem is to give the agent some stake in what happens. With ski pass checkers, the pass-checker receives a monetary bonus for each ski pass they confiscate for ski pass fraud. Without the reward, the pass-checker doesn't have any motivation to deal with the controversy of accusing someone of theft of services.

Bonuses or rewards help realign the incentives of the agent with those of the principal. The same deal is offered to bouncers at bars or night clubs who check whether those looking to gain access to the club are 21 years old. Bars will typically give the bouncers a monetary bonus for each fake ID they confiscate. It's another incentive structure to help overcome the principal-agent problem.

Bonuses and incentives can motivate employees to work harder while they are on the job (fixing the moral hazard problem), they can also fix an adverse selection problem by separating out those who should get the job to begin with. To see this, consider two workers: Larry and Heidi. Larry is a low-quality worker who won't be very productive on the job while Heidi is the high-quality worker who will. When hiring, you can't tell which is the low-quality and which is the high-quality worker. Economists preach that people respond in their own self-interest to the incentives they encounter. If Larry can get away with slacking on the job, he will do it. If you offer a salary of $70,000, both Larry and Heidi will apply.

It's your job to set up a pay structure that will weed out the Larrys. Setting up a pay-for-performance scheme can help do just that.

So instead of paying a flat $70,000 annual salary, you offer a basic salary of $50,000 and an incentive bonus tied to an outcome of another $20,000. The Heidi workers, who know they will put in the high-quality effort and will achieve the performance outcome, will still apply for the job, but the Larrys, whose low-quality effort will make it impossible to get the $20,000 bonus, won't apply. Incentive pay schemes can separate out the low-quality from the start.

Bouncers at a bar aren't the only employees with misaligned incentives between worker and boss. A bartender (agent) who gives free drinks will earn higher tips from their customers. But the cost of those "free" drinks are borne by the bar owner (principal) while the bartender reaps the rewards. It's because of this principal-agent problem that some bars have special lids on their liquor bottles that only pour an exact amount of liquor once the bottle is inserted into a ring. That ring is connected to the bar's computer which records every exact pour. This makes it hard for the bartender to boost their take home pay by giving away the store.

The principal-agent problem is a risk of asymmetric information because the boss can't monitor or supervise each employee during all work hours. Only the employee knows whether they are putting in 100% effort or whether they're looking through their dating app matches on the clock instead.

Sometimes, supervision is the solution as long as supervision isn't too costly. Smartphones and GPS tracking have made some forms of supervision much less costly. In contentious election years, it isn't uncommon to see paid canvassers going door to door to sway votes. Someone has designed smartphone applications to monitor the canvassers' efforts. The app tracks their journey and how many minutes are spent at each doorstep. This prevents the paid canvasser (agent) from slacking on the job and not soliciting votes while under contract with the boss (principal). And sometimes, businesses create mechanisms that turn the customer into the supervisor.

At some fast-food restaurants, you might notice a sign by the cash register that says "If you don't get a receipt, your meal is free." This transforms the role of the customer, who now has an incentive to get a receipt, and that receipt records the transactions that prevent an unscrupulous employee from charging a customer for their burger but actually pocketing the customer's cash.

Avoiding the Market Failure of Imperfect Information

When there is asymmetric information the market can fall apart and the invisible hand cannot do its job. Imperfect information is the fourth example of market failures along with imperfection competition (chapter 4), externalities (chapter 7) and public goods (chapter 8). This chapter discussed approaches to correct information asymmetry:

- provide more information, such as signaling and screening
- extract more information, such as incentive mechanisms, structures, contracts, compensation systems, constraints, institutions, rules, quotas, and policies

All designed to cleverly bridge those information gaps and prevent market failure.

The Supreme Court Justice Oliver Wendell Holmes recognized one of those policies in 1881 when describing why, for centuries, mariners weren't paid until they got their ships' contents safely across the sea. Holmes wrote, "...if the ship perished, if the mariners were to have their wages in such cases, they would not use their endeavors, nor hazard their lives, for the safety of the ship."[144] Holmes didn't use economic terms, but he suggested there was a "plausible explanation of policy" for the no-pay-until-the-cargo-safely-reaches-port rule. We now know that the plausible explanation is moral hazard.

CHAPTER 10:

How Baseball Can Explain Recessions, Keynes, Government Stimulus, and Carrying Couches

I f you've ever watched a baseball game, you might notice a unique tradition that occurs after a strikeout. Once the umpire calls "strike three," you'll often see the catcher pop up out of his squat and snap the ball down to the third baseman. Through this old baseball tradition, the purpose of which is to keep the infielders' arms warm, the ball travels from the catcher to several of the infielders and finally back to the pitcher for the next pitch. In baseball terminology, this is called "throwing the ball around the horn."

Many think the saying comes from a reference to Cape Horn, which is located at the southern tip of South America. Before the Panama Canal was complete, the only passage around the continent sailed around Cape Horn. Like how sailors traveled around Cape Horn, the baseball travels around the infield.

Now imagine what it would look like if the baseball's trip around the diamond were different than normal. This time the first baseman, instead of throwing the ball back to the pitcher, throws it back to the catcher and around the circle again. Then, the catcher grabs another ball and throws it down to third base, with two balls now circulating. Then a third ball, and a fourth, and a fifth until each player is frantically catching and throwing the ball before the next ball arrives. Each player is simultaneously active.

Baseballs zinging around the infield is a metaphor for what economists call the "circular flow of money." Think of baseballs as the cash in the economy, and each player is a consumer who catches the ball (metaphor for working and earning money) and who throws the ball (metaphor for spending their income). One person's spending stimulates another worker's income, just like a player's throwing induces another player's catching. In the well-functioning baseball economy, everyone is simultaneously catching and throwing. Similarly, in a healthy financial economy, everyone is working and spending.

Now imagine what happens when the catcher, instead of throwing the next baseball back down to the third baseman, decides to throw two of the baseballs to a player inside the dugout who holds onto them. With fewer balls in circulation, the infielders aren't working to their full capacity: with five balls all moving around, each player must quickly catch and get rid of the ball before the next one comes their way and again their throwing induces another player's catching. But now, with only three balls in circulation, the shortstop has time to wait before the next ball hits his glove. There is downtime between each catch and throw. A smaller number of throws means fewer catches. Things slow down.

Unemployment exists in the circular flow model. With more and more unemployed players, there is less spending. With lower spending on products, businesses no longer need to hire as many workers. As workers lose their jobs, they have less disposable income to go out and spend in the economy; this means less income earned by the other local businesses. The economy slows down, some workers lose their jobs.

Believe it or not, the metaphor of a bunch of baseballs whizzing around the horn between players is the secret to understanding a lot of macroeconomics. It also helps explain how recessions persist, what the classical economists of the 18th and 19th centuries overlooked, and why economic activity sees up and downs.

Most years see the production of goods and services rise as more people are born, more people get jobs, and technology improves. As the economy produces more and more, it improves people's standard of living. But in some years, this steady growth does not happen. In fact, sometimes we see the reverse. Shops can't sell all their goods, and they cut back on production. As the economy slows, workers lose jobs and unemployment rises. Gross Domestic Product (GDP) slows down and people's incomes fall. These periods are called *recessions*. Economists call the fluctuations in the economy the *business cycle*. Much of the focus of macroeconomics is explaining these economic expansions and contractions.

The baseball metaphor can also explain how an economist during the Great Depression of the 1930s revolutionized economics by developing a school of thought that government intervention can stabilize economy. That economist was John Maynard Keynes (1883-1946).

Economic Thinking Before Keynes and the Great Depression

Dating from Adam Smith (1723-1790), much of economic thinking centered around the logic of scarcity. To a bunch of poor people chasing after a limited number of goods, the way to improve things was to boost the production (i.e., supply) for more of those people to obtain. David Ricardo (1772-1823) stated "demand is only limited by production[145]" and French economist J.B. Say (1767-1832) said, in effect, "supply creates its own demand," often referred to in economics as Say's Law[146]. With this thinking, it was easy to conclude that people will always buy what they make, and so, much of early economics was dedicated to the efficiency of production, focusing on the supply side of things to maximize resources.

The classical economists were also all about equilibrium thinking. Their view wasn't unlike the treatment of gravity in Newtonian Physics. As long as self-interest and free markets existed, economies would head toward equilibrium. Or just like a pendulum pushed one way or another, it would eventually return to its original stationary state. The same logic that we saw in Chapter 1, about how shortages and surpluses are eliminated in the market using our supply and demand analysis, was applied by the classical economists to all markets.

So, if the economy were in a slump, and businesses started laying off workers and shutting down factories, the negative trends gave their own remedy: prices would change. In the labor market, the price of labor is the wage. In short, unemployment drove down wages, and as wages fell, eventually firms would find it profitable to hire more workers. So, if there were a temporary increase in the unemployment rate, wages would fall, making it more attractive for firms to hire more workers; back to equilibrium.

In the same way, if there were idle factories, the price of borrowing (or the interest rate) would fall until entrepreneurs found it worthwhile to take out loans and restart those factories. So, it wouldn't be long until a well-functioning economy would be restored. Or if consumers decided to stop spending their income, consumption spending would fall, but savings would rise. Think of savings as being like any other commodity with its own price; in this case the price of savings is the rate of interest. With an increase in the amount of savings in the economy, that would drive down interest rates; those cheaper interest rates would then induce more businesses to borrow money and ramp up investment spending. With freely adjusting interest rates, savings always equaled investment; back to the stationary state and back to equilibrium.

The consequences of the classical economist's assumptions were that recessions and involuntary unemployment are impossible. The economy was self-correcting. An economic downturn had its own built-in safety switch: if savings increased, then borrowing would become cheaper and the economy would rebound on the backs of business investment spending. Anyone who wanted to work should be able to find work so long as they accepted a lower wage. The prevailing economic doctrine said that free markets would automatically provide full employment in the long run. And this mode of thinking worked pretty well....until it couldn't explain the Great Depression.

Oct. 24, 1929, saw an inflated stock market bubble deflate. The market crashed: by 1932, the Dow was down 90%. The rapid wiping-out of wealth was accompanied by foreclosures on loans and mortgages, which then evolved into a banking crisis.

If the free market provided full employment, why were 13 million Americans (25%) unemployed in 1933? Why had the value of the U.S. economy fallen by almost half between 1929 and 1933? How was there a prolonged economic slump? How do you explain the Great Depression?

In the midst of the massive global economic contraction in the 1930s, existing economic theory was unable either to explain the causes of the severe economic collapse or provide any adequate solutions to jumpstart the economy. There was no room in existing theory about how to boost production and add more jobs. Wages and prices should adjust to get the economy back to equilibrium. Right? Why wasn't that happening? The economy was stuck in stagnation mode despite the many unemployed workers and underutilized plants, machines, and equipment.

This is where Keynes (rhymes with "gains") comes in. Keynes' most famous work, *The General Theory of Employment, Interest, and Money*, published in 1936, got all the attention, but the work that cleared the way was Keynes' *A Treatise on Money*, published six years earlier. It opened up the idea of the disconnect between savings and investment that helped get at the question of why the economy had ups and downs. Keynes showed that it was possible for the free market to settle into a state where workers remained unemployed and machines remained idle for long periods like they were witnessing during the Great Depression.

And before he could espouse his ideas, he first had to show where classical economic theory got it wrong.

Keynes vs. the Classical Economists

The core differences in Keynes' theory compared to those of classical economists like Smith and Ricardo can be summarized as the divergence in the following:

- short run vs. long run
- supply-focused vs. demand-focused
- prices vs. quantities

Let's unpack each of those three.

Keynes suggested that the Great Depression was caused by a lack of total spending in the economy, or what economic textbooks call *aggregate demand*. In classical economic theory, there wasn't any room for the notion that there could be inadequate demand. Resources were limited compared to people's needs, and so there was no room in the economic logic to have a shortage of demand.

Keynes disagreed. In fact, his idea was all about total demand in the economy and how shortages could persist. Keynes pointed out that inadequate demand could cause prolonged periods of unemployment as witnessed in the 1930s. In the Keynesian framework, total spending in the economy on goods and services comes from the sum of three components[147]: consumption (C), investment (I), and government spending (G). If consumers stop spending, and businesses become spooked and don't invest, the government has a role to boost spending and jumpstart the economy.

The classical economist just thought that any increase in demand would quickly cause prices to rise and wouldn't change output, so demand increases couldn't boost employment. Additional government spending would just cause prices to rise; it wouldn't increase the number of jobs. Keynes didn't buy this type of thinking.

Keynes contended that changes in aggregate demand have the largest impact in the short-run on output and employment, not on prices. So, boosts in government spending can increase the number of jobs.

Keynes also questioned the classical economist's automatic movement back to equilibrium and it resulted in one of Keynes's most famous aphorisms. Keynes made a switch from focusing economic analysis from the long run to the short run.[148] One of his better-known quotes is that "….in the long run we are all dead." The full context of the quote is below:

"The long run is a misleading guide to current affairs. In the long run we are all dead. Economists set themselves too easy, to useless a task if in tempestuous seasons they can only tell us when the storm is long past, the ocean will be flat[149]."

In short, Keynes was saying that the long run "steady state" beloved by the classical economists wasn't real: the long run is a series of short runs. We should focus on the short run.

Savings was also a problem to a stalling economy in Keynes' eyes, but not to the classical economists. The classical economists didn't view savings as a problem. Sure, what's saved is a "leakage" from the circular flow model, but that leakage is met with an equal "injection" from investment spending. Returned to the baseball metaphor, any ball that was thrown outside the infield into the dugout (savings) would quickly be thrown right back into the field from the dugout (as investment). Likewise, the classical economists believed that businesses would reinject the money saved in the bank by borrowing and starting or improving new and existing businesses.

Or to quickly contrast the classical economist's way of thinking with what Keynes purported: if a restaurant had vacant tables night in and night out, there'd be no need to borrow money, even at ridiculously cheap interest rates, because what the restaurant really needed was more customers. In this type of situation, the economy would remain in a rut. Having interest-free loans to expand your pizza ovens doesn't really help when customers aren't around to buy your pizzas.

According to the classical economists, the decision to up-grade the pizza oven only depends on how cheaply one can borrow money to make that upgrade. But to Keynes, what really spurred the pizza owner to make an investment in a new oven was a feeling of optimism, not a low interest rate.

Keynes used the term "animal spirits" to describe the public's wave of pessimism and optimism. When households and businesses are pessimistic, they cut back on spending. When households and businesses are optimistic, they boost their spending and investment. Pessimism results in reduced demand, a slower economy, and more unemployment. Keynes' dismaying conclusion was to reject the classical economists' automatic safety mechanism that would turn around an economic slowdown. Said another way, Keynes showed how an economy in a depression could remain there.

Keynesian Economics
If you only knew the following three points about Keynesian Economics, you'd be ahead of most people:
- Demands drives economies in the short-run
- Economies can fall into lengthy slumps.
- The government can sustain demand during times of slumps.

Keynes' medicine for a sick economy suffering from inadequate demand was active fiscal and monetary policy. Both had the same objective: to encourage consumers and businesses to spend and invest again so that the economy's production capacity doesn't just sit there. The Keynesian remedy is direct government spending, cutting taxes, lowering interest rates, and making borrowing easier.

What really distinguishes Keynes' theory from those of his contemporaries is his belief in active policies to mitigate economic downturns. Direct government spending can lead to unbalanced government budgets, but instead of worrying about deficit spending, Keynes advocated for countercyclical fiscal policies to wind back the wrong direction of a business cycle, such as labor-intensive infrastructure projects to stimulate employment during recessions/depressions.

This idea was central to the series of programs, public works projects, regulations, and banking reforms under President Franklin Roosevelt's New Deal. Agencies like the Civilian Conservation Corps (CCC) took unemployed men and provided them with shelter, food, clothing, and a wage in exchange for manual labor related to conservation projects and development of the country's natural resources. One such project has been used by the Beatles, Bon Jovi, and Justin Bieber. And it is a short drive from Denver Colorado.

Red Rocks Amphitheater, in Morrison, Colorado, is a product of the New Deal infrastructure projects. An outdoor concert venue, where audience seats are sandwiched by two massive iconic rock walls, is so spectacular that after winning Pollstar Magazine's award for best small outdoor venue for the 11th time, the concert industry magazine decided to name the award the "Red Rocks Award" and disqualified the amphitheater from the running.

The Multiplier

A central element to Keynesian theory is the idea of the "multiplier,"originally conceived by Richard Kahn to describe a type of echo mechanism.[150] John R. Hicks gets the credit of translating Keynes' idea into the quantitative interpretation that has been taught for generations to millions of undergraduate macroeconomics students.[151] Hicks took Keynes' idea and distilled it into an orderly and mathematical version that is easily digestible, which can partially be credited to Keynesian teaching's longstanding influence.

Keynes' ideas were extremely captivating but also, at times, impenetrable. And without everyday examples for people to follow, those captivating ideas can be lost. A case in point occurred when Keynes met with President Roosevelt in May 1934.

Keynes submerged the president in an esoteric explanation of how the multiplier works. He was hoping to show how borrowing to pay for public works should be considered an investment because the public works would soon pay for themselves through the taxation of the freshly employed.

But like a college economics 101 student whose eyes glaze over when they see too much jargony math, Keynes' wonky , mathematical-laden rendition didn't land with the president. Roosevelt later stated that Keynes "let a whole rigamarole of figures. He must be a mathematician rather than a political economist."

Keynes should have used some "in-other-words" words.

According to Frances Perkins, FDR's labor secretary, Keynes used a simplified example with her that abandoned the theoretic mumbo jumbo for an everyday description: "a dollar spent on relief by the government was a dollar given to the grocer, by the grocer to the wholesaler, and by the wholesaler to the farmer, etc. With one dollar paid out for relief or public works or anything else, you have created four dollars' worth of national income.[152]"

It works like this.

Any government stimulus gives money to consumers, which they then spend. Each dollar of government stimulus becomes income to someone who turns around and spends a portion of that dollar. The fraction of that dollar that is spent is called the marginal propensity to consume (MPC). The original spending by the government feeds back into a second round of spending as the consumers go out and spend a portion of the stimulus in the local economy. This round of spending becomes income for yet more people who then turn around and spend a portion of it. And so on.

Mathematically, the sum of these rounds of spending is equal to 1/(1-MPC) which we call the *Keynesian multiplier*. The sum of all the rounds of spending may be much larger than the original government expenditure. The size of the multiplier depends upon how much of each dollar is spent verses saved.

Think back to the baseball analogy from the beginning of the chapter. If baseballs are "leaked" from the circular flow, they don't stimulate another player's catching. In the same way, as more of the spending is saved, it means less income for consumers in later rounds of spending. Every dollar earned derives from money that was spent by someone else.

Consider this example. On the mountain path he was hiking, Jace finds a $10 bill which he uses to buy spaghetti from Patrick's Pasta Palace. This is where the ripple effect happens. Patrick the pasta-maker is great with marinara sauce but not with scissors, so he uses $8 of that $10 to have his hair cut by Brett the barber. Brett celebrates his additional customer at the end of the day by buying a $6.40 margarita with salt from Barbara the barkeep, who then treats herself to a $5.12 cappuccino at Kathy's Coffeehouse before studying late at night for her midterm exam.

This process continues as each seller spends 80% of their income (MPC of 0.8) and saves the rest. The Keynesian multiplier is 5, meaning that initial $10 created $50 of spending. (1/(1-0.8) = 5).

But what happens if people save a higher portion of their income? What if each person decided to only turn around and spend 50% of their income (MPC of 0.5)? Then the Keynesian multiplier is 2, which means that the initial $10 turned into

$20 of spending in the economy. Higher spending creates a greater stimulus. Higher savings means less stimulus. Savings reduces the multiplier. Consumption increases it.

The multiplier can work the other way as well. For each dollar people cut from consumption, it means subsequent rounds of cuts, resulting in a much larger drop in economic activity attributable to the initial drop in consumption.

If people spooked by a downturn in the economy start saving more—they go out to eat less, forgo their new back-country ski purchase, and delay their furnace upgrade—the restaurant, ski equipment industry, and home HVAC industry all get less business. As those industries get less business, they are forced to lay off workers. Unemployment rises, causing a negative feedback loop. People become even more concerned about the future and even more reticent to spend and instead save even more. Uncertainty hurts consumer confidence and they spend less. The downturn amplifies. This is Keynes' multiplier in reverse. The initial $100 saved by one weary consumer causes a fall in spending of $200 or $300.

So, while Roosevelt didn't get the "rigamarole" Keynes presented, FDR summed up Keynes' sensitivities nicely when he said, "The only thing we have to fear is fear itself."

Saving during a recession might be prudent for one individual but doesn't do well for the whole economy. For one person, it makes sense to cut back on spending and save in preparation for uncertainty during a recession. But when everybody tries to save more, the overall level of spending in the economy falls. As the slowdown increases, production slows and people lose jobs, quite possibly leading to a drop in savings as well. Keynes called this the "paradox of thrift."

Think back to the baseball metaphor: if the third baseman decides to hoard the baseball instead of throwing it to the shortstop, the shortstop doesn't have a ball to throw to the second baseman and so on. Keynesian economics says that only way to reverse this process is for someone else to spend more: and that someone else was the government. This is a central tenet of Keynesian Economics: a cure for a recession is government stimulus.

Nasar has a concise and comprehensive explanation of Keynes's revolutionary ideas:

> What made the General Theory so radical was Keynes's proof that it was possible for a free market economy to settle into states in which workers and machines remained idle for prolonged periods of time. . . The only way to revive business confidence and get the private sector spending again was by cutting taxes and letting business and individuals keep more of their income so they could spend it. Or, better yet, having the government spend more money directly, since that would guarantee that 100 percent of it would be spent rather than saved. If the private sector couldn't or wouldn't spend, the government would have to do it.[153]

What Keynesians Economics Is Not

Keynes is often mischaracterized as "anti-capitalist" while some even confuse Keynesian Theory with the philosophy of Karl Marx. Marxism and Keynesianism are not the same thing, not by a long shot, although they are linked by the year 1883, the year Keynes was born and the year Marx died. Marxism is also a major political tradition that opposes capitalism. Keynes was attempting to improve capitalism, not to overturn it.[154]

Keynes himself made efforts to distinguish his theory from Marxism. Keynes, unlike Marx and some socialists, said he was not arguing that the government replace private industry. Keynes wrote, "The important thing for Government is not to do things which individuals are doing already, and to do them a little better or a little worse, but to do those things which at present are not done at all." [155]

It's also wrong to say that Keynesian economics is all about "big government" and perpetual government deficits. Keynes believed governments should deficit spend during a recession but build up savings during boom times and then finance the spending it does during bad times with the money it saved up during good times. Nor was Keynes a tax-and-spend proponent. On the contrary, he wondered whether a government that takes more than 25% was a good thing.

Introductory Macroeconomics students only get the C + I + G version of Keynes, that is, the textbook Keynesian model developed by Sir John Hicks (1904-1989) and Franco Modigliani (1918-2003). To be fair, Keynes's influence and his corpus of writing covered topics from Hitler to the gold standard.

One of his most prescient works was the *Economic Consequences of the Peace* (1919) that castigated the overly burdensome penalties imposed on Germany after WWI and its detriment of the overall economic well-being of Europe. In this polemic, Keynes, who was a delegate from Great Britain at the Paris Peace Conference, predicted that the penalties of the Versailles Treaty imposed on Germany would lead to another war. His work on exchange rates and the gold standard had massive influence on international monetary policy and international trade, which helped lead to the creation of the International Monetary Fund and the World Bank.

The Heyday of Keynesian Economics, Its Fizzle, and Its Return in a Pinch

Much of the motivation for *The General Theory* was to reduce mass unemployment during an economic downturn. By the mid-1940s, Keynes' prescription for fighting unemployment became standard policy in many counties. His death in 1946 didn't slow down the Keynesian revolution. In that same year, America's Employment Act of 1946 took federal responsibility in maintaining full employment. The law made the executive branch responsible for the economy, and in so doing, gave the administration new powers.

It seemed there was no turning back to the old days when the economy was allowed to manage itself. Eisenhower used Keynesian tools and Johnson cut taxes, which were both followed by economic growth. Keynesianism was the wonder drug. As a testament to Keynesianism winning the day, the December 1965 edition of *Time* magazine gave the "Man of the Year" award to John Maynard Keynes.

In 1971, even President Nixon declared himself a Keynesian in economics. During this time, Keynesian economists relied on data first collated by A.W.H. "Bill" Phillips that showed the inverse relationship between unemployment and inflation. The Phillips Curve, as macroeconomics students are taught, implied that unemployment could be reduced if policymakers were willing to deal with a little inflation.

But as the 1970s went along, the Phillips Curve seemed to break down. Inflation jumped to double digits, yet unemployment didn't fall. Even worse, unemployment went up. Rising prices and rising unemployment became known as *stagflation*.

It seemed the wonder drug was overused and losing its potency. The Keynesians couldn't explain what was happening as the stagflation of the 1970s caused a crack in the fine-tuning-the-economy-via-government armor. And through that crack came the revival of conservative economics.

The charge was led by Nobel Prize winning economists Milton Friedman and Robert Lucas, and it was endorsed by President Ronald Reagan and Prime Minister Margaret Thatcher. Their brand of economics put a greater emphasis

317

on the free market, fewer regulations, lower taxes, and less government intervention. Yet it wasn't too long into Reagan's presidency, despite his anti-government rhetoric, that he was fighting the economic slowdown of 1981 with some old-fashioned Keynesian stimulus. The spending came in the form of substantial military expenditures and broad tax cuts, a central feature of the Economic Recovery Tax Act of 1981.

It seems when economic hard times come back, governments—regardless of their ideologies—almost always reach for the Keynesian cure. Economist Robert Lucas once remarked, "I guess everyone is a Keynesian in the foxhole.[156]"

Reagan had a stimulus package in 1981. George W. Bush's administration had two stimulus packages, in 2001 and 2008. Barack Obama introduced one in 2009, and the Trump administration created a massive stimulus program to fight the COVID-19 pandemic in 2020. When the economy stumbles and people start to lose jobs, policymakers inevitably pivot back to Keynes' prescriptions and what can be done to boost spending.

The recession of 2001 and the Bush Tax Cuts

President George W. Bush opened the Keynesian playbook. In 2001, a recession occured that was caused by three big shocks to aggregate demand: the end of the dot-com bubble, the terrorist attacks on Sept. 11, 2001, and corporate accounting scandals.

After a run-up in stock prices of high-tech companies in the 1990s, stock prices fell 25% from August 2000 to August 2001. The reduction harmed household wealth and reduced consumer spending as well as harming the profitability of businesses, which also saw a decrease in investment spending. In the weeks after 9/11, the stock market fell 12% (its biggest weekly loss since the Great Depression in the 1930s)[157].

The uncertainty caused by the terrorist attacks also dampened household spending and business plans. At about the same time, Enron and WorldCom were misleading the public about their profitability. When the scandals were revealed, the companies' stocks prices plummeted along with other business stocks. And, unemployment in the U.S. jumped from 3.9% in October 2000 to 6% in April 2002.

The Bush administration responded quickly by passing a tax cut in 2001 officially called the *Economic Growth and Tax Relief Reconciliation Act of 2001*,[158] which included an immediate tax rebate. The tax policy change included modifications to tax brackets and adjusted the estate tax. Rebate checks were mailed to millions of Americans ranging from $300 for single tax filers, $600 for married tax filers and $500 for single parents. Estimates said that 92 million Americans would get the rebate check, dispersing $38 billion. To put those rebates into perspective, the median family income in 2000 was $41,000. So, a $600 rebate was equal to 1.5% of the household income in the exact middle of income distribution; as a portion of after-tax household income the rebates were an even greater share.[159] And we will see in a second why Bush should have named those "rebates" something else.

How "stimulating" would these stimulus checks be? How much of the rebate checks would be saved and how much would be spent?

The goal of immediate stimulus is to encourage spending (think adding more balls into our infield). The enemy of this is savings: a $300 check that gets put right into the bank doesn't jumpstart the circular flow. Two economists, Matthew Shapiro and Joel Slemrod, wondered about the same question back in 2001, and so they surveyed 1,506 Americans asking them about how they'd spend their stimulus checks.

What they found was very disappointing from a stimulus standpoint.

They asked survey respondents, "Thinking about your family's financial situation this year, will the tax rebate lead you mostly to increase spending, mostly to increase savings, or mostly to pay off debt?"

Only 22% of households planned to spend their rebate checks; a vast majority of them decided to save it.[160] What did that mean for its stimulus power? Not much. The rebate was added to the 2001 tax bill with the explicit intention of providing a short-term jolt to economic spending. But a spending rate of 22% suggests the tax rebate had a very small impact on aggregate demand. In order for the stimulus to "work," people have to go out and spend it: it has to increase consumption.

Economists then asked, "why such a low level of spending?" Americans typically have a hard time saving for retirement from their regular paychecks, yet Americans had no problem saving this stimulus income. Why the reluctance to spend it? Then the behavioral economists licked their lips, thinking that the lessons from experimental economics could provide a reason why. Could it be that it was framed poorly and therefore didn't induce immediate spending? Could those stimulus checks be "framed" differently to motivate us non-robot-brained humans to spend it more readily?

Classical economics says that money is completely fungible. Put another way, it means money is consumed without regard to its context or where it came from: $600 is $600. The behavioral economists say that's not so. The behavioral concepts of *mental accounting* and *framing* influence how consumers decide to use stimulus money. For instance, how a person spends casino gambling winnings looks different than how they spend expected or earned income.[161] Maybe behavioral economics could devise a better stimulus?

This goes back to the research that purports that people divide their income into different mental accounts, each with their own different ways and portions of spending (think marginal propensity to consume.) Said another way, a "rebate" sounds like a returned loss, but a "bonus" sounds like extra, unexpected money. So, if people think the stimulus money is a "bonus" they will spend more of it.

Framing matters to non-robot-brained humans. We saw some of this in chapter 3. A "bonus" sounds like a windfall, like extra unexpected money won from a gamble. A "rebate" sounds like money that just returns you to the same wealth you already had. For example, when I bought new tires for my Jeep for $600, I received a $60 mail-in rebate that I received several weeks later. That $60 didn't feel like a windfall; it just felt like my own money being paid back to me. I mentally coded it as returned income, not additional income. It didn't cause me to splurge. I saved most of it.

How do you test the hypothesis that we spend "bonus" money more readily than "rebated" money?

Well, you start by giving $50 to a bunch of college students, which was one of several experiments that Nicholas Epley, Dennis Mak, and Lorraine Chen Idson performed to show that people spend income framed as a gain differently than income framed as a return to a prior state.

They took those suddenly-richer-by-50-dollars college students and later asked them how they spent that money. In the experiment, there was a control group and a test group. Some students were told that the $50 was coming from a laboratory funded by students' tuition dollars through the university's operating budget. These students saw wording that said, "You are receiving this tuition rebate because our lab has a surplus of funds…we will contact you in one week to ask you some questions about your tuition rebate…"

Others had that $50 framed differently. These students saw the identical wording but with a slight twist: "tuition rebate" was replaced with "bonus income." They read, "You are receiving this bonus income because our lab has a surplus of funds…we will contact you in one week to ask you some questions about your bonus income…"

Tax rebate   Bonus check

On average, the students who had their $50 framed as a "rebate" spent $9.55 of the $50 while students whose $50 was framed as a "bonus" spent $22.04. Think about that; by changing one word, "rebate," into "bonus," students more than doubled their spending.

The rebate group was also much more likely to save all the money. In fact, 73% of participants in the rebate group reported spending none of the $50 — saving all of it, compared to 36% in the bonus group. It seems that students were more eager to spend when money was mentally coded as a "bonus."

The authors set up a similar experiment to see if they could frame the Bush tax rebates as returned income vs. additional income. Six months after those rebate checks were mailed out, some Boston residents were greeted by a researcher asking them how they spent their Bush Tax Rebates.

Participants read one of two descriptions of the 2001 Tax Relief Act during their questionnaire. This is where the test and control groups came in. One description would frame the Bush stimulus checks as bonus money, and one would code it as money-retuned-to-a-prior-level.

Those randomly assigned to the rebate group read: "proponents of this tax cut argued that the government collected more tax revenue than was needed to cover its expenses, resulting in a tax surplus" that should be returned "*as withheld income.*"

The other group of participants read "proponents of this tax cut argued that the costs of running the government were lower than expected, resulting in a budget surplus" that should be retuned "*as bonus income.*"

All participants were then asked how much money they received from the Bush stimulus checks and what percentage of it they saved and spent.

Participants in the bonus condition group recalled spending much more than the rebate group. Of the bonus group, 87% reported spending it while only 25% of the rebate condition reported spending it. More evidence that "bonuses" are stimulating because they aren't saved.

Not only did the behavioral economists blame the "tax rebate" label for low spending, much of President Bush's own rhetoric might have also sparked a "better save this" mentality with Americans that could explain the high savings rate. Bush described the rebates as a surplus that "should be returned to the taxpayers who earned" because "it's the people's money and government ought to be passing it back after it's met priorities.[162]" Bush made it sound a lot like returned money, back to the status-quo, and not an unexpected windfall. But if the goal is spending, you want people to think of it as a windfall.

So we learned that if you're giving stimulus money out in a lump sum, it should be called a "bonus." Subtle framing of stimulus checks has a dramatic effect on spending and the power of stimulus to jumpstart a flailing economy. This type of framing has all sorts of policy implications the behavioral economists were eager to test out. For instance, If I give you $400 right now, how much of it would you spend? What if I gave you $40 a month for the next 10 months? Would you spend more or less of it compared to the $400 lump sum? Behavioral economists were itching to know if the delivery method of a stimulus would influence consumer spending and saving decisions.

And they didn't have to wait too long. The next natural American federal government stimulus experiment would come seven years later when a housing bubble burst and the sub-prime mortgage crisis morphed into a full-fledged financial crisis.

2008 Great Recession

The bankruptcy of Lehman Brothers in September 2008 is often viewed as the climax of the sub-prime mortgage crisis, but the trouble was building for several years. American housing prices rose 124% between 1997 and 2006. Home prices, which for a long time remained around three times the average wage, were 4.6 times that average wage in 2006.[163] As the housing bubble burst in 2005 and 2006, housing prices fell, and homeowners couldn't make their mortgage payments.

Many bank loans made to "subprime" mortgage borrowers, those with poor chances of repayment, were bundled together and sold as securities to banks around the world. When house prices fell and home buyers abandoned their mortgages, those securities also rapidly fell in value. Suddenly investment banks had sinking assets on their balance sheets causing what looked like an old fashion bank run on all the big investment banks. With banks wary to lend to businesses and consumers paying down debt, the drop in spending led to the Great Recession, officially lasting 18 months. Unemployment doubled from the start of 2008 at 5% to 10% by the end of 2009.

To combat the slowdown, there were several rounds of stimulus. In May 2008, the Bush Administration sent another round of checks to individuals in amounts between $300 to $600, depending on the individual's income (double for couples), just like it did in 2001.

Less than a year later in February 2009, President Obama signed a $787 billion stimulus bill into law that provided a mixture of tax cuts, infrastructure spending, and emergency spending for unemployment benefits among other programs. Part of the stimulus package was the Making Work Pay tax credit: a tax cut of up to $400 for taxpayers or $800 for couples.

But this time it wasn't mailed out in a check as a one-time payment like the Bush rebates were. This time it was disbursed in several installments through workers' paychecks.

Why do it this way instead of a lump sum check all at once?

It got to workers faster because they didn't have to wait for checks to arrive: with a tweak to their paycheck withholdings, workers could see the benefit right away. But the biggest reason was that behavioral economists said to do so!

The idea was that by giving people the sense that their paychecks had grown, they'd be more likely to spend that extra money. Remember, a stimulus ain't a stimulus unless it gets spent.

There was a growing body of behavioral economics literature to support that. Several intriguing studies of Israelis who received reparation payments from Germany after WW2 found that those who got the biggest payments spent very little of the money (only about 17%) while those who received small payments spent most of it (80%).[164]

Work from behavioral economist Richard Thaler (we saw him in chapter 3) suggests that people spend windfalls differently depending on whether they view that new money as wealth or as income. If it's wealth, people will save it. If it's income, people are more likely to spend it.

So, what does this mean for the delivery method of stimulus dollars?

One big check won't make people spend it because it is more likely that people will see it as an increase in wealth and stash it in the bank. But a steady increase in people's paychecks will be perceived as income and more readily spent. The idea was that if you have an extra $10 a week, you wouldn't think twice about splurging on an extra latte or add the extra guacamole on your burrito---people would spend it.

So which method induced more spending: the 2008 check-in-the-mail approach or the 2009 more-in-the-paycheck approach?

At first glance, the one-time payment was the winner. The flow of payments method of 2009 was only half as good as the lump sum. Survey respondents said they spent 13% of the more-in-paycheck stimulus compared to 25% of the lump sum.[165]

But wait: President Bush was explicit about advertising the rebate checks, and people notice a check in the mail. Did people notice if the bottom line of their pay stub grew by $10 a week?

What if the low level of spending occurred because people didn't notice it? Did the people who did know about it spend more of it? That's the question Marilyn Spencer and Valrie Chambers set out to answer.

They found that only 20% of the 2008 lump sum rebates was spent, in line with other studies. They also confirmed that many taxpayers did not know they had received the 2009 tax rebate through their paychecks; the authors used the term "stealth stimulus" and "stealth rebate." They found that only about half of Americans even knew they had gotten it. But those who noticed their 2009 monthly installment rebate (about $38 extra each month on average from their survey recipients) spent 60% of it—three times as much as the 2008 lump sum.[166] So, maybe the steady drip method is better in getting consumers to go out and spend, as long as they are aware of it.

But questions like this are never settled.

The debate among economists on the effectiveness of fiscal policy to stimulate the economy still continues. Which basically means a bunch of economists are still arguing about the size of their multipliers.

Classical economists contend that government purchases will just cause prices to increase, and forward-looking individuals will see borrowing today by the government as higher taxes in the future, which means they cut back spending today. Thus, the classical economists argue that multipliers are small or nonexistent. The Keynesians, on the other hand, believe multipliers can be quite large under the right conditions— like when interest rates are already near zero and ineffectual monetary policy can't induce business investment. In other words, fiscal policy is most powerful during recessions when it's needed most.

Obama's economists believed that direct government spending (like improvements to highways and bridges) had more stimulating power than tax cuts. And the reason for this can be explained by savings. If the government gives $100 in tax cuts to Dominique, who saves 30%, only $70 is injected into the economy. If the government directly spends $100 on construction projects, the full $100 is initially injected. This explains why the Obama administration went with only a third of the stimulus package in the form of tax cuts.

John Maynard Keynes, who believed in using government fiscal policy to help manage the economy, would have been proud of Obama. Keynes suggested the target of government spending should be useful public works projects like the construction of schools, parks, hospitals, and infrastructure. Government stimulus on infrastructure projects, in addition to "priming the pump" and injecting spending into an economy in a rut, also have a secondary benefit of providing long term benefits. Keynes, however, acknowledged that politics would get in the way of such government infrastructure projects.

Keynes used a flippant example that the government could inject spending into a sluggish economy by burying bottles filled with cash in unused coalmines and then allowing people to dig them up.

If the Treasury were to fill old bottles with banknotes, bury them at suitable depths in disused coalmines which are then filled up to the surface with town rubbish, and leave it to private enterprise on well-tried principles of laissez-faire to dig the notes up again ... there need be no more unemployment.... It would, indeed, be more sensible to build houses and the like; but if there are political and practical difficulties in the way of this, the above would be better than nothing[167].

Keynes then addressed the idea that the general public finds some forms of government spending more palatable than others, even if the forms they find more palatable are in fact known to be more wasteful. Keynes suggests that there is a tendency to analyze such spending on buildings and bridges as a business proposition, but spending on something like the military is exempted from such cost-efficient scrutiny because no one expects military spending to be a wise business proposition in the first place. Thus, the public accepts wastefulness when it comes to fighter jets, but not solar power. Keynes wrote:

It is curious how common sense, wriggling for an escape from absurd conclusions, has been apt to reach a preference for wholly 'wasteful' forms of loan expenditure rather than for partly wasteful forms, which, because they are not wholly wasteful, tend to be judged on strict 'business' principles[168].

I wondered whether the tools of experimental economics could be used to test Keynes' assertion. I was initially drawn to this question back in 2011 while stimulus packages were calling deficit spending to the public's attention. Then I read Paul Krugman's column entitled "Bombs, Bridges, and

Jobs." In the New York Times op-ed, Krugman discusses the idea of "weaponized Keynesians," which he defined as people who believe "that the government does not create jobs when it funds the building of bridges or important research or retrains workers, but when it builds airplanes that are never going to be used in combat, that is, of course, economic salvation."

Krugman suggests that there are politicians who accept that government spending in a depressed economy can create jobs while simultaneously opposing government spending on infrastructure projects, which begs the question: "Why is government spending on destruction more palatable than spending on things such as bridges and high-speed railways?" Does the public view different types of government spending through different lenses?

I wondered whether the experiments of behavioral economics could shed some light on that question. And that's when I remembered the couch-carrying experiment---a study by James Heyman and Dan Ariely that would give me my inspiration for my own experiment.[169]

Suppose you were out for a walk and you come across a stranger trying to load a sofa into a van. How likely would you be to help out if the stranger offered to pay you 50 cents for your assistance? Would you be more likely to risk throwing your back out if the stranger paid you $5 to lift the couch? What if the stranger asked for your help without offering to pay you anything? Would you do it out of the kindness of your heart? Unsurprisingly, Heyman and Ariely found that more people would move the couch for $5 than for half a dollar, that is, a higher the level of payment corresponded with a higher level of effort.

What was a surprise, however, was that people were more likely to help lift the sofa if they were paid nothing than if they were paid 50 cents. So, paying a small incremental amount of money compared to no money actually decreased the likelihood of getting someone to help move the couch. Their experiment showed that people exhibit less effort when they receive a small wage compared to receiving no wage at all. Such action is difficult to explain in the standard economic framework; a small wage should always be better than no wage.

To help explain why, first contemplate this scenario.

Consider a young man on a first date at an Italian restaurant. After two hours of great conversation—appreciation of his corny jokes, general interest in his mountain-climbing stories, delicious wine, salad, pasta, and dessert—the young man is optimistic that this date could turn into a worthwhile relationship. Then the bill comes. He scans the itemized bill and begins to complain to his date about how expensive her salad was and starts grumbling about how much the house wine cost.

Why is the young man now in a sinking ship?

He brought the norms that govern business into a dating situation, where norms are governed by different criteria. Instead of viewing the dinner as an altruistic gesture, she now sees it as more of a business transaction. Mentioning the dollar cost induces her to start doing the cost/benefit analysis of her own. He is now subject to much harsher scrutiny when being evaluated through a cost/benefit lens than when he is being scrutinized through a lens by which social/dating norms act. The lens through which the young man is evaluated could be the difference between a second date or never seeing her again.

The premise underlying this scenario stems from the psychological field of relationship theory which purports that there are a few basic types of social relationships. The modes/

customs/mores of one domain of life are often different from another domain. The way one interacts with one's boss while she is paying you an hourly wage is completely different from the way one acts when helping a stranger jump-start a car battery. You expect your boss to pay a wage for your work effort because business principles govern this type of domain. On the other hand, helping a stranger whose car battery has died doesn't have a business principle attached.

Heyman and Ariely suggest that we live simultaneously in two different worlds: one where social norms prevail and one where market norms take charge. Cost-benefit analysis is the primary motivation under the market norm. Effort and payment are directly related in this world. You get what you pay for. But under social norms, strong community ties inhabit this relationship. Instant paybacks are not necessary. Friendly requests are common under the social ethos.

They found that people's work effort responds differently depending on whether their reward is viewed as a wage (i.e., from a market standpoint) or as an altruistic gesture (social standpoint). Standard economic theory says the appraisal of compensation levels should go in this order:
1. Performing task for a large wage
2. Performing task for a small wage
3. Performing task for free

Instead, performing a task for free is preferred to performing a task for a small wage. This quirk is reconciled because of the lens (either social or market) through which they evaluate the situation. When people volunteer (for free), they bring with them a sense of altruism and good-will from helping someone out. However, when monetary compensation is offered, it has a tendency to eliminate that good-will feeling.

And so, a small wage doesn't fully compensate people for the lost good-will feeling.

I wanted to see if norms could explain if and why people would prefer completely wasteful government stimulus spending over partially wasteful spending, as Keynes suggested, in the same way Heyman and Ariely showed that low payments get less workers than no payment.

So, I surveyed 300 undergraduate students at the University of Denver asking them to rank on a scale of 1 to 9 whether the following was a good idea:

In order to fight unemployment during a recession and jump-start consumer spending, your government decides to hire a bunch of unemployed construction workers for the year to build a second bridge into the city that will cut the commute time of 1 million daily commuters from 50 minutes to 20 minutes.

There were multiple versions of the survey. The only variation between low, medium, and high waste was the number of daily commuters and the number of minutes saved. Some students saw a "low-waste" scenario that reduced commute time from 50 to 20 minutes of a million commuters. Some students saw a scenario that reduced commute time from 50 to only 40 minutes for half a million commuters. The high waste scenario's bridge project only impacted 100 commuters cutting travel time from 50 to 45 minutes.

Still other students saw a different version that didn't have a new bridge saving commute being built. Instead, they saw:

In order to fight unemployment during a recession and jump-start consumer spending, your government decides to hire a bunch of unemployed construction workers for the year to tear down old, unused bridges.

I found that hiring unemployment construction workers to tear down an unused bridge was preferred to building an additional bridge that only reduced commute time for 100 workers by five minutes. Students were more favorable to the complete waste scenario than the high waste scenario. This result is very difficult to explain in the standard economic theory model, in the same way it has difficulty explaining how receiving zero dollars can sometimes be preferred over receiving $1. However, relationship theory reconciles this inconsistency. We scrutinize things from a market lens harder than we scrutinize things from a social lens, and government stimulus projects that look very "business-like" tend to be analyzed from a market lens and projects that look wasteful and "unbusiness-like" tend to be judged from a social lens. This was further strengthened by my survey questions that asked how likely the survey participants were influenced by the usefulness of the project vs. community well-being. The idea was to test whether seeing the numbers of daily commuters affected and time saved would trigger a market norms way to evaluating. My experiment said that it did. Wastefulness can sometimes be preferred … just as Keynes thought.

And not only did he basically invent the study of macroeconomics, but Keynes also penned one of the best definitions of why economists should have a wide knowledge from many fields. Keynes wrote the following in a 1924 obituary for the economist Alfred Marshall:

...Yet good, or even competent, economists are the rarest of birds. An easy subject, at which very few excel! The paradox finds its explanation, perhaps, in that the master-economist must possess a rare combination of gifts. (S/)He must reach a high standard in several different directions and must combine talents not often found together. (S/)He must be mathematician, historian, statesman, philosopher—in some degree. (S/)He must understand symbols and speak in words. (S)He must contemplate the particular in terms of the general, and touch abstract and concrete in the same flight of thought. (S/)He must study the present in the light of the past for the purposes of the future. No part of man's (or woman's) nature or his institutions must lie entirely outside his/her regard...[170]

In other words, the best economists draw from a wide range of disciplines and modes of thinking. You should too. You can see it in this chapter as the tools of the behavioral economists, which adopted modes of thinking from psychologists, were used to influence public policy (i.e. the design of government stimulus), which then impacted the whole economy. I hope this book helped you learn the economic concepts to unlock the mysteries of human behavior and that sometime in the future, you'll be able to impress your friends by applying some arcane economic idea to explain a real-world oddity. Be sure to throw in some "in-other-words words" when you do it.

Author's Note

A huge thanks to Tim Hoover, who edited every chapter and whose writing is always armed with wit and clever examples. I owe special thanks to many of my friends, family, and colleagues who graciously helped edit the manuscript and give feedback: Shawn Adrian, Nancy Kriek, Martin Cronkhite, Hallie Hoffman, Jace Jackson, Maxwell Tejera, Sophie Mariam, Caroline Nutter, Rachel Siegel, Matt Valeta, Volker Grzimek, Brian Mahoney, and Anders Fremstad.

About the Author

Christopher Stiffler is an economics professor and senior economist at the Colorado Fiscal Institute in Denver, Colorado. But he's also worked as a high school Latin teacher, trained as a professional wrestler and climbed all of Colorado's 14,000-foot peaks. He is a burro racer, public speaker, thru-hiker of the Colorado Trail and dabbles in things like ice climbing, stand-up comedy and cowboy poetry. He does his best writing after weekend trips backpacking into Colorado's wilderness away from cell service. Christopher got his start explaining economics in 2009, writing an explanatory economics column for his small hometown newspaper in Bedford, Pennsylvania. The column was geared at explaining complicated economic concepts in simple metaphorical terms that everyone can understand. His other published works include the children's books titled "An Igloo Half-Made" and "A Burro Named Bedford."

Contact him at Christopher.Stiffler.author@gmail.com

Endnotes

1 Kishtainy, Niall. (2017) A Little History of Economics. New Haven: Yale University Press. page 31

2 Heilbroner, Robert L. (1961). The worldly philosophers; the lives, times, and ideas of the great economic thinkers. New York :Simon and Schuster page 55.

3 Ibid page 70.

4 Dwight David Eisenhower, "The Chance for Peace," speech given to the American Society of Newspaper Editors, Apr. 16, 1953

5 Harford, T. (2006). The undercover economist: Exposing why the rich are rich, the poor are poor--and why you can never buy a decent used car!. Oxford: Oxford University Press.

6 See Mosselmans, Bert. Marginalism (2018) Agenda Publishing.

7 Kishtainy, Niall. (2017) A Little History of Economics. New Haven: Yale University Press. Page 42.

8 *Marshall, Alfred, 1842-1924. Principles of Economics; an Introductory Volume. London: Macmillan, 1920.*

9 Canterbury, E. Ray (2011). A Brief History of Economics : Artful Approaches to the Dismal Science (2nd ed.)

10 Marshall wasn't the first to invent the supply and demand cross diagram, but he did develop the most complete and systematic version of it. For a history of the origins of the supply and demand diagram see Thomas M. Humphrey, 1992. "Marshallian Cross Diagrams and Their Uses Before Alfred Marshall : The Origins of Supply and Demand Geometry," Economic Review, Federal Reserve Bank of Richmond, vol.

78(Mar), pages 3-23.

11 Cuellar, S., Karnowsky, D., & Acosta, F. (2009). The Sideways Effect: A Test for Changes in the Demand for Merlot and Pinot Noir Wines. Journal of Wine Economics, 4(2), 219-232.

12 Wheelan, Charles. J. (2002). Naked Economics : Undressing the Dismal Science. New York :Norton. Page 116

13 Adam Smith, The Wealth of Nations Book IV, Section ii, 12

14 Irwin, Douglas, A. (1996). Against the tide: an intellectual history of free trade. Princeton, N.J. : Princeton University Press. Page 89.

15 Torrens, Robert. (1815). An Essay on the External Corn Trade. London: J. Hatchard.

16 See James Buchanan and Yong Yoon (Winter 2002). "Globalization as Framed by the Two Logics of Trade," The Independent Review, v. VI, n.3, pp. 399-405

17 That percentage was adjusted upward to account for underreporting.

18 I relied heavily on the 2009 paper by Kilmer and Pacula: Kilmer, B. and Pacula, R.L. (2009) "Estimating the Size of the Global Drug Market: A Demand-Side Approach — Report 2" Santa Monica, CA: RAND Corporation, TR-711-EC.

19 Nisbet, Charles T and Vakil, Firouz (1972). "Some Estimates of Price and Expenditure Elasticities of Demand for Marijuana Among U.C.L.A. Students." The Review of Economics and Statistics, vol. 54, issue 4, 473-75

20 Maynard, Leigh J., 2000. "Empirical Tests Of The Argument That Consumers Value Stable Retail Milk Prices," Journal of Agribusiness, Agricultural Economics Association of Georgia, vol. 18(2), pages 1-18.

21 Pacula RL, Grossman M, Chaloupka FJ, O'Malley P, Johnston LD, Farrelly MC, (May 2000). Marijuana and Youth. Working Paper 7703 http://www.nber.org/papers/w7703NATIONAL BUREAU OF ECONOMIC RESEARCH

22   van Ours JC, Williams J. (2007). Cannabis prices and dynamics of cannabis use. J Health Econ; 26:578-96

23   Caulkins J, Pacula R. (2006). Marijuana markets: Inferences from reports by the household population. Journal of Drug Issues. 36

24   Clements K, Zhao X.(2009). Economics and marijuana. Cambridge University Press; Cambridge, UK.

25   See Colorado Legislative Council's memo at https://leg. colorado.gov/agencies/legislative-council-staff/marijuana-taxes%C2%A0

26   Morris, Michael. (December 2014). "Gasoline prices tend to have little effect on demand for car travel" U.S. Energy Information Administration available at https://www.eia.gov/todayinenergy/detail.php?id=19191

27   Fare Elasticity and Its Application for Forecasting Transit Demand, American Public Transit Association, 1991 available https://www.apta.com/wp-content/uploads/Resources/resources/reportsandpublications/Documents/Pham_Linsalata_Fare_Elasticity_1991.pdf

28   Franklin, J, Niemeier, D. (1998). Discrete Choice Elasticities For Elderly and Disabled Travelers Between Fixed-route Transit and Paratransit. Transportation Research Record, Vol. 1623, p. 31-36.

29   David Gillen (1994), "Peak Pricing Strategies in Transportation, Utilities, and Telecommunications: Lessons for Road Pricing," Curbing Gridlock, TRB (www.trb.org), pp. 115-151

30   Lawrence Frank, et al. (2008), "Urban Form, Travel Time, And Cost Relationships With Tour Complexity And Mode Choice," Transportation, Vol. 35, No. 1, January, pp. 37-54

31   Balcombe, R. and Mackett, R. and Paulley, N. and Preston, J. and Shires, J. and Titheridge, H. and Wardman, M. and White, P. (2004) The demand for public transport: a practical guide. Technical report. Transportation Research Laboratory

Report (TRL593). Transportation Research Laboratory, London, UK.

32   Wardman, Mark. (2012). 'Review and Meta-Analysis of U.K. Time Elasticities of Travel Demand.' Transportation 39(3): pp 465-90

33   Dowling, Richard Gerhard and Reinke, David (2008). Multimodal Level of Service Analysis for Urban Streets. National Cooperative Highway Research Program Transportation Research Board.

34   See the story from Leo Rosten in Cialdini, R. B. (1993). *Influence: Science and practice.* New York: Harper Collins College Publishers.

35   Levitt, S. D., & List, J. A. (2008). Homo economicus evolves. *Science,* 319(5865), 909-910

36   Ariely, Dan. (2010). The Upside of Irrationality: The Unexpected Benefits of Defying Logic at Work and at Home. New York: Harper.

37   Luigino Bruni & Robert Sugden, (2007). "The road not taken: how psychology was removed from economics, and how it might be brought back," Economic Journal, Royal Economic Society, vol. 117(516), pages 146-173, January.

38   Simon, Herbert A., (1955). "A Behavioral Model of Rational Choice", *Quarterly Journal of Economics,* 69(1): 99–118.

39   Friedman, M. (1953). Essays in Positive Economics. Chicago, Ill.: University of Chicago Press.

40   Thaler, Richard H., Behavioral Economics: Past, Present and Future (May 27, 2016). Available at SSRN: https://ssrn.com/abstract=2790606 or http://dx.doi.org/10.2139/ssrn.2790606

41   Fox, Justin. "From 'Economic Man' to Behavioral Economics. A short history of modern decision making" https://hbr.org/2015/05/from-economic-man-to-behavioral-economics

42   Thaler, R. H., & Sunstein, C. R. (2009). Nudge: improving

decisions about health, wealth, and happiness. Rev. and expanded ed. New York: Penguin Books.

43   Thaler, Richard H., Behavioral Economics: Past, Present and Future (May 27, 2016). Available at SSRN: https://ssrn.com/abstract=2790606 or http://dx.doi.org/10.2139/ssrn.2790606

44   Thaler, R. H. (2015). Misbehaving: The making of behavioral economics. W W Norton & Co.

45   Lowenstein, Roger. "Exuberance Is Rational" The New York Times Magazine

46   Camerer, Colin & Loewenstein, George. (2004). Behavioral Economics: Past, Present, Future. Advances in Behavioral Economics.

47   Thaler, R. (1983). Transaction utility theory. *Advances in Consumer Research, 10,* 229-232

48   Epley, N., & Gilovich, T. (2006). The anchoring-and-adjustment heuristic: Why the adjustments are insufficient. Psychological Science, 17, 311-318

49   Kahneman, Daniel. Thinking, Fast and Slow. New York: Farrar, Straus and Giroux, 2011

50   Ariely, D., Loewenstein, G., Prelec, D., 2003. Coherent arbitrariness: stable demand curves without stable preferences. Quarterly Journal of Economics 118, 73–105

51   Corr, P. J., & Plagnol, A. C. (2019). Behavioral economics: The basics. Page 121.

52   Whitney, R.A., Hubin, T., & Murphy, J.D. (1965). *The new psychology of persuasion and motivation in selling.* Englewood Cliffs, NJ: Prentice-Hall.

53   Ariely, Dan. Predictably Irrational: the Hidden Forces That Shape Our Decisions. New York: Harper Perennial, 2010.

54   Robson, D. (2019, August 1). The trick that makes you overspend. *BBC Worklife.* https://www.bbc.com/worklife/article/20190801-the-trick-that-makes-you-overspend

55   See Dan Ariely's TED Talk "Are we in control of our decisions?"

56   See Anderson, Chris 2009, "Free, How Today's Smartest Businesses Profit by Giving Something for Nothing"

57   Iyengar, S. S., & Lepper, M. R. (2000). When choice is demotivating: Can one desire too much of a good thing? *Journal of Personality and Social Psychology, 79*(6), 995–1006.

58   Ariely, D. (2008, May 5). 3 main lessons of Psychology. Retrieved from https://danariely.com/3-main-lessons-of-psychology/

59   "The Default Choice, So Hard to Resist" New York Times (Online), New York: New York Times Company. Oct 15, 2011.

60   See Samuelson, W., & Zeckhauser, R. J. (1988). Status quo bias in decision making. *Journal of Risk and Uncertainty, 1*, 7-59.

61   Kahneman, Daniel, Jack L. Knetsch, and Richard H. Thaler (1990), "Experimental Tests of the Endowment Effect and the Coase Theorem," Journal of Political Economy, 98 (December),1325–1348.

62   Heberlein, Thomas A. and Richard C. Bishop (1985), "Assessing the Validity of Contingent Valuation: Three Field Experiments," paper presented at the International Conference on Man's Role in Changing the Global Environment, Venice, Italy Ziv Carmon & Dan Ariely, *Focusing on the Forgone: How Value Can Appear So Different to Buyers and Sellers*, 27 J. Consumer Res. 360, 360 (2000).

63   Bar-Hillel, Maya and Efrat Neter (1996), "Why Are People Reluctant to Exchange Lottery Tickets?" Journal of Personality and Social Psychology, 70 (January), 17–27

64   Norton, M. I., Mochon, D., & Ariely, D. (2012). The IKEA effect: When labor leads to love. Journal of Consumer Psychology, 22, 453-460.

65   Shapiro, L. (2004). Something from the oven: Reinventing dinner in 1950s America. New York: Viking

66   Wason, Peter (1960). "On The Failure to Eliminate Hypotheses in a Conceptual Task". Quarterly Journal of Experimental Psychology. 12 (3): 129–140.

67   Lord, C. G., Ross, L., & Lepper, M. R. (1979). Biased assimilation and attitude polarization: The effects of prior theories on subsequently considered evidence. Journal of Personality and Social Psychology, 37(11), 2098–2109.

68   The first to use the term "confirmation bias" was in Mynatt, C. R., Doherty, M. E., & Tweney, R. D. (1977). Confirmation bias in a simulated research environment: An experimental study of scientific inference. Quarterly Journal of Experimental Psychology, 29(1), 85-95.

69   Read, Daniel, George Loewenstein, and Shobana Kalyanaraman (1999), "Mixing Virtue and Vice: Combining the Immediacy Effect and the Diversification Heuristic" Journal of Behavioral Decision Making,12,257-273.

70   Fortitude American Resilience in the Era of Outrage. Crenshaw, Dan (2020) Hachette Book Group, Inc. page 74

71   The prize was shared with Vernon Smith, another pioneer of experimental economics, and would have been shared with Amos Tversky if he were still alive.

72   Tversky, A. and Kahneman, D. 1981. The framing of decisions and the psychology of choice. Science, 211: 453–458.

73   Kahneman, Daniel, and Amos Tversky. "Prospect Theory: An Analysis of Decision under Risk." Econometrica, vol. 47, no. 2, 1979, pp. 263–291

74   Pope, Devin G., and Maurice E. Schweitzer. 2011. "Is Tiger Woods Loss Averse? Persistent Bias in the Face of Experience, Competition, and High Stakes." American Economic Review, 101 (1): 129-57.

75   Elmore, Ryan and Urbaczewski, Andrew, Loss Aversion in Professional Golf (January 7, 2019). Available at SSRN: https://papers.ssrn.com/sol3/papers.cfm?abstract_id=3311649

76   Simon Gachter & Henrik Orzen & Elke Renner & Chris Starmer, 2007. "Are experimental economists prone to

framing effects? A natural field experiment," Natural Field Experiments 00331, The Field Experiments Website.

77   Voss, C., & Raz, T. (2017). Never split the difference. Random House Business Books. Page 129

78   City of Longmont Local Transit Pass Program 2018 Memo provided by Boulder County.

79   You can do a similar calculation by first taking the difference between price and ATC, the per-unit profit. If you multiply this difference by q* you will arrive at profit in a slightly different formula (P*-ATC) X q* = Profit

80   I've purposefully glossed over *variable cost* and the *average variable cost curve*. Both are important in the firm's decision whether to shut down. We learned that the firm will make zero profit once the market price falls below ATC-minimum (break even point), but there is a range of prices where the firm will still operate in the short run at a loss because it can cover some of its fixed costs. For example, losing $600 in the short-run by operating is better than the alternative of shut-downing and losing all the fixed costs of $1,000. That important "shutdown price" occurs at the minimum of the average variable cost curve.

81   It is also possible for a monopolist to suffer losses depending on its costs.

82   Arthur Cecil Pigou. (1920) The Economics of Welfare Macmillan, London.

83   Campbell, P. (2021, July). Why Tinder's Charging Older Users More, and Why It Makes Perfect Sense. Available at: https://www.priceintelligently.com/blog/why-tinders-charging-older-users-more-and-why-it-makes-perfect-sense

84   Which Laws Do Your Marketers Know? Some Legal Issues on Price Discrimination. (2015) Koku

85   Rank, Jessica (2005) "Is Ladies' Night Really Sex Discrimination?: Public Accommodation Laws, De Minimis Exceptions, and Stigmatic Injury," Seton Hall Law Review:

Vol. 36 : Iss. 1 , Article 6.

86 Koire v. Metro Car Wash, 707 P.2d 195, 204 (Cal. 1985)

87 City of Clearwater v. Studebaker's Dance Club, 516 So.2d 1106, 1109 (Fla. App. 1987)

88 Mattioli, D. (2012, Aug). On Orbitz, Mac Users Steered to Pricier Hotels. *The Wall Street Journal.* Available at https://www.wsj.com/articles/SB10001424052702304458604577488822667325882

89 Schumpeter, J. (2016, Jan) Flexible Figures. *The Economist* available at https://www.economist.com/business/2016/01/28/flexible-figures

90 See a detailed discussion in McAdams, D. (2014). *Game-changer: Game theory and the art of transforming strategic situations.*

91 Hamilton, James L, 1972. "The Demand for Cigarettes: Advertising, the Health Scare, and the Cigarette Advertising Ban," The Review of Economics and Statistics, MIT Press, vol. 54(4), pages 401-411, November.

92 Cassidy, J. (2015, May 27). The Triumph (and Failure) of John Nash's Game Theory. *The New Yorker.* http://www.newyorker.com/news/john-cassidy/the-triumph-and-failure-of-john-nashs-game-theory

93 Poundstone, W. (1993) Prisoner's Dilemma. Oxford University Press

94 Poundstone, W. (1993) Prisoner's Dilemma. Oxford University Press. page 106.

95 A. W. Tucker. (June 1983) "The Mathematics of Tucker: A Sampler." The Two-Year College Mathematics Journal Vol. 14, No. 3 pp. 228-232

96 Zinman, Jonathan and Zitzewitz. Eric, (2016). "Wintertime for Deceptive Advertising?" American Economic Journal: Applied Economics, 8(1): 177–192.

97   See the following paper that documents dating site lying: Jeffrey T. Hancock, Catalina Toma, and Nicole Ellison, (2007) "The Truth about Lying in Online Dating Profiles," CHI'07 *Proceedings of the SIGCHI Conference on Human Factors in Computing Systems:* 449-452

98   Schelling, T. C. (1960). The strategy of conflict. Harvard University Press. and Schelling, T.C. (1965) Arms and Influence. Yale University Press.

99   Bernstein, Ross. (2006). The Code: the unwritten rules of fighting and retaliation in the NHL. Triumph Books

100 Page xiv to ibid.

101 Visuals of the *Golden Balls* payout matrices were inspired by Talwalkar, Presh. (2014). The Joy of Game Theory: An Introduction to Strategic Thinking.

102 Jersey Shore was a reality TV show from 2009 to 2012 airing on MTV.

103 I discovered this example from Talwalkar, Presh. (2014). The Joy of Game Theory: An Introduction to Strategic Thinking. Masterson, Teresa. "No Backsies! Designers Unload Competitors' Swag on Snooki." NBC 10 Philadelphia. NBCUniversal Media, 20 August 2010.

104 J. E. Meade, External Economies and Diseconomies in a Competitive Situation, 52 Econ. J. 54 (1952) (The author won the Nobel Prize in economics in 1977 but not for this work).

105 Francis M. Bator (1958). "The Anatomy of Market Failure," Quarterly Journal of Economics, 72(3) pp. 351–79

106 McLaughlin, M. (2016). Ban, Fee, Take-Back/Recycle: which Approach Wins out in the End? (Master's Thesis). University of New Hampshire.

107 Convery, F., McDonnell, S., & Ferreira, S. (2007). The most popular tax in Europe? Lessons from the Irish plastic bags levy. Environmental Resource Economics, 38, 1-11.

108 Armstrong, L. and Chapman, E.O. City of Aspen Single Use Bag Study. Journal of Sustainability Education Vol. 16, December 2017 available at http://www.susted.com/wordpress/wp-content/uploads/2018/01/Armstrong-JSE-Fall-2017-General-PDF.pdf

109 Frédéric Bastiat. A 200-year-old's libertarian insights remain both relevant and amusing. (2001, July 19). The Economist. https://www.economist.com/finance-and-economics/2001/07/19/frederic-bastiat

110 Dougan, William R. and Thomas, Charles J, (2014) Coase, Hayek, Pigou, and Walras: Taxes vs Permit Auctions in Environmental Policy

111 Henry Sidgwick, The Principles of Political Economy 406 (3rd ed. 1901, 1st ed. 1883).

112 Bitong, Anna (2018, April 3). Mamihlapinatapai: A Lost language's untranslatable legacy. BBC. https://www.bbc.com/travel/article/20180402-mamihlapinatapai-a-lost-languages-untranslatable-legacy

113 Rapoport, Anatol "Experiments with N-Person Social Traps I." In *Journal of Conflict Resolution* 32 (1988): 457-72

114 Samuelson, Paul A. (1954), The Theory of Public Expenditure, in: Review of Economics and Statistics 36, pp. 386–389

115 *Lloyd, W. F. (1833). Two Lectures on the Checks to Population*

116 Kenney, Andrew (2017, January 10). Dog waste and traffic are forcing a major rethink of Elk Meadow, Colorado's greatest dog park. Denverite. https://denverite.com/2017/01/10/500-pounds-dog-poop-forcing-major-rethink-elk-meadow-colorados-greatest-dog-park/

117 Poundstone, W. (1992): Prisoner's Dilemma, New York: Double Day. page 203-204.

118 Ober, Josiah 2001. "Thucydides Theoretikos/Thucydides Histor: Realist Theory and the Challenge of History." Pp.

273-306 in Democracy and War: A Comparative Study of the Korean War and the Peloponnesian War, edited by D.R. McCann, B.S. Strauss. Armonk, N.Y. and London: M.E. Sharpe

119   David M. Pritchard (editor) 2011 War, Democracy and Culture in Classical Athens

120   The History of the Peloponnesian War by Thucydides; translated by Richard Crawley from Project Gutenberg.

121   See Elinor Ostrom's 8 Principles for Managing a Commons

122   Ostrom, E. (1990). Governing the commons: The evolution of institutions for collective action. Cambridge University Press

123   Rules, Games, and Common-Pool Resources (1994). Elinor Ostrom, Roy Gardner, and James Walker with Arun Agrawal, William Blomquist, Edella Schlager, and Shui Yan Tang. Ann Arbor. The University of Michigan Press.

124   Wooten, J. (2018). Economics media library. The Journal of Economic Education, 49(4), 364-365. https://econ.video/tag/curb-your-enthusiasm/

125   Akerlof, G. (1970) The market for "lemons": Qualitative uncertainty and the market mechanism. Quarterly Journal of Economics, 84, 488-500.

126   Graphic below inspired by "The Joy of Game Theory; An Introduction to Strategic Thinking," by Presh Talwalkar.

127   Michael Spence (1973). "Job Market Signaling." Quarterly Journal of Economics. 87 (3): 355–374

128   Bram, Uri. How Game Theory Improves Dating Apps, (2016, November 17) The Economist. https://www.1843magazine.com/culture/the-daily/how-ga,me-theory-improves-dating-apps

129   Soohyung Lee & Muriel Niederle, 2015. "Propose with a rose? Signaling in internet dating markets," Experimental Economics, Springer; Economic Science Association, vol. 18(4), pages 731-755, December.

130   The Theory of "Screening," Education, and the Distribution of Income Stiglitz, Joseph. The American Economic Review, Jun 1, 1975, Vol.65(3), p.283

131   Winter, R. A., 2000, Optimal Insurance Under Moral Hazard, in: G. Dionne, ed., Handbook of Insurance (Boston: Kluwer), pp. 15

132   Ducat, A.C., 1865, *The Practice of Fire Underwriting*, 4th edition (Hardford: Ward & Co.)

133   Dembe, A. E., and L. I. Boden, 2000, Moral Hazard: A Question of Morality?, New Solutions: A Journal of Environmental and Occupational Health Policy 10:257-279.

134   A History of the Term "Moral Hazard" David Rowell and Luke B. Connelly: The Journal of Risk and Insurance, Vol. 79, No. 4 (December 2012), pp. 1051-1075

135   Lewis and Short (eds) 1879, *A Latin Dictionary: Founded on Andrews' Edition of Freund's Latin Dictionary, Reviewed and in Great Part Rewritten by Charlton T. Lewis and Charles Short* (Oxford: Clarendon)

136   Dembe AE, Boden LI. Moral Hazard: A Question of Morality? NEW SOLUTIONS: A Journal of Environmental and Occupational Health Policy. 2000;10(3):257-279.

137   David Rowell & Luke B. Connelly, 2012. "A History of the Term "Moral Hazard"," Journal of Risk & Insurance, The American Risk and Insurance Association, vol. 79(4), pages 1051-1075, December.

138   See the *decretal Naviganti* from 1234 by Pope Gregory IX

139   Baker, Tom. "On the Genealogy of Moral Hazard." Texas Law Review Vol. 75, number 2, December 1996

140   McClintock, E., 1892, *On the Effects of Selection* (New York: Mutual Life Insurance Company of New York).

141   Arrow, Kenneth J. (1963). Uncertainty and the welfare economics of medical care. The American Economic Review Vol. 53, No. 5, pp. 941-97

142   The Economics of Moral Hazard: Comment Mark V. Pauly *The American Economic Review* Vol. 58, No. 3, Part 1 (Jun., 1968), pp. 531-537 (7 pages)

143   Queen, Jack (2017, March 17). Breckenridge ski pass frauds see spring break uptick. *Vail Daily*. https://www.vaildaily.com/news/crime/breckenridge-ski-pass-frauds-see-spring-break-uptick/

144   The Project Gutenberg EBook of The Common Law, by Oliver Wendell Holmes, Jr. from 1881

145   Ricardo, David, 1772-1823. (1817). *On the principles of political economy and taxation*. London: John Murray. Chapter 21

146   Say, Jean-Baptiste. (1803). *A Treatise on Political Economy (Traité d'économie politique)*: Grigg and Elliott.

147   We are ignoring exports here.

148   Skidelsky, Robert. 2009. *Keynes: the return of the master*. London: Allen Lane. p.79

149   Keynes, J.M. (1923) *A Tract on Monetary Reform*, Macmillan Ch. 3, p. 80

150   Kahn, Richard F. 1931. "The Relation of Home Investment to Unemployment." *Economic Journal* 41(162):173-98.

151   Hicks, John R. 1937. "Mr. Keynes and the 'Classics': A Suggested Interpretation." *Econometrica* 5(1):147-59.

152   Frances Perkins. (1946). *The Roosevelt I knew*. Viking Press, New York. p. 226.

153   Sylvia Nasar (2011) *Grand Pursuit: The Story of Economic Genius*. New York: Simon & Schuster. P.330

154   See Keynes's Sidney Ball lecture in *Collected Writings*, vol. 19: *Activities* 1922-9, pages 267-272.

155   John Maynard Keynes, 2010. "The End of Laissez-Faire," Palgrave Macmillan Books, in: Essays in Persuasion, chapter 2, pages 272-294, Palgrave Macmillan.

156   Quoted in Justin Fox, "The Comeback of Keynes," *Time*, 27

January 2009.

157 Mankiw, N.G. (2003). Principles of Economics 3rd Third Edition p. 746-747

158 There was a second round called the *Jobs and Growth Tax Relief Reconciliation Act of 2003* as well.

159 Shapiro, Matthew, D., and Joel Slemrod. 2003. "Consumer Response to Tax Rebates." American Economic Review, 93 (1): 381-396.

160 Shapiro, M. & Slemrod, J. (2003) Did the 2001 tax rebate stimulate spending? Evidence from taxpayers surveys. In J. Poterba (Ed.), *Tax policy and the Economy.* Cambridge: MIT Press.

161 Arkes, H.R., Joyner, C.A., Pezzo, M.V.,Nash, J.G., Siegel-Jacobs, K., & Stone, e. (1994). The psychology of windfall gains. *Organizational Behavioral and Human Decision Processes,* 59, 331-347.

162 Transcript of President Bush's White House News Conference. *New York Times,* February 23, 2001. P. A10.

163 Skidelsky, Robert. 2009. *Keynes: the return of the master.* London: Allen Lane. p.5

164 Bodkin, Ronald G. "Windfall Income and Consumption," The American Economic Review, Sep., 1959, Vol. 49, No. 4 (Sep., 1959), pp. 602-614 Mordechai E. Kreinin. "Windfall Income and Consumption: Additional Evidence." The American economic review, 1961-06-01, Vol.51 (3), p.388-390 Landsberger, M. "Windfall Income and Consumption: Comment," The American Economic Review, Jun., 1966, Vol. 56, No. 3 (Jun., 1966), pp. 534-540

165 Sahm, Claudia R., Matthew D. Shapiro, and Joel Slemrod. 2012. "Check in the Mail or More in the Paycheck: Does the Effectiveness of Fiscal Stimulus Depend on How It Is Delivered?" American Economic Journal: Economic Policy, 4 (3): 216-50

166 National Heuristic Shift toward Saving Any Form of Tax Rebate, Marilyn K. Spencer; Valrie Chambers Accounting and the Public Interest (2012) 12 (1): 106–136

167 Keynes, John Maynard, 1883-1946. The General Theory of Employment, Interest and Money. London: Macmillan, 1936.

168 Keynes, John Maynard, 1883-1946. The General Theory of Employment, Interest and Money. London: Macmillan, 1936.

169 Heyman, James and Ariely, Dan (2004). "Effort for Payment; a Tale of Two Markets." Psychological Science, 15, p787-793

170 Alfred Marshall, 1842-192: J. M. Keynes, The Economic Journal, Vol. 34, No. 135 (Sep., 1924), pp. 311-372; alternative pronouns added.